Imagined
Human Beings
*A Psychological Approach
to Character and Conflict
in Literature*

Bernard J. Paris

NEW YORK UNIVERSITY PRESS
New York and London

NEW YORK UNIVERSITY PRESS
New York and London

Library of Congress Cataloging-in-Publication Data
Paris, Bernard J.
Imagined human beings : a psychological approach to character and
conflict in literature / Bernard J. Paris.
p.   cm.—(Literature and psychoanalysis ; 9)
Includes bibliographical references and index.
ISBN 0-8147-6655-2 (clothbound : alk. paper).—ISBN
0-8147-6656-0 (paperbound : alk. paper)
1. Literature—Psychological aspects.   2. Psychology in
literature.   3. Psychoanalysis and literature.   4. Characters and
characteristics in literature.   5. Motivation (Psychology) in
literature.   I. Title.   II. Series.
PN56.P93P38   1997
809'.93353—dc21   97-4879
CIP

New York University Press books are printed on acid-free paper,
and their binding materials are chosen for strength and durability.

Manufactured in the United States of America
10 9 8 7 6 5 4 3 2 1

112598-2610XII

For Shirley
still my inspiration

Contents

Preface

What fascinates me most about literature is its portrayal of human beings and their relationships. For many years I have been developing a psychological approach in which I try to understand the behavior of realistically drawn characters in the same way that we understand the behavior of real people. These characters are not flesh and blood creatures, of course, but are imagined human beings who have many parallels with people like ourselves. Numerous critics have maintained that it is inappropriate or impossible to explain the behavior of fictional characters in motivational terms, but I argue in chapter 1 that the rejection of psychological analysis has been a major critical error.

One reason why I find it possible to analyze literary characters psychologically is that I employ the theories of Karen Horney, which explain behavior in terms of its function within the present structure of the psyche rather than in terms of infantile origins. While literature gives little or no information about infancy, it reveals a great deal about the adult. A Horneyan approach does not force us to invent a character's early history but permits us to utilize exactly the kind of information that literature supplies. For the benefit of those who are unfamiliar with Horney, I provide an account of her ideas in chapter 2.

Among the virtues of Horney's theory are that it is free of arcane terminology and is readily intelligible. I have aspired to the same virtues in this book. I have written it not only for fellow critics, but also for all students, teachers, and lovers of literature who are drawn to novels and plays because of their human interest. For the sake of readability, I have chosen not to become a combatant in the theory wars that are raging in the fields of psychoanalysis and literary studies these days. I have discussed Karen Horney's place in psychoanalytic thought in my 1994 biography of her, and I have defended various aspects of my psychological approach to literature in previous critical works (Paris 1974, 1978b, 1986a, 1991a, 1991b).

I have entitled this book *Imagined Human Beings* because it is largely about mimetic characters who can be understood in psychological terms. As the subtitle suggests, it is also about various kinds of conflict. There are conflicts, first of all, within and between the characters. In part 2, I analyze the inner divisions of the central characters and the dynamics of their relationships in works by Sophocles, Chaucer, Shakespeare, Ibsen, and Barth. I want to show not only the ability of the Horneyan approach to yield clarifying readings of controversial texts but also its range of application.

Perhaps because the title of her first book was *The Neurotic Personality of Our Time,* some people have the impression that Horney's theory is limited to the time and place in which she wrote. It is not a universal theory, of course (no theory is), but it deals with human needs and defenses that are portrayed in the literature of many periods and cultures. While not ignoring cultural differences, a Horneyan approach enables us to see an underlying similarity in human experience. It can help us to understand the behavior of characters in literature from the past, to enter into their feelings, and to enrich our knowledge of ourselves and others through an understanding of their inner conflicts and relationships.

There are other kinds of conflict that I explore as well. I argue in part 3 that in realistic literature there is usually conflict between plot and rhetoric on the one hand and mimesis on the other. When concretely drawn characters are understood in psychological terms, they tend to escape their roles in the plot and to subvert the view of them advanced by the rhetoric. I look at two patterns of action in particular, the education and vindication plots. When I examine the protagonists of education plots from a Horneyan perspective, they do not seem to have matured but to have switched from one defensive strategy to another. In vindication plots, noble characters are unappreciated at the outset but eventually receive the admiration they deserve. From a Horneyan perspective, these characters appear less admirable than the vindication pattern requires them to be.

There is almost always conflict between an author's interpretations and judgments, which are part of what I mean by "rhetoric," and the mimetic portrait of a character. Authors tend to glorify characters who embody the defensive strategies they favor while accurately portraying their behavior as damaging to themselves or others. A Horneyan approach helps us not only to see disparities between rhetoric and mimesis but also to understand the forces in the implied author's personality that generate them. There are sometimes inconsistencies within the rhetoric itself, as the author presents conflicting interpretations and judgments. A Horneyan approach can help us to make sense of such inconsistencies by seeing them as a product of the inner divisions of the implied author.

The conflicts between rhetoric and mimesis that are a consequence of realistic characterization can be either exacerbated or reduced by the choice of narrative technique. In part 3, I compare six novels that employ a variety of narrative techniques and try to show that the problems created by both omniscient and first person narration are illuminated by a Horneyan approach and resolved by the use of multiple narrators, such as Emily Brontë employs in *Wuthering Heights*.

This book is a product of the continuing evolution of the psychological approach to literature that I have been unfolding since 1964. It illustrates some of applications of the approach that I have discussed before, but it emphasizes some things that my previous books do not, such as plot and narrative technique, and it applies the approach more systematically and to a wider range of literary issues and texts. It provides distinctive readings, I think, of a dozen major works of Western literature. If read in conjunction with part 1, each chapter can be understood by itself, but the chapters are connected to each other by a series of comparisons and are part of an unfolding story that reaches its climax in my discussion of *Wuthering Heights*. In the concluding chapter, I review what I have done here and elsewhere and suggest additional applications of the approach.

I have been working out the interpretations presented here in my classes for several decades, and I have found the Horneyan approach a joy to teach, at both the undergraduate and graduate levels. Perhaps my greatest debt is to the students at Michigan State University and the University of Florida who challenged me with their questions and bore with me as I groped for answers. In some cases it took me decades to arrive at a reading with which I felt satisfied.

I have chosen to summarize preceding criticism rather than to document it in detail, but I hasten to say that I am deeply indebted to the critics who have gone before me. I believe that my interpretations are substantially different from theirs, but I have benefited greatly from engaging with their points of view, as I hope others will benefit by engaging with mine. Critical controversies have often alerted me to contradictory elements in literary works that I might not have seen on my own.

I have profited from having presented papers on some of the works discussed in this book. I formulated the earliest version of my reading of *Madame Bovary* for a conference on Flaubert that was organized by Herbert Josephs at Michigan State University. I presented a paper on *The End of the Road* at a meeting of the Popular Culture Association, in a session chaired by Branimir Rieger, and a partial version of my reading of *Hedda Gabler* at a conference of the International Karen Horney Society. I later presented fuller versions of my reading of this play to a seminar at Trinity College, University of Toronto, and to the Group for the Application of Psychology, University of Florida. I presented an early version of my interpretation of *A Doll's House* at a scientific meeting of the Association for the Advancement of Psychoanalysis and a later version to the Literature and Psychoanalysis Group of the Toronto Psychoanalytic Society. All of these presentations were followed by discussions from which I learned a great deal, and I wish to thank those who participated in them.

I have received particular help with my chapter on "The Clerk's Tale" from Marie Nelson, my medievalist colleague at the University of Florida, and astute comments on my chapter on *The End of the Road* from Andrew Gordon, my Americanist colleague and fellow member of the Institute for Psychological Study of the Arts at UF. Diane Hoeveler and Beth Lau made valuable suggestions for improving the much briefer version of my reading of *Jane Eyre* that was published in the MLA volume they edited on approaches to the teaching of that novel (Paris 1993a).

Other portions of the present book have also been previously published. Chapter 1 draws on "A Horneyan Approach to Literature" (Paris 1991c) and the Introduction of *Third Force Psychology and the Study of Literature* (Paris 1986a). Chapter 2 draws on *Karen Horney: A Psychoanalyst's Search for Self-Understanding* (Paris 1994a). Part of the discussion of *A Doll's House* in chapter 3 was published in *The American Journal of Psychoanalysis* (Paris 1978a), and a version of chapter 6 was published in the same journal (Paris 1989b). A preliminary version of my reading of *Madame Bovary* was published in *The Literary Review* (Paris 1981), and a modified version of the present chapter on that novel was published in *The American Journal of Psychoanalysis* (Paris 1997). A portion of chapter 13 was published in *Women and Literature* (Paris

1982) and another portion in "Third Force Psychology and the Study of Literature, Biography, Criticism, and Culture" (Paris 1986b). The Conclusion draws on *Third Force Psychology and the Study of Literature* (Paris 1986a), "A Horneyan Approach to Literature" (Paris 1991c), *Bargains with Fate* (Paris 1991a), and *Karen Horney: A Psychoanalyst's Search for Self-Understanding* (Paris 1994a). I wish to thank the journals and presses that have previously published portions of this book for allowing me to include this material here.

I wish to extend my deepest thanks to Jeffrey Berman, the General Editor of the New York University Press's Literature and Psychoanalysis series, and to my wife, Shirley. This book probably would not have been written without Jeffrey Berman's invitation, and he has given me sound advice and encouragement at every stage. It was a great help having him in mind as my reader as I sat at my word processor. As always, Shirley has lived through the process of creation with me and has given me the benefit of an immediate perceptive response. She has been my first and best critic and my most precious source of support. I dedicated my first book to her in 1965. It is time for me to dedicate another book to my very dear wife.

PART I

Introduction

1

Applications of a
Horneyan Approach

It is not difficult to see why psychoanalytic theory has been widely used in the study of literature. Psychoanalysis deals with human beings in conflict with themselves and each other, and literature portrays and is written and read by such people. What is confusing is that there are so many psychoanalytic theories, each with its claims and proponents. It clearly makes sense to use psychoanalysis in literary study, but which theory should we employ?

I do not believe that literature should be placed on the Procrustean bed of any one theory. Human psychology is inordinately complex and can be approached in many ways. A number of theories have accurately described certain aspects of it, but none has the whole truth or is universally applicable. Many theorists have derived global models of human nature from the limited range of phenomena they understand well, or have tried to explain too much with too limited a repertory of motives. We need a wide range of theories to do justice to the richness and diversity of human experience and to the literature that expresses it. Some theories are highly congruent with certain works and some with others, and often several can be employed in studying the same text or aspect of literature. There is a large body of Freudian and Jungian criticism; and the ideas of Alfred Adler, Otto Rank, Wilhelm Reich, Melanie Klein, D. W. Winnicott, R. D. Laing, Fritz Perls, Heinz Kohut, Jacques Lacan, and others have also been profitably used in literary studies.

Another psychoanalyst with an important contribution to make is Karen Horney. Her theory fits numerous works from a wide range of periods and cultures and illuminates a variety of literary issues. It yields a distinctive set of insights and is a valuable critical tool.

When I first read Horney in 1959, at the suggestion of a colleague in psychology, I was deeply impressed by her theory. She not only described my behavior in an immediately recognizable way, but she seemed to have invaded my privacy and to have understood my insecurities, inner conflicts, and unrealistic demands on myself. Above all, she enabled me to comprehend a mysterious change that had taken place in me since the completion of my dissertation.

I was originally a specialist in Victorian fiction who was trained at Johns Hopkins in the explication of texts and the history of ideas. In my doctoral dissertation, I examined George Eliot's thought in relation to her time and her novels in relation to her ideas. While I was working on my dissertation, I felt that George Eliot had discovered the answer to the modern quest for values, and I expounded her Religion of Humanity with a proselytizing zeal. When I completed the dissertation, I found that although I still felt my reading of George Eliot to be accurate, I was no longer enthralled by her ideas. I could not understand my loss of enthusiasm, which had left me feeling painfully disoriented and uncertain about my beliefs.

Reading Karen Horney helped me to understand what had happened. Horney correlates belief systems with strategies of defense and observes that when our defenses change, so does our philosophy of life. I had had great difficulty writing my dissertation, for reasons that therapy later made clear, and had frequently felt hopeless about completing the Ph.D. Faced with the frustration of my academic ambitions, I found George Eliot's Religion of Humanity to be exactly what I needed: we give meaning to our lives by living for others rather than for ourselves. But when I finished my dissertation and was told that it ought to be published (Paris 1965), I could once again dream of a glorious career. Since I no longer needed to live for others in order to give meaning to my life, George Eliot's philosophy lost its appeal. In Horneyan terms, my inability to write my dissertation forced me to abandon my expansive ambitions and to become self-effacing, but on triumphantly completing it, I became expansive once more, and George Eliot's ideas left me cold. This was an unconscious process of which I first became aware through my reading of Horney and that I understood more fully in the course of psychotherapy.

While in therapy in the early 1960s, I read a great deal of psychoanalytic theory, often using it as an aid to self-analysis. I did not connect it to the study of literature until one memorable day in 1964 when I was teaching Thackeray's *Vanity Fair*. Again it was Horney who helped me to understand what was mystifying me. While arguing that the novel is full of contradictions and does not make sense thematically, I suddenly remembered Horney's statement that "inconsistencies are as definite an indication of the presence of conflicts as a rise in body temperature is of physical disturbance" (1945, 35). In the next instant I realized that the novel's contradictions become intelligible if we see them as part of a system of inner conflicts. I have been unfolding the implications of that "aha" experience ever since, with profound effects on my view of literature.

As we shall see when examining *The Awakening,* there are other works like *Vanity Fair* in which thematic contradictions make it impossible to understand the text in its own terms. Literary critics have often defended the artistic unity of such works by suppressing awareness of inconsistencies or by rationalizing contradictions as part of a controlled structure of tension, irony, and paradox. More recently they have tended to delight in contradictions as evidence of the tendency of all linguistic structures to deconstruct themselves. With the help of Horney's theory we are often able both to recognize inconsistencies as genuine problems and to understand them as parts of an intelligible structure of psychological conflict. Long before the advent of deconstruction, I was showing how literary works almost always contain elements that subvert their dominant themes, but after this deconstructive move I was able to reconstruct them by showing that they still make sense in psychological terms (Paris 1974; see de Beaugrande 1986).

After accounting for the thematic contradictions of *Vanity Fair* as part of a structure of inner conflicts, I realized that Horney also works well with the major characters in the novel—William Dobbin, Amelia Sedley, and Becky Sharp. As I taught other nineteenth-century novels with Horney in mind, I came to see that they, too, contain highly individualized characters whose motivational systems can be understood with the help of her theory. This recognition eventually led to my first book using Horney—*A Psychological Approach to Fiction: Studies in Thackeray, Stendhal, George Eliot, Dostoevsky, and Conrad* (1974). Characterization was not my only concern, but I gave a large part of each chapter to a detailed analysis of major figures in *Vanity Fair, The Red and the Black, The Mill on the Floss, Notes from Underground,* and *Lord Jim.* In subsequent books, I have taken a Horneyan approach to all of Jane Austen's and all of Shakespeare's major characters (Paris 1978b, 1991a,

1991b). The fact that Horney works well with literature from a wide variety of periods and cultures tells us something about both the power of her theory and the enduring features of human behavior.[1]

Like most students of literature, I had been taught to analyze literary characters primarily in formal and thematic terms. When I looked at realistically drawn characters from a Horneyan perspective, I came to see that there was an immense amount of psychological detail that literary criticism had simply ignored. These characters were not simply functions in a text or encoded messages from the author but were imagined human beings whose thoughts, feelings, and actions made sense in motivational terms. I had not been taught that literature is about human beings, human relationships, and human experiences; but outside of the academy one of the primary appeals of great literature has always been its portrayal of characters who seem to be of the same nature as ourselves. A psychological understanding of these characters makes them all the more fascinating.

When I began discussing the psychology of literary characters, I quickly encountered a great deal of resistance to this procedure among my fellow critics. It has become a dogma of modern theory that literary characters do not belong to the real world in which people have internal motivations but to a fictional world in which everything they are and do is part of a larger structure whose logic is determined by purely artistic considerations. The most recent schools of criticism continue to see characters in primarily functional terms, with many of them attacking the whole concept of a self that can be represented.

I believe that the rejection of the idea that literary characters can be analyzed in ways similar to those in which we analyze real people has been an enormous critical error (for fuller accounts of my argument, see Paris 1974 and 1991b). The objections to this procedure apply to some kinds of characters but not to others. It is essential to recognize that there are different types of characterization requiring different strategies of interpretation.

A useful taxonomy is that of Scholes and Kellogg (1966), which distinguishes between aesthetic, illustrative, and mimetic characterization. Aesthetic characters are stock types who may be understood primarily in terms of their technical functions and their formal and dramatic effects. Illustrative characters are "concepts in anthropoid shape or fragments of the human psyche parading as whole human beings." We try to understand "the principle they illustrate through their actions in a narrative framework" (88). Behind realistic literature there is a strong "psychological impulse" that "tends toward the presentation of highly individualized figures who resist abstraction and generalization" (101). When we encounter a fully drawn mimetic character, "we are justified in asking questions about his motivations based on our knowledge of the ways in which real people are motivated" (87). A mimetic character usually has aesthetic and illustrative functions, but numerous details have been called forth by the author's desire to make the character lifelike, complex, and inwardly intelligible, and these will go unnoticed if we interpret the character only in functional terms.

One of the most frequent objections to motivational analysis is that it takes characters out of the work and tries to understand them in their own right. Given the nature of mimetic characterization, this is not an unreasonable procedure. Mimetic characters are part of the fictional world in which they exist, but they are also autonomous beings with an inner logic of their own. They are, in E. M. Forster's phrase, "creations inside a creation" (1927, 64) who tend to go their own way as the author becomes absorbed in imagining human beings, motivating their behavior, and supplying their reactions to the situations in which they have been placed.

There has been a great deal of resistance among critics not only to regarding literary characters as imagined human beings, but also to using modern psychoanalytic theories to analyze them. One objection has been that earlier authors could not possibly have conceived of their characters in the terms we are using to talk about them. My reply to this is that the authors had to make sense of human behavior for themselves, as we all do, and that they drew upon the conceptual systems of their day. To see their characters in terms of those systems is to recover what may have been the authors' conscious understanding of them, but that does not do justice to their mimetic achievement or make the characters intelligible to us. To interpret Hamlet in terms of humors psychology does not explain his behavior to me.

We cannot identify our authors' conceptions of their characters with the characters they have actually created, even if we could be certain of what their conceptions were. One of the features of mimetic characters is that they have a life independent of their creators and that our understanding of them will change, along with our changing conceptions of human behavior. Even though the characters will outlive every interpretation, each age has to make sense of them for itself, using its own modes of explanation. Any theory we use will be culture-bound and reductive; still, we must use some theory, consciously or not, to satisfy our appetite for conceptual understanding.

I believe that psychoanalytic theory has much to contribute to our understanding of literature and that it permits a conceptual clarity that cannot be derived from literature alone. But literature has a contribution of at least equal importance to make to the theories that help us to understand it. There is a reciprocal relation, I propose, between psychoanalytic theory and the literary presentation of the phenomena it describes. Theory provides categories of understanding that help us to recover the intuitions of the great writers about the workings of the human psyche, and these intuitions, once recovered, become part of our conceptual understanding of life. We gain greater insight into human behavior because of the richness of artistic presentation. Even the most sophisticated theories are thin compared to the complex portrayals of characters and relationships that we find in literary masterpieces, and they are thinner yet, of course, when compared with the density of life. While discussing an aspect of vindictiveness in *Neurosis and Human Growth*, Karen Horney observed that "great writers have intuitively grasped [this phenomenon] and have presented it in more impressive forms than a psychiatrist can hope to do" (198). Taken together psychoanalytic theory and literature give us a fuller grasp of human experience than either provides by itself.

The analyst and the artist often deal with the same phenomena, but in significantly different ways. Psychoanalytic theory gives us *formulations about* human behavior, whereas literature gives us *truth to* experience. Because of its concrete, dramatic quality, literature enables us not only to observe people other than ourselves but also to enter into their mental universe, to discover what it feels like to *be* these people and to confront their life situations. We can gain in this way a phenomenological grasp of experience that cannot be derived from theory alone, and not from case histories either, unless they are also works of art. Because literature provides this kind of knowledge, it has a potentially sensitizing effect, one that is of as much importance to the clinician as it is to the humanist. Literature offers us an opportunity to amplify our experience in a way that can enhance our empathic powers, and because of this it is a valuable aid to clinical training and personal growth.

Another major source of resistance to the psychoanalytic study of character has been its reliance on infantile experience to account for the behavior of the adult. Since literature usually provides little information about early childhood, psychoanalytic critics tend to infer early experience from adult behavior, which they then account for in terms of infantile origins. Crucial explanatory material is generated out of the premises of their theory, with no corroborating literary evidence except the supposed results of the invented experiences, which were inferred from these results to begin with.

A Horneyan approach is not subject to this difficulty. Although Horney, like Freud, sees psychological problems as originating in early childhood, she does not see the adult as simply repeating earlier patterns, and she does not explain adult behavior through analogies with childhood experience. Once a child begins to adopt defensive strategies, his or her particular system develops under the influence of external factors, which encourage some strategies and discourage others, and of internal necessities, whereby each defensive move requires others in order to maintain its viability. The character structure of the adult has its origins in early childhood, but it is also the product of a complicated evolutionary history, and it can be understood in terms of the present constellation of defenses. Such a synchronic or structural approach is highly suitable for the analysis of literary characters, since we are often supplied with ample information about their existing defenses, however sketchy their childhoods may be. Because it describes the kinds of phenomena that are actually portrayed in literature, it permits us to stick to the words on the page, to explicate the text.

As I have continued to look at literature from a Horneyan perspective, one discovery has led to another, about both the nature of literature and the possible applications of the approach. I began by using the theory to make sense of thematic contradictions but soon came to appreciate its power to illuminate character. Recognizing the psychological complexity of many of the protagonists of nineteenth-century fiction led me to change my ideas about characterization; and as I read and taught works from a variety of periods and national literatures, I found that mimetic characterization is more widespread than generally thought and that Horney's theory works well with writers from many cultures. My selection of texts in part 2 of this book is designed to show, among other things, that a Horneyan approach is applicable to works from *Antigone* to *The End of the Road*.

Employing a Horneyan approach to character has led me to perceive that the great mimetic creations almost always subvert their aesthetic and thematic functions. As we have seen, E. M. Forster describes "round" characters as "creations inside a creation." They "arrive when evoked," he says, "but full of the spirit of mutiny. For they have these numerous parallels with people like ourselves, they try to live their own lives and are consequently engaged in treason against the main scheme of the book" (1927, 64). That seems exactly right to me. As wholes in themselves, imagined human beings can be understood in terms of their inner motivational systems, and when they are so understood, they appear to be inharmonious toward the larger whole of which they are a part. They are in conflict with their roles in the plot and with the author's rhetorical treatment of their experience.

When I first became aware of the incongruities between form and theme on the one hand and mimesis on the other, I felt that they were failures of art, but I have found them to be almost inescapable in realistic literature and have come to regard them as a concomitant of great characterization. Round characters create a dilemma for their creators. If they "are given complete freedom," says Forster, "they kick the book to pieces, and if they are kept too sternly in check, they revenge themselves by dying, and destroy it by intestinal decay" (1927, 64). The artists' character-creating impulses work against their efforts to shape and interpret experience, and they must choose between allowing their characters to come alive and kick the book to pieces or killing their characters by subordinating them to the main scheme of the work. The great realists choose fidelity to their psychological intuitions over the demands of theme and form, usually without knowing that they are doing so.

There are a number of reasons why realistic characterization is almost bound to subvert a work's formal and thematic structures. As Northrop Frye observes, there are "two poles of literature," the mimetic, with its "tendency to verisimilitude and accuracy of description," and the mythic, with its "tendency to tell a story . . . about characters who can do anything" (1957, 51). Western literature has moved steadily from the mythic to the mimetic pole, but the movement toward mimesis has affected only content; literary form is derived from mythic patterns. Thus even in the most realistic works, "we see the *same* structural principles" that we find in their pure form in myth (136). There is a built-in conflict between myth and mimesis: "the realistic writer soon finds that the requirements of literary form and plausible content always fight against each other" (Frye 1963, 36).

Literary form and realistic characterization involve incompatible canons of decorum and universes of discourse. Realistic characterization aims at verisimilitude; it follows the logic of motivation, of probability, of cause and effect. But, as Frye observes, when judged by the canons of probability, "every inherited convention of plot in literature is more or less mad" (1963, 36). Form and mimesis arouse different sets of expectations within the reader. Mimetic characters create an appetite for a consistently realistic world. We want their behavior to make sense and their fates to be commensurate with the laws of probability. Realism does not round out a shape, however, and mimetic characters are often set into manipulated plots that arrive at rather arbitrary conclusions. One of our cravings, either for realism or closure, tends to be frustrated at the end.

In many realistic works, the formal pattern is closed, despite the improbabilities this creates, and the characters remain true to life, subverting that closure. In Jane Austen's novels, for example, the happy endings demanded by the comic structure seem much less satisfactory when we become aware of her protagonists' unresolved psychological problems and the deficiencies in their relationships (see Paris 1978b). One of the most common formal patterns in fiction is the education plot, based on the archetype of the fortunate fall, in which the protagonists err because of their flaws, suffer because of their errors, and achieve wisdom and maturity because of their suffering. When we analyze the characters in Horneyan terms, we usually find that their growth is an illusion and that if they have undergone a great change it is from one destructive solution to another. The education plot and mimetic characterization are usually at odds with each other. This often gives rise to critical controversies, the sources of which can be understood through a Horneyan approach.

It is important to distinguish between the psychological portrait of a character and the rhetoric by which the character is surrounded. By rhetoric I mean what we normally think of as theme and a good deal more besides. The rhetoric consists of all the devices an author employs to influence readers' moral and intellectual responses to a character, their sympathy and antipathy, their emotional closeness or distance (see

Booth 1961). When we understand mimetic characters in motivational terms, we usually find ourselves responding in ways that are different from those that the rhetoric seeks to induce and taking issue with the author's interpretations and judgments.

The great psychological realists have the capacity to see far more than they can conceptualize. Their grasp of inner dynamics and of interpersonal relations is so subtle and profound that concrete representation is the only mode of discourse that can do it justice. When they comment on what they have represented or assign their characters illustrative roles, they are limited by the inadequacy of abstractions generally and of the conceptual systems available to them. Their interpretations of their characters are often wrong and almost always oversimple, in contrast to their intuitive grasp of the characters' psychology. The more we recover their intuitions and do justice to their mimetic achievement, the more disparities we perceive between their representation of human behavior and their interpretation of it.

Psychological analysis leads us to judgments that are in conflict with those of the author because it enables us to see the destructiveness of the solutions that have been glorified by the rhetoric. Writers tend to validate characters whose defensive strategies are similar to their own and to satirize those who have different solutions. The rhetoric of the work and sometimes even the action are designed to gain sympathy for the life-styles and values of the favored characters. Changes from a condemned defensive strategy to an approved one are celebrated as education and growth, although the new solution is often as unhealthy as the one that has been discarded. Insofar as the characters are mimetically portrayed, we are given an opportunity to understand them in our own terms and to arrive at our own judgments. When we arrive at different interpretations and judgments, the author's spell is broken, the characters are seen to rebel, and we experience a disparity between rhetoric and mimesis.

To be more precise, we experience a disparity between the author's interpretations and judgments and our own. The mimetic component of literature can never be definitively interpreted, by the author or anyone else. By virtue of its richness, it escapes all conceptual schemes, and conceptual schemes are constantly changing. I employ a Horneyan approach because it satisfies my appetite for clarity here and now. I am aware of the epistemological problems, but I choose to make as much sense of things as I can, according to my best lights, rather than to dwell on the uncertainty of knowledge. Although I shall not be constantly calling attention to the fact, let it be understood that I know that I am presenting my version of reality, which I hope will be of use to some others in the construction of theirs.

Once psychological analysis of mimetic characters led me to resist authorial rhetoric, I began to interpret the rhetoric itself from a psychological perspective and to see it (along with much else) as a reflection of the psyche of the implied author. When the rhetoric consistently glorifies characters who embrace a particular solution while criticizing those who have adopted others, it reveals the implied author's own defenses, repressions, and blind spots. In works where the rhetoric is inconsistent, such as *Vanity Fair* or *The Awakening,* it reveals the implied author's inner conflicts. It is possible to psychoanalyze not only the implied authors of individual texts but also the authorial personality that can be inferred from many or all of a writer's works. I have done this with Thomas Hardy (Paris 1976a), Jane Austen (Paris 1978b), and William Shakespeare (Paris 1991a). The next step would be psychobiography, in which texts could be used as a source of insight into the inner life of their creator. Karen Horney's theory has been employed in this way by Lawrance Thompson in his monumental biography of Robert Frost (1966, 1970, 1976), and many other writers would be illuminated by Horneyan analysis.

As I have said, a Horneyan approach has led me to see that there are almost bound to be disparities between rhetoric and mimesis. I have come to realize that these disparities can be either exacerbated or reduced by the choice of narrative technique. Omniscient narration tends to exacerbate them because although omniscient narrators present themselves as authoritative sources of interpretation and judgment, they are not. First person narration reduces the disparities because the interpretations and judgments belong to a character and therefore are clearly subjective. First person narration creates other problems, however, such as those of reliability. How do we know the degree to which the narrator's perspective is endorsed by the implied author? How do we know whether the narrator's interpretations and judgments are trustworthy? And, most perplexing, how do we know if the narrator's *accounts* of self and others are accurate? In omniscient narration, we believe what the narrator *shows* us about the characters, even if we are skeptical about what we are *told*. But in first person narration, can we believe the narrator's accounts of self and others, even when they are presented dramatically? The perceptions and recollections of an anxious, defensive, insecure narrator may well be distorted.

I have found that both omniscient and first person narrators require psychological analysis. The omniscient narrator's interpretations and judgments are a reflection of the character structure of the implied author, who has a vested interest in giving a certain rhetorical spin to the story. First person narrators are usually characters with profound psychological problems who are engaged in various forms of self-punishment and self-justification. Understanding their needs and defenses can go a long way toward helping us to detect their distortions and assess their reliability. As I have suggested, a Horneyan approach to narration often gives us a great deal of insight into the psyche of the implied author.

Some works, such as *Wuthering Heights,* employ multiple narrators. First person narrators often seem to be speaking for the author, but the use of multiple narrators tends to relativize the narration, especially when the narrators have differing perspectives. Techniques such as this that lead to the disappearance of the author can diminish or eliminate the disparity between rhetoric and mimesis, since the rhetorical stance of the implied author becomes difficult or impossible to define. The implied author may be recovered through psychological analysis, however, if we see the multiple narrators as expressing conflicting components of the author's psyche and consider the motives behind this choice of narrative technique.

The studies of individual works in the body of this book will illustrate most of the applications of a Horneyan approach that I have discussed, and I shall suggest others in the conclusion. In part 2, I shall examine characters and relationships in works by Ibsen, Barth, Chaucer, Shakespeare, and Sophocles. The texts I have selected display most of the defensive strategies Horney describes and show the forms they have taken in various periods and cultures. These works are bound together by a number of recurring motifs, such as living through others, morbid dependency, suicide or suicidal tendencies, and searching for glory, all of which Horney's theory illuminates. I shall not consider the works chronologically but in an order that facilitates comparison.

In part 3, I shall continue to examine characters, relationships, and recurring motifs, but I shall also consider the protagonists in relation to rhetoric and plot and shall explore the ways in which mimesis functions as a subversive force. I shall focus on six novels: *Great Expectations,*

Jane Eyre, The Mayor of Casterbridge, Madame Bovary, The Awakening, and *Wuthering Heights.* Some of these novels display the education pattern that I have described above, while others have a vindication pattern, based on the Cinderella archetype, in which a virtuous but persecuted protagonist finally achieves the status and approval he or she deserves. Both of these patterns are supported by the rhetoric and undermined by the mimesis, which (as I interpret it) shows the educated characters to be compulsive and immature and the vindicated characters to be less deserving of glorification than the author would have us believe.

I shall compare the novels in terms of these formal patterns and also in terms of their narrative techniques. *Great Expectations* and *Jane Eyre* have unreliable first person narrators, *The Mayor of Casterbridge* and *The Awakening* have problematic omniscient narration, and *Madame Bovary* has an omniscient narrator who is not as invisible as many, including the author, have claimed. *Wuthering Heights* avoids most of the difficulties found in the other novels by its use of multiple narrators. The problem here is to locate the implied author and to get some sense of where she stands in relation to the characters and their values. I believe that a Horneyan approach can help us to solve this problem.

In my discussions of literature, I shall use Horney's theory as a source of insight rather than as a grid upon which to lay texts. Although influenced by Horney, the readings I offer are mine. They are not the inevitable result of the application of her theory; indeed, I sometimes disagree with her analysis of a literary character.

I believe that psychoanalytic theory illuminates literature, that literature enriches theory, and that combining theory and literature enhances both our intellectual and our empathic understanding of human behavior. This process involves not just theory and literature but also our own personalities and our insight into ourselves. There is a triangular relationship between literature, theory, and the individual interpreter. Our literary and theoretical interests reflect our own character, the way in which we use theory depends on the degree to which it has become emotionally as well as intellectually meaningful to us, and what we are able to perceive depends on our personality, our theoretical perspective, and our access to our inner life.

I have found Horney's theory to be a powerful instrument of analysis, and I am eager to share this discovery with others so that their under-standing of literature and life might also be enriched by it. I know, however, that no one will entirely agree with my readings, just as I never entirely agree with anyone else's, and that the application of Horney's theory might yield different results in other hands.

For those unfamiliar with Horney or with my previous expositions of her ideas, I provide an account of her mature theory in the following chapter. Those who know her theory well may wish to proceed directly to chapter 3.

2

Horney's Mature Theory

Born in a suburb of Hamburg in 1885, Karen Horney (née Danielsen) attended medical school in Freiburg and completed her studies at the universities of Göttingen and Berlin. She married Oskar Horney in 1909, was in analysis with Karl Abraham in 1910–12, had three daughters between 1911 and 1916, received her M.D. in 1915, and became a founding member of the Berlin Psychoanalytic Institute in 1920. She separated from Oskar in 1926 and accepted Franz Alexander's invitation to become founding Associate Director of the Chicago Psychoanalytic Institute in 1932. In 1934, she moved to New York, where she joined the faculties of the New York Psychoanalytic Institute and the New School for Social Research. Because of her critique of orthodox theory, Horney was forced to resign from the New York Psychoanalytic in 1941, whereupon she founded the American Institute for Psychoanalysis, of which she was dean until her death in 1952.[1]

Horney's thought went through three stages. In essays she wrote between 1923 and 1935, she tried to revise Freud's phallocentric view of feminine psychology while remaining within the framework of classical theory. These essays were largely ignored during her lifetime, but since their republication in *Feminine Psychology* in 1967, Horney has been widely recognized as the first great psychoanalytic feminist.

Exposed to new ideas and to patients with different problems after she moved to the United States, Horney began to question libido theory, the universality of stages of psycho-sexual development, and many other basic tenets of psychoanalysis. In *The Neurotic Personality of Our Time* (1937) and *New Ways in Psychoanalysis* (1939), she replaced biology with culture and disturbed human relationships when explaining the origins of neuroses, and she shifted to a predominantly structural paradigm in which she sought to account for behavior in terms of its current function.

In her last two books, *Our Inner Conflicts* (1945) and *Neurosis and Human Growth* (1950), Horney described in a systematic way the interpersonal and intrapsychic strategies of defense that people develop in order to cope with the frustration of their psychological needs. While each stage of Horney's thought is important, I believe that her mature theory represents her most significant contribution. It provides explanations of human behavior in terms of currently existing constellations of defenses and inner conflicts that we can find nowhere else. It is this aspect of her thought that I have found to be of most value for the study of literature and that I shall describe here.

According to Horney, we are not simply tension-reducing or conditioned creatures but have present in us an "evolutionary constructive" force that urges us "to realize" our "given potentialities" (1950, 15). We each have a biologically based inner nature, a "real self," that it is our object in life to fulfill. Horney would have agreed with Abraham Maslow's account of the basic psychological needs that must be met if we are to actualize our potentialities. These include physiological survival needs, needs for a safe and stable environment, needs for love and belonging, needs for esteem, and the need for a calling or vocation in which we can use our native capacities in an intrinsically satisfying way (Maslow 1970).

Horney sees healthy human development as a process of self-realization and unhealthy development as a process of self-alienation. If our basic needs are relatively well met, we shall develop "the clarity and depth of [our] own feelings, thoughts, wishes, interests . . . .; the special capacities or gifts [we] may have; the faculty to express [ourselves], and to relate [ourselves] to others with [our] spontaneous feelings. All this will in time enable [us] to find [our] set of values and [our] aims in life" (1950, 17). If our psychological needs are seriously frustrated, we shall develop in a quite different way. Self-alienation begins as a defense against "basic anxiety," which is "a profound insecurity and vague apprehensiveness" (18) generated by feelings of isolation, helplessness, hostility, and fear. As a result of this anxiety, we "cannot simply like or dislike, trust or distrust, express [our] wishes or protest against those of another, but [we have] automatically to devise ways to cope with people and to manipulate them with minimum damage to [ourselves]" (Horney 1945, 219). We cope with others by developing the interpersonal strategies of defense that I shall examine next, and we seek to compensate for our feelings of worthlessness and inadequacy by an intrapsychic process of self-glorification. These strategies constitute our effort to fulfill our now insatiable needs for safety, love and belonging, and esteem. They are also designed to reduce our anxiety and to provide an outlet for our hostility.

According to Horney, we try to overcome feelings of being unsafe, unloved, and unvalued in a potentially hostile world by moving *toward, against,* or *away from* other people. These moves give rise to the neurotic solutions of compliance, aggression, and detachment. Whereas healthy people move flexibly in all three directions, compulsive people are "driven to comply, to fight, to be aloof, regardless of whether the move is appropriate in the particular instance" (Horney 1945, 202). Each solution involves its own constellation of behavior patterns and personality traits, its own conception of justice, and its own set of beliefs about human nature, human values, and the human condition. Each involves also a deal or bargain with fate in which obedience to the dictates of that solution is supposed to be rewarded (see Paris 1991a).

In each defensive move, one of the feelings involved in basic anxiety is overemphasized: helplessness in the compliant solution, hostility in the aggressive solution, and isolation in the detached solution. Since all of these feelings are bound to arise under adverse conditions, we make all three defensive moves compulsively and are torn by inner conflicts, since the moves are incompatible with each other. To gain some sense of wholeness, we emphasize one of the moves and become predominantly compliant, aggressive, or detached. Which move we emphasize will depend on a combination of temperamental and environmental factors.

The other trends continue to exist but operate unconsciously and manifest themselves in disguised and devious ways. The conflict between the moves has not been resolved but has gone underground. If the submerged trends are for some reason brought closer to the surface, we experience severe inner turmoil and may become paralyzed, unable to move in any direction at all. When impelled by a powerful influence or the collapse of our predominant solution, we may embrace one of our repressed defensive strategies. Although often experienced as conversion or education, this is merely the substitution of one solution for another.

Horney calls the major solutions compliance, aggression, and detachment in *Our Inner Conflicts* and self-effacement, expansiveness, and resignation in *Neurosis and Human Growth,* where she combines the interpersonal and the intrapsychic. The two sets of terms clearly overlap and can often be used interchangeably. In *Neurosis and Human Growth,* there are three distinct expansive solutions: the narcissistic, the perfectionistic, and the arrogant-vindictive. There are thus a total of five major solutions: compliance or self-effacement, narcissism, perfectionism, arrogant-vindictiveness, and detachment or resignation. The aggressive solution of *Our Inner Conflicts* corresponds closely to the arrogant-vindictive solution of *Neurosis and Human Growth,* and, as with the other pairs, I shall use whichever term seems most appropriate in a given context.

Self-effacing people often grew up under the shadow of someone—perhaps a preferred sibling, a beautiful mother, or an overbearing father—and sought love and protection through a self-subordinating devotion. They may have had a fighting spirit at one time, but the need for affection won out and they "became compliant, learned to like everybody and to lean with a helpless admiration" on those they "feared most" (Horney 1950, 222).

The strategies they adopted in childhood evolve into a constellation of character traits, behaviors, and beliefs in the adults. They try to overcome their anxiety by gaining affection and approval and by controlling others through their dependency on them. They need to feel part of something larger and more powerful than themselves, a need that often manifests itself as religious devotion, identification with a group or cause, or morbid dependency in a love relationship. Love appears "as the ticket to paradise, where all woe ends: no more feeling lost, guilty, and unworthy; no more responsibility for self; no more struggle with a harsh world" for which they feel "hopelessly unequipped" (Horney 1950, 240).

In order to gain the love, approval, and support they need, basically compliant people develop certain qualities, inhibitions, and ways of relating. They seek to attach other people by being good, loving, self-effacing, and weak. They become " 'unselfish,' self-sacrificing," "over-considerate," "overappreciative, overgrateful, generous" (Horney 1945, 51). Appeasing and conciliatory, they tend to blame themselves and feel guilty when they quarrel with another, experience disappointment, or are criticized. They are severely inhibited in their self-assertive and self-protective activities and have powerful taboos against "all that is presumptuous, selfish, and aggressive" (Horney 1950, 219). They glorify suffering and use it to manipulate others and justify themselves.

The compliant defense brings with it not only certain ways of feeling and behaving, but also a special set of values and beliefs. The values "lie in the direction of goodness, sympathy, love, generosity, unselfishness, humility" (Horney 1945, 54). These can be admirable values, but compliant people embrace them because they are necessary to their defense system rather than as genuine ideals. They must believe in turning the other cheek, and they must see the world as displaying a providential order in which people like themselves are rewarded. Their bargain is that if they are generous, loving people who shun pride and do not seek their own gain or glory, they will be well treated by fate and other people. If their bargain is not honored, they may despair of divine justice, they may conclude that they are at fault, or they may have recourse to belief in a higher justice that transcends human understanding. They need to believe not only in the fairness of the world order but also in the goodness of human nature, and here, too, they are liable to disappointment.

In compliant people, says Horney, there are "a variety of aggressive tendencies strongly repressed" (1945, 55). They are repressed because experiencing them or acting them out would clash violently with their need to be good and would radically endanger their whole strategy for gaining love, protection, and approval. It would undermine their bargain with fate. Compliant people's strategies increase their buried hostility since they invite abuse but also make them afraid of expressing anger or fighting back.

Because of their need for surrender and a safe outlet for their aggression, compliant people are often attracted to their opposite, masterful expansive people whose "egotism, ambition, callousness, unscrupulousness" and "wielding of power" they may consciously condemn but secretly admire (Horney 1945, 54). Merging with such people allows them "to participate vicariously in the mastery of life without having to own it" to themselves (Horney 1950, 244). This kind of relationship usually develops into a morbid dependency that exacerbates compliant people's difficulties. When the love relationship fails them, they will be terribly disillusioned and may feel that they did not find the right person, that something is wrong with them, or that nothing is worth having.

There are numerous predominantly compliant or self-effacing characters in literature who have been analyzed in Horneyan terms. Starting with Shakespeare, these include Helena in *A Midsummer Night's Dream*, Viola in *Twelfth Night*, Hamlet, Desdemona, Duke Vincentio in *Measure for Measure*, Timon of Athens, Prospero (Paris 1991a), the poet in

Shakespeare's sonnets (Lewis 1985; Paris 1991a), and Antony in *Antony and Cleopatra* (Paris 1991b). In later writers, there is Fanny Price in Jane Austen's *Mansfield Park* (Paris 1978b), Thackeray's Dobbin and Amelia (Paris 1974), Esther Summerson in Dickens's *Bleak House* (Eldredge 1986), Maggie Tulliver in George Eliot's *The Mill on the Floss* (Paris 1974), Tess in Hardy's *Tess of the d'Urbervilles* (Paris 1976a), Conrad's Charley Marlow (Paris 1974, 1993b), the priest in Graham Greene's *The Power and the Glory* (Straub 1986), Saul Bellow's Moses Herzog (Paris 1976b), Alice Mellings in Doris Lessing's *The Good Terrorist* (Eldredge 1989), and George Bailey in Frank Capra's *It's a Wonderful Life* (Gordon 1994). As is true for characters exemplifying each of the major solutions, most have inner conflicts and manifest other trends. There are many more characters displaying each solution than I shall cite here, since I am mentioning only prime examples who have already been discussed in print.

People in whom expansive tendencies predominate have goals, traits, and values that are the opposite of those of self-effacing people. What appeals to them most is not love, but mastery. They abhor helplessness, are ashamed of suffering, and need to achieve success, prestige, or recognition. There are three expansive types: the narcissistic, the perfectionistic, and the aggressive or arrogant-vindictive.

The arrogant-vindictive solution is in many ways the opposite of the self-effacing one. Arrogant-vindictive people usually have had a particularly harsh childhood in which they have encountered "sheer brutality, humiliations, derision, neglect, and flagrant hypocrisy." Like the survivors of concentration camps, they go through "a hardening process in order to survive." As children, they "may make some pathetic and unsuccessful attempts to win sympathy, interest, or affection but finally choke off all tender needs." Since affection is unattainable, they scorn it or conclude that it does not exist. Thus they have no incentive to please and can give free rein to their bitter resentment. The desire for love is replaced by ambition and a drive toward "vindictive triumph." They live for the "day of reckoning" when they will prove their superiority, put their enemies to shame, and show how they have been wronged. They dream of becoming the great hero, "the persecutor, the leader, the scientist attaining immortal fame" (Horney 1950, 202–3).

As adults, arrogant-vindictive people are ferociously competitive: they "cannot tolerate anybody who knows or achieves more . . . , wields more power, or in any way questions [their] superiority" (Horney 1950,

198). They have to drag their rivals down or defeat them. They retaliate when injured by hurting their enemies more than they have hurt them. They are ruthless and cynical in their relations with others, seeking to exploit and outsmart everyone. They trust no one and are out to get others before others get them. They avoid emotional involvement and dependency and use the relations of friendship and marriage to enhance their position. They want to be hard and tough and regard all manifestations of feeling as sloppy sentimentality.

Whereas self-effacing people tend to be masochistic, arrogant-vindictive people are often sadistic. They want to enslave others, to play on their emotions, to frustrate, disparage, and humiliate them. Horney does not explain this behavior in sexual terms but sees it partly as their way of retaliating for injuries and partly as a response to their sense of the emptiness and futility of their lives. They develop a pervasive envy of everyone who seems to possess something they lack, whether it be wealth and prestige, physical attractiveness, or love and devotion. The happiness of others "irritates" them. If they "cannot be happy," "why should [others] be so?" The arrogant-vindictive person must "trample on the joy of others" because if they "are as defeated and degraded as he, his own misery is tempered in that he no longer feels himself the only one afflicted" (Horney 1945, 201–2).

Aggressive people regard the world as "an arena where, in the Darwinian sense, only the fittest survive and the strong annihilate the weak." A "callous pursuit of self-interest is the paramount law" (Horney 1945, 64). There are no values inherent in the order of things except that might makes right. Considerateness, compassion, loyalty, unselfishness are all scorned as signs of weakness, "as restraints on the path to a sinister glory" (Horney 1950, 203). Those who value such qualities are fools just asking to be exploited. Aggressive people are sometimes drawn toward compliant types, however, because of their submissiveness and malleability—and also because of their own repressed self-effacing tendencies.

Just as self-effacing people must repress their aggressive impulses in order to make their solution work, so for arrogant-vindictive people any "attitude of compliance would be incompatible" with their "whole structure of living" and would "shake its foundations." They need to fight their softer feelings: "Nietzsche gives us a good illustration of these dynamics when he has his superman see any form of sympathy as a sort of fifth column, an enemy operating from within" (Horney 1945, 69–

70). They fear the emergence of compliant trends because this would make them vulnerable in an evil world, would cause them to feel like fools, and would threaten their bargain, which is essentially with themselves. They do not count on the world to give them anything but are convinced they can reach their ambitious goals if they remain true to their vision of life as a battle and do not allow themselves to be seduced by the traditional morality or their own compliant tendencies. If their predominant solution collapses, powerful self-effacing trends may emerge.

Predominantly arrogant-vindictive characters who have been discussed in Horneyan terms include Iago (Rosenberg 1961, Rabkin and Brown 1973, Paris 1991a), Edmund, Goneril, Regan, Lady Macbeth, and Macbeth after the murder (Paris 1991a), and Richard III and Cassius (Paris 1991b) in Shakespeare; Julien Sorel in Stendhal's *The Red and the Black* (Paris 1974); Becky Sharp in *Vanity Fair* (Paris 1974); Count Guido in Browning's *The Ring and the Book* (Lewis 1986); Raskolnikov in Dostoevsky's *Crime and Punishment* (Paris 1978c, 1991c, 1994b); and Joe Christmas in Faulkner's *Light in August* (Haselswerdt 1986).

Predominantly narcissistic people also seek mastery, but their childhoods are quite different from those of arrogant-vindictive people, as are their strategies of defense. Whereas arrogant-vindictive people have usually been subject to abuse, narcissistic people were often "favored and admired" children who were "gifted beyond average" and "early and easily won distinctions" (Horney 1950, 194). The goal of aggressive people is to prove their superiority to their detractors through achievement; the goal of narcissistic people is to maintain the sense of being exceptional that they imbibed in childhood. "Healthy friction with the wishes and will of others" (18), which Horney regards as an essential condition of sound development, and the need to earn a sense of worth through achievement, are missing in their early experience. They develop an unrealistic sense of their powers and importance, and this creates anxiety of a different kind from that experienced by those toward whom the world has been begrudging. They are afraid of other people whose genuine accomplishments or refusal to indulge them call their inflated conception of themselves into question. Note that Horney does not posit a primary narcissism, as do many other theorists, but rather sees narcissism, like aggression, as a reaction to an unhealthy environment.

As adults, narcissists seek to master life "by self-admiration and the exercise of charm" (Horney 1950, 212). They have an "unquestioned belief in [their] greatness and uniqueness" that gives them a "buoyancy and perennial youthfulness." The narcissist "has (consciously) no doubts; he *is* the anointed, the man of destiny, the great giver, the benefactor of mankind." He feels that there is "no one he cannot win" and is adept at charming people "with a scintillating display of feeling, with flattery, with favors and help—in anticipation of admiration or in return for devotion received." His insecurity is manifested by the fact that he "may speak incessantly of his exploits or of his wonderful qualities and needs endless confirmation of his estimate of himself in the form of admiration and devotion" (194).

Like arrogant-vindictive people, narcissists use people and do "not seem to mind breaking promises, being unfaithful, incurring debts, defrauding" (Horney 1950, 195). But they are not "scheming exploiters"; rather, they feel that their needs are "so important that they entitle [them] to every privilege." They expect unconditional love from others, no matter how much they "trespass on their rights."

Because their imagination is captivated by "the glory of the dramatic," narcissists resent "the humble tasks of daily living" as "humiliating." They have fantasies of "quick and glamorous achievement," avoid consistent effort and attention to detail, and quickly lose interest as a face-saving device if they encounter obstacles (Horney 1950, 313–15). When disillusioned they may give up their ambitions, telling themselves that they would have accomplished something great if they had decided really to try.

On the surface narcissistic people are "rather optimistic" and "turn outward toward life," but "there are undercurrents of despondency and pessimism" (Horney 1950, 196). They see the world as a fostering parent, expect continual good luck, and demand the fulfillment of their wishes by fate and other people. Their bargain is that if they hold onto their dreams and their exaggerated claims for themselves, life is bound to give them what they want. Since life can never match their expectations, they feel, in their weaker moments, that it is full of tragic contradictions.

Predominantly narcissistic characters who have been discussed in Horneyan terms include King Lear (Paris 1991a) and Richard II (Paris 1991b) in Shakespeare, Jane Austen's Emma Woodhouse (Paris 1978b), Mathilde de la Mole in *The Red and the Black* (Paris 1974), and Conrad's Lord Jim (Paris 1974).

In *Neurosis and Human Growth,* Horney gives the least amount of attention to the perfectionistic solution, but she discusses it also in *New Ways in Psychoanalysis,* where she argues that an adherence to "rigid and high moral standards" and a "drive toward rectitude and perfection" (1939, 207) are not products of an instinctually based superego but special needs of individuals who have had a certain kind of childhood. They were made to feel worthless or guilty if they did not live up to their parents' demands, but by conforming to expectations they could put themselves beyond reproach and gain a feeling of superiority. Perfectionists do not revel in a sense of being wonderful, like narcissists, but derive a sadistic satisfaction from their rectitude because it shows others "how stupid, worthless, and contemptible they are." They want to "strike others with righteous indignation from the height of their infallibility," to "inflict the same injury" on others that their parents inflicted on them (218–21).

As adults, perfectionists feel superior because of their "high standards, moral and intellectual, and on this basis look down on others" (Horney 1950, 196). They easily feel guilty but regard this as a virtue because it proves their "high sensitivity toward moral requirements." If the analyst points out that their self-recriminations are exaggerated, they may feel that the analyst is inferior and "cannot possibly understand" them (Horney 1939, 220). Unlike narcissists, perfectionists work hard and pay obsessive attention to details. What really matters is not the details themselves "but the flawless excellence of the whole conduct of life" (Horney 1950, 196). Only this will reduce their anxiety, make them feel superior to others, and give them a sense of controlling their own destiny.

Since they are pursuing the impossible, perfectionists must find ways to defend themselves against failure and its consequences. One defense is to equate "standards and actualities—*knowing* about moral values and *being* a good person" (Horney 1950, 196). While they deceive themselves in this way, they may insist that others live up to their standards and "despise them for failing to do so. [Their] own self-condemnation is thus externalized." The imposition of their standards on others leads to admiration for a select few and a critical or condescending attitude toward most people.

The bargain of the perfectionist is based on a legalistic conception of the world order: "Because he is fair, just, dutiful, he is entitled to fair treatment by others and by life in general. This conviction of an infallible justice operating in life gives him a feeling of mastery" (Horney 1950, 197). Success is not a matter of luck, of being the favorite of fortune, as it is for the narcissist, or of superior shrewdness, talent, and ruthlessness, as it is for the arrogant-vindictive person; rather, it is a proof of virtue. Ill fortune may mean that he is not really virtuous or that the world is unjust. Either conclusion shakes him "to the foundations of his psychic existence," invalidating "his whole accounting system" and conjuring up "the ghastly prospect of helplessness." If he recognizes "an error or failure of his own making," self-effacing trends and self-hate may come to the fore.

Predominantly perfectionistic characters who have been analyzed in Horneyan terms include Brutus and Coriolanus (Paris 1991b), Othello, Cordelia, and Macbeth before the murder (Paris 1991a) in Shakespeare; Samuel Richardson's Clarissa Harlowe (Eldredge 1982); and three characters in Jane Austen—Elinor Dashwood in *Sense and Sensibility,* Knightly in *Emma,* and Anne Elliot in *Persuasion* (Paris 1978b).

People who are predominantly resigned or detached usually have had a childhood in which there were "cramping influences" against which they "could not rebel openly, either because they were too strong or too intangible." Demands were made for love, understanding, conformity, or emotional support that threatened to "engulf" them. They felt that they had to submit to these demands in order to obtain love, but they also wanted to rebel against "the bonds put around" them. They handled this situation by withdrawal. Putting "an emotional distance between [themselves] and others," they no longer wanted affection nor did they want to fight. This helped them preserve their individuality, but they had to put a check on their feelings and "retract all those wishes and needs which would require others for their fulfillment." While retracting their wishes made them more independent, it also sapped their "vitality and maim[ed their] sense of direction" (Horney 1950, 275–76).

Whereas self-effacing people crave love and expansive people seek mastery, detached people worship freedom and independence. They want to be left alone, to have nothing expected of them, to be subject to no restrictions. They have a *"hypersensitivity to influence, pressure, coercion or ties of any kind"* (Horney 1950, 266, emphasis in original). They may react with anxiety to physical pressure from clothing, closed spaces, long-term obligations, the inexorability of time, the laws of cause and effect, traditional values and rules of behavior, or, indeed, anything that interferes with their absolute freedom. They want to do what they please when they please, but since they are alienated from their spontaneous desires, their freedom is rather empty. It is a *freedom from* what they feel as coercion rather than a *freedom to* fulfill themselves. Their desire for freedom may take the form of a craving for serenity, which means for them "simply the absence of all troubles, irritations, or upsets" (263).

Detached people disdain the pursuit of worldly success and have a profound aversion to effort. They have a strong need for superiority and usually look on their fellows with condescension, but they realize their ambition in imagination rather than through actual accomplishments. They make themselves invulnerable by being self-sufficient. This involves not only living in imagination but also restricting their desires. In order to avoid being dependent on the environment, they try to subdue their inner cravings and to be content with little. They cultivate a "don't care" attitude and protect themselves against frustration by believing that "nothing matters."

Detached people withdraw from both other people and themselves. They seek privacy, shroud themselves "in a veil of secrecy," and, in their personal relations, draw around themselves "a kind of magic circle which no one may penetrate" (Horney 1945, 75–76). They withdraw from themselves by suppressing or denying their feelings. Their resignation from active living gives them an "onlooker" attitude that often enables them to be excellent observers both of others and of their own inner processes. Their insight divorced from feeling, they look at themselves "with a kind of objective interest, as one would look at a work of art" (74).

Their withdrawal from themselves is in part an effort to resolve their inner conflicts. In this solution, says Horney, the subordinated trends are not deeply repressed; they are visible to the trained observer and are rather easily brought to awareness. Because detached people are likely to entertain the attitudes of the subordinated solutions, their values are highly contradictory. They have a "permanent high evaluation" of what they regard "as freedom and independence" and cultivate individuality, self-reliance, and an indifference to fate. But they may at one time "express an extreme appreciation for human goodness, sympathy, generosity, self-effacing sacrifice, and at another time swing to a complete jungle philosophy of callous self-interest" (Horney 1945, 94).

In order to reduce their vulnerability, detached people believe, "consciously or unconsciously, that is it *better* not to wish or expect anything.

Sometimes this goes with a conscious pessimistic outlook on life, a sense of its being futile anyhow and of nothing being sufficiently desirable to make an effort for it" (Horney 1950, 263, emphasis in original). They do not usually rail against life, however, but accept their fate with ironic humor or stoical dignity. They try to escape suffering by being independent of external forces, by feeling that nothing matters, and by concerning themselves only with things within their power. Their bargain is that if they ask nothing of others, they will not be bothered; if they try for nothing, they will not fail; and if they expect little of life, they will not be disappointed.

Predominantly detached characters who have been analyzed in Horneyan terms include Horatio in *Hamlet,* Thersites in *Troilus and Cressida,* and Apemantus in *Timon of Athens* (Paris 1991a); Mr. Bennet in Jane Austen's *Pride and Prejudice* (Paris 1978b); Dostoevsky's underground man (Paris 1974); and Quentin Compson in Faulkner's *Absalom, Absalom!* and *The Sound and the Fury* (Butery 1989). The detached solution is particularly prevalent in twentieth-century literature, and much work remains to be done with characters who manifest it.

Horney describes childhood experiences typical for those who have adopted each of the major solutions, but most children have a combination of these experiences and develop a combination of defenses. Conflicts between the solutions cause oscillations, inconsistencies, and self-hate. One of the most significant features of Horney's theory is that it permits us to make sense of contradictory attitudes, behaviors, and beliefs by seeing them as part of structure of inner conflicts. Horneyan theory has a dynamic quality: solutions combine, conflict, become stronger or weaker, need to be defended, generate vicious circles, and are replaced by others when they collapse. This quality of the theory is difficult to convey in exposition, but it will become evident in our discussions of literature.

While interpersonal difficulties are creating the movements toward, against, and away from people, and the conflicts between these moves, concomitant intrapsychic problems are producing their own defensive strategies. To compensate for feelings of self-hate and inadequacy, individuals create, with the aid of their imagination, an "idealized image" of themselves that they endow with "unlimited powers" and "exalted faculties" (Horney 1950, 22). The idealized image, in turn, generates neurotic claims, tyrannical "shoulds," and neurotic pride, all of which ultimately increase self-hate.

The content of the idealized image is much influenced by our predominant solution and the attributes it exalts. The idealized image of self-effacing people "is a composite of 'lovable' qualities, such as unselfishness, goodness, generosity, humility, saintliness, nobility, sympathy" (Horney 1950, 222). Arrogant-vindictive people see themselves as masters of all situations who are smarter, tougher, more realistic than other people. Narcissists see themselves as prophets and benefactors of mankind who have unlimited energies and are capable of magnificent achievements, effortlessly attained. Perfectionists regard themselves as models of rectitude who achieve a flawless excellence in the whole conduct of life. The idealized image of detached or resigned people "is a composite of self-sufficiency, independence, self-contained serenity, freedom from desires" and "stoicism" (277). In each solution, the idealized image may be modeled in whole or in part on a religious or cultural ideal or an example from history or personal experience.

The creation of the idealized image leads to additional inner conflict. The conflict between the interpersonal strategies is imported into the idealized image, which reflects not only the predominant solution but also the subordinated ones. Since each solution glorifies a different set of traits, the idealized image has contradictory aspects, all of which demand to be actualized. A conflict also arises between pride and self-hate. Individuals can feel worthwhile only if they live up to their idealized image, deeming everything that falls short to be worthless. As a result, they develop a "despised image" of themselves that becomes the focus of self-contempt. A great many people shuttle, says Horney, "between a feeling of arrogant omnipotence and of being the scum of the earth" (1950, 188).

The idealized image evolves into an idealized self and the despised image into a despised self, as people become convinced they really are the grandiose or awful beings they have imagined themselves to be. Horney posits four selves competing with each other: the real self, the idealized self, the despised self, and the actual self. The real (or possible) self is based on a set of biological predispositions that require favorable conditions for their actualization. The idealized (or impossible) self is an imaginary creation that is unrealistically grandiose, and the despised self is unrealistically worthless and weak. The actual self is what a person really is—a mixture of strengths and weaknesses, health and neurosis.

The distance between the actual and real selves will vary, depending on the degree of self-alienation. It will be small in self-actualizing people.

With the formation of the idealized image, the individual embarks upon a "search for glory," as "the energies driving toward self-realization are shifted to the aim of actualizing the idealized self" (Horney 1950, 24). What is considered to be glorious depends on the major solution. Horney does not see the search for glory, the quest of the absolute, the need to be godlike as essential ingredients of human nature but as reactions to the frustration of basic needs. It is when people feel themselves to be nothing that they must claim to be all.

For many people the search for glory is the most important thing in their lives. It gives them the sense of meaning and feeling of superiority they so desperately crave. They may experience depression or despair if they feel that their search for glory will never succeed. They fiercely resist all encroachments on their illusory grandeur and may prefer death to the shattering of their dreams. The search for glory is a "private religion" the rules of which are determined by the individual's neurosis, but glory systems are also a prominent feature of every culture. They include organized religions, various forms of group identification, wars and military service, and competitions, honors, and hierarchical arrangements of all kinds.

The creation of the idealized image produces not only the search for glory but the whole structure of phenomena that Horney calls the pride system. We take an intense pride in the attributes of our idealized selves and on the basis of this pride make "neurotic claims" on others. At the same time, we feel that we *should* perform in a way that is commensurate with our grandiose conception of ourselves. If the world fails to honor our claims or we fail to live up to our shoulds, we become our despised selves and experience agonizing self-hate. As with our idealized image, the specific nature of our pride, shoulds, claims, and self-hate will be influenced by our predominant solution and by the conflicts between it and subordinate trends.

Our need to actualize our idealized image leads us to impose stringent demands and taboos upon ourselves, a phenomenon Horney calls "the tyranny of the should." The function of the shoulds is "to make oneself over into one's idealized self: *the premise on which they operate is that nothing should be, or is, impossible for oneself*" (Horney 1950, 68). The shoulds are characterized by their coerciveness, disregard for feasibility, imperviousness to psychic laws, and reliance on willpower for fulfillment

and imagination for denial of failure. There is a good deal of externalization connected with the shoulds. We often feel our shoulds as the expectations of others, our self-hate as their rejection, and our self-criticism as
their unfair judgment. We expect others to live up to our shoulds and
displace onto them our rage at our own failure to do so. The shoulds are
a defense against self-loathing, but, like other defenses, they aggravate
the condition they are employed to cure. Not only do they increase self-
alienation, but they also intensify self-hate, since the penalty for failure
is a feeling of worthlessness and self-contempt. This is why the shoulds
have such a tyrannical power. "It is the threat of a punitive self-hate"
that "truly makes them a regime of terror" (85).

The shoulds are impossible to live up to because they are so unrealistic: we should love everyone; we should never make a mistake; we
should always triumph; we should never need other people, and so forth.
The shoulds always demand the repression of needs, feelings, and wishes
that cannot be repressed. The shoulds are also impossible to live up to
because they reflect our inner conflicts and are at war with each other.
They are generated by the idealized image, but the idealized image is a
composite of various solutions, each of which produces its own set of
demands. As a result, we are often caught in a crossfire of conflicting
shoulds. As we try to obey contradictory inner dictates, we are bound to
hate ourselves whatever we do, and even if, paralyzed, we do nothing at
all. The crossfire of conflicting shoulds is a powerful concept that explains much inertia and inconsistency.

Another product of the idealized image is "neurotic claims," which
are our demands to be treated in accordance with our grandiose conception of ourselves. Claims also involve the expectation that we will get
what we need in order to make our solution work. Generally speaking,
neurotic claims are unrealistic, egocentric, and vindictive. They demand
results without effort, are based on an assumption of specialness or
superiority, deny the world of cause and effect, and are "pervaded by
expectations of magic" (Horney 1950, 62).

Neurotic claims do not achieve their objective, which is confirmation
of our idealized image and our predominant solution. If the world fails
to honor our claims, as is often the case, it is saying that we are not who
we think we are and that our strategy for dealing with life is ineffective.
We may react with rage, despair, and self-hate, but we may also reaffirm
our claims, which are extremely tenacious, since we depend on them for
self-aggrandizement and a sense of control over our lives.

The claims are what we feel entitled to according to the conception of justice that is part of our predominant solution. Although specific expectations will vary from solution to solution, the essential conception of justice remains the same. In a just world, our claims will be honored; if they are not, life is absurd. Since our solution will collapse if the universe is not organized as it is supposed to be, we have a powerful vested interest in preserving our belief system in face of contrary evidence. If we become convinced that the world has belied our expectations, we may go to pieces or switch to another solution with a different conception of the universe.

An important part of the justice system in each solution is what Horney calls a "deal" and what I have called a bargain with fate, the specifics of which will vary with the solution, as I have shown. The bargain is that if we obey our shoulds, our claims will be honored, our solution will work, and our idealized conception of ourselves will be confirmed. I have made a detailed study of this phenomenon in *Bargains with Fate: Psychological Crises and Conflicts in Shakespeare and His Plays* (1991), where I argue that the leading characters of the major tragedies are thrown into a state of psychological crisis by precipitating events that challenge their bargains with fate.

It is important to recognize that the bargain with fate involves not only an expectation that our claims will be honored if we live up to our shoulds, but also a conviction that we will be punished if we violate them. The justice system of our solution can turn against us, as it does against Macbeth. In some cases, conflicting solutions generate conflicting bargains, ethical codes, and conceptions of justice.

Neurotic pride, says Horney, is "the climax and consolidation of the process initiated with the search for glory" (1950, 109). It substitutes for realistic self-confidence and self-esteem a pride in the attributes of the idealized self, in the successful assertion of claims, and in the "loftiness and severity" of the inner dictates. Since pride turns the compulsive behaviors of the various solutions into virtues, anything can be a source of pride. There is commonly a great pride in the mental processes of imagination, reason, and will, since "the infinite powers" we ascribe to ourselves "are, after all, powers of the mind." The mind must work incessantly at "maintaining the private fictitious world through rationalizations, justifications, externalizations, reconciling irreconcilables—in short, through finding ways to make things appear different from what they are" (91–94).

Pride is a vitally important defense, but since it is based on illusion and self-deception, it increases our vulnerability. Threats to pride produce anxiety and hostility; its collapse results in self-contempt. We are especially subject to feelings of shame (when we violate our own pride) and humiliation (when our pride is violated by others). We react to shame with self-hate and to humiliation with a vindictive hostility ranging "from irritability, to anger, to a blind murderous rage" (Horney 1950, 99).

There are various devices for restoring pride. These include retaliation, which reestablishes the superiority of the humiliated person, and loss of interest in that which is threatening or damaging. They also include various forms of distortion, such as forgetting humiliating episodes, denying responsibility, blaming others, and embellishing. Sometimes "humor is used to take the sting out of an otherwise unbearable shame" (Horney 1950, 106). We also protect our pride by avoidances, such as not trying, restricting wishes and activities, and refusing to become involved in any serious pursuit or relationship.

Self-hate is usually the end product of the intrapsychic strategies of defense, each of which tends to magnify the individual's feelings of inadequacy and failure. Self-hate is essentially the rage the idealized self feels toward the self we actually are for not being what it "should" be. Self-hate is in large part an unconscious process, since it is usually too painful to be confronted directly. The chief defense against awareness is externalization, which takes active and passive forms. Active externalization "is an attempt to direct self-hate outward, against life, fate, institutions or people." In passive externalization "the hate remains directed against the self but is perceived or experienced as coming from the outside." When self-hate is conscious, there is often a pride taken in it that serves to maintain self-glorification: "The very condemnation of imperfection confirms the godlike standards with which the person identifies himself" (Horney 1950, 114–15). Horney sees self-hate as "perhaps the greatest tragedy of the human mind. Man in reaching out for the Infinite and Absolute also starts destroying himself. When he makes a pact with the devil, who promises him glory, he has to go to hell—to the hell within himself" (154).

As we turn to look at literature from a Horneyan perspective, it is important to keep in mind that we shall find neither characters in books nor people in life who correspond exactly to Horney's descriptions. Her types are composites, drawn from her experience with people who share certain dominant trends but who differ from each other in many important ways. The Horneyan typology helps us to see how certain traits and behaviors are related to each other within a psychological system, but once we have identified a person's predominant solution, we must not assume the presence of all the characteristics Horney ascribes to that solution. It is also important to remember, as Horney observes, that "although people tending toward the same main solution have characteristic similarities, they may differ widely with regard to [their] level of human qualities, gifts, or achievements" (1950, 191). The situation is further complicated by the fact that people experience inner conflicts and display behaviors, traits, and beliefs that belong to more than one solution. Quoting William James to the effect that " 'most cases are mixed cases' " and that " 'we should not treat our classifications with too much respect,' " Horney concludes: "It would be more nearly correct to speak of directions of development than of types" (1950, 191).

If we forget these qualifications, we are liable to put people into categories instead of grasping their individuality, and our analysis will be little more than a reductive labeling. Horney allows for infinite variations and combinations of defenses and recognizes other components of the personality as well. In a brief description, her theory seems highly schematic, but when properly employed it is quite flexible.

PART II

Characters and Relationships

3

A *Doll's House* and *Hedda Gabler*

The first person to look at literature from a Horneyan perspective was Karen Horney herself. She taught courses at the New School for Social Research that were focused on literary works, and she frequently used literature for illustrative purposes in her writings. An admirer of Henrik Ibsen, she cited his works more often than those of any other author. This is not surprising, for Ibsen is the greatest psychological dramatist next to Shakespeare, and there is a remarkable congruence between his plays and her theory. Many of Ibsen's characters seem to have stepped from the pages of *Our Inner Conflicts* and *Neurosis and Human Growth*. I could easily devote a book to a Horneyan study of Ibsen, but I shall confine myself here to two of his most famous and enigmatic characters, Nora Helmer and Hedda Gabler. At the center of Ibsen's plays, there is often a relationship, the psychodynamics of which are portrayed with remarkable subtlety. I shall analyze Nora's relationship with her husband, Torvald, and Hedda's with Ejlert Lövborg.

Although Horney initially devoted herself to the study of feminine psychology, she stopped writing on this topic in the mid-1930s and developed a theory that she regarded as gender-neutral. She did not see any defensive strategies as essentially masculine or feminine but felt that all were employed by members of both sexes. The greater incidence of self-effacement in women and aggression in men is a product, she felt, of culture. Horney's position is borne out by the study of literature. Self-effacement is more common in female characters and aggression in males, but there are many aggressive women and self-effacing men.

One of the major objectives of women's liberation movements has been to free women from the cultural demand for self-effacement and to establish their right to full human development. At the thematic level, this seems to be what *A Doll's House* is about. In the first two acts of the play, Nora Helmer is a striking example of feminine compliance, while in the last act she rebels against her doll-like role and asserts her claim to full humanity.

Indeed, the most difficult thing to understand about Nora is the speed of her transformation from a submissive, self-sacrificing woman who lives only for love and family into a self-assertive person who rejects all responsibility to her husband and children in the name of her duty to herself. At the end Nora seems so different from her earlier self that some have felt that Ibsen sacrificed consistent characterization to his thematic concerns. Nora learns that she has been unjustly treated by a male-dominated society and that she must rebel against the conventional view of her nature if she is to realize herself. "You and Father have done me a great wrong," she tells Torvald. "You've prevented me from becoming a real person" (act 3).[1] She decides that she must leave home if she is to have a chance of discovering what she really thinks and who she really is. Nora's speeches are stirring, but has Ibsen put words into her mouth that are inconsistent with her previously drawn character? Is her transformation psychologically plausible? How, exactly, does her disillusionment with Torvald produce her amazing turnabout? Can a woman who intended to drown herself near the beginning of the last act become as strong a person as Nora seems to be at the end?

I believe that Nora is a well-drawn mimetic character whose transformation is intelligible if we understand her defensive strategies and the nature of her relationship with her husband. She never becomes a mere mouthpiece but remains an inwardly motivated character, full of inconsistencies and blind spots that are psychologically realistic. Her transformation is plausible when we recognize that with the collapse of her predominant solution, her previously repressed tendencies emerge.

Nora experiences genuine growth at the end of the play, but she is not as clear-headed as she thinks she is. She fails to see, for example, that she has also participated in the creation of her destructive relationship with her husband and that Torvald has been no more of a real person for her than she has been for him. She informs Torvald that she must leave home because he has not treated her as a real person, but she also says that she stopped loving him when the wonderful thing did not happen. If Torvald had behaved heroically on the receipt of Krogstad's letter, Nora would have been delighted, but such behavior on his part would not have shown respect for her as a person. Nora seems unaware of this, and of much else besides. She says that she has never been more sure of herself, but she is full of self-doubt, and her flight from Torvald and her children is compulsive. Turning against her failed self-effacing solution, Nora is now driven by defensive needs for aggression and withdrawal, as well as by her newly awakened desire for self-actualization.

Nora initially develops into a predominantly self-effacing person not only because of the attitudes toward women in her society but also because of the particular conditions of her childhood. She has no mother, and her father is a domineering man who wants her to remain a "doll-child" and who would be "displeased" if she expressed any ideas contrary to his own (act 3). Nora cannot afford to rebel; she is strongly attached to her father and does her utmost to please him. She retains the childlike playfulness and docility that he finds so charming and either adopts his opinions or remains silent. It seems likely that the absence of a mother increases her dependence on her father; she has no one else to turn to for love and protection. Moreover, she has no model of mature womanhood to emulate, and she acquires few skills on which to base her self-esteem. When she becomes a mother herself, she depends on her old nurse, Anne-Marie, to care for her children, whom she treats as playmates. Nora's father rewards her compliance with fondness and indulgence, and she grows up feeling that the way to gain safety, love, and approval is to please a powerful male.

In Torvald Helmer, Nora finds a man who is much like her father, and she relates to him in a similar way. She is content to be his "lark," his "squirrel," his "doll-baby," his "little featherbrain," his "crazy little thing" (act 1). Nora does not feel demeaned by these epithets, as we feel her to be, although at an unconscious level they are destructive. She lives, as she says, "by performing tricks" for Torvald, and she is proud of her ability to keep him charmed. For Torvald there is "something very endearing about a woman's helplessness" (act 3), and Nora is at great pains to conceal the fact that she has saved his life and almost paid off a large loan by her own efforts: "Torvald could never bear to think of owing anything to me! It would hurt his self-respect—wound his pride. It would ruin everything between us." It is important to Nora to preserve Torvald's feeling of mastery, for this is the price of his love and protection. She is keeping her heroic effort "in reserve," however, for the day when she is "no longer so pretty and attractive . . . when it no longer amuses him to see [her] dance and dress-up and act for him" (act 1).

In the meantime, it gives her "something to be proud and happy about." She is proud partly because "working like that and earning money" has given her a feeling of strength, has made her "feel almost like a man" (act 1), but mostly because it fulfills her need to be good and loving. Like Mrs. Linde, and most women in her culture, Nora glorifies sacrificing self for others, and she reveals her secret only when Mrs. Linde makes her feel inferior by contrasting Nora's easy life with her own noble suffering.

Nora also has needs for power and mastery, which she fulfills in a typically self-effacing way by identifying with Torvald. She exults in the fact that "all the employees at the Bank [will] be dependent on Torvald now": "What fun to think that we—that Torvald—has such power over so many people" (act 1). She bristles when Krogstad speaks disrespectfully of her husband because she participates in Torvald's glory, and any threat to his status is a threat to her own. Her identification is so intense that she is ready to commit suicide to preserve her husband's high position.

Nora begins to think of suicide as soon as Krogstad threatens to reveal that she has obtained a loan from him by forging her father's signature. She becomes panic-stricken when, ignoring her pleas, Torvald dismisses Krogstad, saying that he will bear "the whole burden" of any retaliation. "He'd do it too! He'd do it—in spite of anything!" she exclaims to Dr. Rank. "But he mustn't—never, never! Anything but that!" (act 2). Nora is convinced that Torvald loves her so "deeply" and "intensely" that "he wouldn't hesitate for a moment to give up his life for [her] sake." She thinks that one way of saving him would be to pay off her debt, thereby securing the incriminating papers. She considers asking Dr. Rank for the money, but when Rank declares his love, she can accept nothing from him, even though the alternative is so terrible. Apparently, her romanticism is so intense that she would rather commit suicide than taint her devotion to Torvald. She is afraid to kill herself, however, until Krogstad boasts that within a year he will be Torvald's "right hand man. It'll be Nils Krogstad, not Torvald Helmer, who'll run the Joint Stock Bank." "I have the courage for it now," Nora declares (act 2).

Nora's relationship with her husband is based on a bargain she has made in her own mind. She will be a charming, obliging, self-sacrificing wife, and Torvald will love and protect her. Nora delights in being babied, coddled, and indulged. Everything Torvald does for her shows how valuable she is to him and assures her that she will be taken care of. She does not mind being weak as long as his strength is at her service. She controls him through her dependency. When he becomes director of the bank, she does not regret the fact that she will no longer have to earn money secretly but is overjoyed that there will be "no more trouble! No more worry! I'll be able to play and romp about with the children" (act 1). She does expect to be rewarded for her years of devotion, however. Some day, somehow, Torvald is going to make a magnificent sacrifice for her, and then she will see how strong and noble he is and how much he loves her. This is the "wonderful thing" that will validate her bargain and make her dream of glory come true.

Nora is certain that when Torvald opens Krogstad's threatening letter, the wonderful thing will happen. Torvald is too brave, too noble to submit to Krogstad's demands. In order to protect her from prosecution, he will take responsibility for the forgery on himself. In Nora's romantic fantasy Torvald is her knight and she is his lady. Just before he reads the letter, he tells her: "Do you know something, Nora. I often wish you were in some great danger—so I could risk body and soul—my whole life—everything, everything for your sake" (act 3). Torvald's equally romantic version of their relationship reinforces Nora's. She believes his professions and is convinced that he will sacrifice himself for her. Nora wants the wonderful thing to happen, but she is terrified of it as well, for Torvald will become a social outcast, like Krogstad. He will lose his power and position, and life will become unbearably bleak and mean. A ruined Torvald could satisfy neither Nora's compliant needs for care and protection nor her expansive needs for power and glory.

The severity of Nora's neurosis is clearly revealed by her determination to kill herself. By committing suicide she will prevent Torvald from taking the blame on himself. Her heroic sacrifice will forestall his. Instead of having to endure guilt and self-hate for having ruined Torvald, she will save his career as she had earlier saved his life. The reward will be his undying gratitude and devotion. She will be enshrined forever in his memory and will not have to fear the loss of his love when she is no longer so attractive. Her suicide will secure Nora from the ravages of time and the vicissitudes of fortune. She will die in full possession of the two things she values most, Torvald's love and his glory.

In a relationship of morbid dependency, such as that between Nora and Torvald, there is a turning point, says Horney, for the self-effacing partner, "as the stake she is gambling for fails to materialize" (1950, 252). The turning point for Nora comes with Torvald's reactions to

Krogstad's letter. He neither praises her for having earned so much money and saved his life nor offers to take the blame for her forgery on himself. Instead he calls her a hypocrite, a liar, and a criminal and tells her that she "won't be allowed to bring up the children" (act 3). "All thought of happiness" between them is over. She has put him in Krogstad's power, and he "must find some way to appease him." If we have understood what has been going on in Nora up to this moment, we can see why Torvald's reactions have such a tremendous impact upon her. Her dream has been shattered; her image of Torvald, her bargain, her hopes are all exploded illusions. Her sense of injustice is overwhelming, since she has been ready to die for him, and he is thinking only of himself. Enraged, she feels now that she does not love Torvald and that he has never loved her. Nothing he says could possibly repair the relationship; she has lost all faith in his assurances and regards him with contempt.

With the collapse of her self-effacing solution, hitherto repressed trends in Nora's personality begin to emerge. All the time she was submitting to Torvald and her father, she was unconsciously resenting their constraints and hating them for making her self-abandonment the price of their love. She rebelled in small ways, such as sneaking macaroons, and was aware of a desire to say, in front of Torvald, "Damn!— damn!—damn it all!" (act 1). Now that there is no prize to be won by compliance, she cannot bear the thought of continuing to be treated in degrading, patronizing ways. Nor can she repress her resentment any longer. She accuses both Torvald and her father of having grievously wronged her and seems to want Torvald to suffer. When he says that he "can't endure the thought" of parting with her, she replies: "All the more reason it should happen" (act 3).

Torvald is not the only object of Nora's rage; she is angry with herself and full of self-hate. Her self-effacing side is horrified at the thought that she has been "living here for eight years with a stranger" and that she has "borne him three children": "I can't bear to think about it! I could tear myself to pieces!" (act 3). By leaving immediately she removes herself from sexual temptation and restores her pride in herself as a woman who is intimate only with a man she loves. She sees her bargain in a new light, and now, to avoid feeling that she has sold herself, she must reject Torvald's help: "I can't accept anything from strangers." Torvald's attack on her moral character exacerbates her doubts about her fitness as a mother.

A good deal of self-hate is generated also by Nora's emerging aggressive trends. She perceives that in many ways Torvald is right when he calls her a child and tells her that she has "no understanding of the society we live in" (act 3). She had been content to be a pampered darling who was unfit to cope with the world, but now she hates her weakness and is determined to stand on her own feet. Here, too, the defense of her pride requires that she leave home. She feels that she is of no use to her children partly because she is so childlike herself. Nora defends herself against her self-hate by putting the whole blame on Torvald and her father and by resolving to become different. Anything that stands in the way of her determination to change, any claim of love or duty, she ruthlessly rejects: "This is something I *must* do."

It seems likely that Nora becomes aggressive, rather than wallowing in self-pity and despair, because her earlier experience of working has given her a feeling that she *can* earn money like a man. Without this in her background, she might have reacted quite differently to the collapse of her romance. As it is, she gives up her belief in the miraculous power of love and transfers her expansive pride from Torvald to herself. She is going to prove that she is as good as a man and does not need anybody to take care of her! She has very little sense of what she is going to do, but she must escape the dependency she now so despises. Her belief in Torvald seems to have been replaced by a faith in the magic power of her will.

Aggressive trends are not the only hitherto suppressed components of Nora's personality to surface at the end. A person living in a suffocating environment like Nora's is bound to develop tendencies toward detachment, to have strong urges to run away, to get free of the constant pressure on her thoughts and feelings. Nora insists that she must be alone if she is to "think things out" for herself. She rejects all responsibility toward others and refuses Torvald's help partly because she is afraid of anything that will interfere with her independence: "You mustn't feel yourself bound any more than I shall. There must be complete freedom on both sides" (act 3). Torvald wants to write to her, but Nora anxiously pleads with him not to. She expresses no interest in hearing about the children and makes no effort to see them before she departs.

Nora's detachment is not only a response to past oppression but also a defense against present conflicts. She has to be callous toward her husband and children, she has to run away from them, because they threaten to rouse up her self-effacing side, of which she is now afraid.

There is something decidedly cold-blooded about Nora at the end. She is not allowing herself to be aware of the complexities of her situation, to feel a sense of loss, or to experience tender emotions.

Although part of Nora's transformation involves the adoption of new defenses, there are signs of genuine growth. Nora has seen the severity of her self-alienation and has understood some of its causes. She wants to find herself, to discover her own thoughts and feelings, and to grow from this authentic center of her being. She sees that her humanity has been stunted and is determined to become a capable, functioning, fully responsible person. Her insistence that she has a sacred duty to herself is healthy self-assertion.

How far Nora can grow is a question on which we can only speculate. In the absence of a supportive environment, her prospects do not seem promising. It will be very difficult for her to arrive at a true knowledge of herself and the world around her. She has made contact with previously repressed feelings, such as rage and the desire to throw off her bonds, but this is not the same thing as getting in touch with her real self. Her discovery of her self-alienation is an essential first step, but it is difficult to see how she can recognize and relinquish her defenses without help, and none is available. At the end of the play Nora is like a person in an early stage of therapy who is so afraid of losing contact with her new perceptions and so determined that nothing shall interfere with her growth that she cannot be worried about doing justice to others or caring about their feelings. It is at this stage, of course, that many marriages break up.

If Nora continued to grow, there might be a chance for her marriage, for she would come to see both Torvald and herself more clearly. She would relinquish her over-simple perception of him as a detestable tyrant or a contemptible weakling and recognize that his defenses had complemented hers in many ways but had also been in conflict with them. Nora and Torvald have had such an intensely romantic relationship because they have satisfied each other's neurotic needs. Nora needed to merge with a powerful, dominant male, and Torvald loved being master. She was excited by his strength and he by her weakness and dependency. She wished to be possessed and Torvald was extremely possessive. She dreamt of being cherished and protected and he of rescuing her from peril. Each was the center of the other's existence. Torvald was as emotionally dependent on Nora as she on him; at the end, it is he who cannot bear the thought of their separation. Each was "in love" with an idealization of the other rather than with the real person.

When Torvald's illusory version of Nora is shattered, he cries out, "God! What an awakening!" (act 3). The play has been building toward this moment. We see from the beginning that Nora and Torvald have different attitudes toward borrowing money, social responsibility, and scrupulousness in the management of their affairs. Although she knows that Torvald is opposed to being in debt, Nora proposes that they borrow on the promise of his new job in order to splurge for Christmas. When Torvald asks what would happen if "on New Year's Eve a tile blew off the roof and knocked my brains out," Nora replies that under such circumstances it would not matter if she owed money (act 1). "But," Torvald asks, "what about the people I'd borrowed from?" "Who cares about them?" replies Nora. "After all they're just strangers." Torvald dismisses her response as a joke, but Nora is serious. When Krogstad asks if it had not occurred to her that she was not being honest with him when he lent her money on the basis of her father's signature, Nora answers: "I really couldn't concern myself with that. You meant nothing to me."

The Helmers have not had a great deal of money because as a lawyer Torvald has refused "to handle any cases that are in the least bit—shady" (act 1). Nora tells Mrs. Linde that she "agree[s] with him, of course," but she does not observe his code of rectitude herself and seems to feel that he is too strict. Governed by the values of her self-effacing solution, Nora feels justified in doing whatever is necessary to care for the members of her family. She cannot imagine that "a daughter has no right to spare her dying father worry and anxiety" or that "a wife has no right to save her husband's life." Nora's claims are that she cannot be adversely judged because she acted out of love and that there "won't be any trouble" because she has "three little children" (act 2).

Her belief system is shaken, however, when Torvald attacks Krogstad at the end of act 1. After committing a forgery, Krogstad had escaped punishment through "tricks and evasions." When a man behaves like that, says Torvald, "his life becomes a tissue of lies and deception. He's forced to wear a mask—even with those nearest to him—his own wife and children." Krogstad "has been deliberately poisoning his own children for years, by surrounding them with lies and hypocrisy." Nora recognizes herself in this description, since her life is a tissue of lies and deception. She, too, has committed forgery, and she has deceived Torvald about the loan. She lies habitually, about eating macaroons, about what she does with the money Torvald gives her, about what she is doing with the time she spends working, and so on. She justifies many of these lies as being in a good cause and required by Torvald's rigidity, but after Torvald's speech about Krogstad she becomes terrified. Afraid that she is harming her family and corrupting her home, she begins to withdraw from her children and to contemplate going away. The self-hate and self-doubt thus activated remain with her through the rest of the play.

It is because Mrs. Linde is appalled by the "deceit and subterfuge" on which Nora's relationship with Torvald is based that she insists on exposing Nora's secret, even though Krogstad is willing to take back his threatening letter. She feels that Nora and Torvald must come "to a thorough understanding," that "Helmer must know the truth" (act 3). She tells Nora that she has "nothing to fear from Krogstad" but that she "must speak out." Nora's reaction to this is remarkable: "Now I know what I must do"—that is, she must commit suicide. Why? If she has nothing to fear from Krogstad, she does not have to kill herself to save Torvald's career and prevent the wonderful thing from happening. Does she want to die so as to avoid a confrontation with Torvald? Does she sense what his reaction will be? Does she fear that he will despise her, as he does Krogstad.

Torvald's denunciation of Krogstad had been extraordinarily passionate: "It would have been impossible for me to work with him. It literally gives me a feeling of physical discomfort to come in contact with such people" (act 1). The perfectionistic Torvald is pursuing a flawless excellence in the whole conduct of life, and he discharges onto Krogstad the contempt he would feel for himself should he behave as Krogstad has done. Krogstad is, in effect, his despised image, what he cannot bear to be, and he finds his very presence disturbing, especially when Krogstad, an old school friend, treats him with familiarity. His repudiation, condemnation, and defiance of Krogstad confirm his high standards and solidify his sense of identity.

Nora dreads Krogstad partly because her father had been attacked in the newspapers, and she fears that Krogstad will attack Torvald. Confident of his rectitude, Torvald dismisses her fears: "My dear Nora, there is a distinct difference between your father and me. Your father's conduct was not entirely unimpeachable. But mine is; and I trust it will remain so" (act 2). Torvald feels that his strength is the strength of ten because his heart is pure. His bargain is that he will ultimately triumph and have nothing to fear as long as his conduct is unimpeachable. At the beginning of the play, his bargain seems to be working. He suffered financially because he would not take shady cases, but he has received a splendid new appointment as the reward of his virtue.

Torvald's reaction to Krogstad's letter is so intense because his well-earned success has been poisoned, and he has been put in the power of a man he detests. Since he will be in a false position whatever he does, the flawless excellence of his life has been lost forever. Perhaps the greatest blow for him is that his idealized image of Nora and their relationship has been shattered. He has awakened after eight years to discover that the woman who had been his "pride and joy" is "lawless" and "unprincipled" (act 3). He has had intimations of the conflict between his values and Nora's before, but he has dismissed them because of his need to hold onto his exalted image of her and their relationship. When he catches her in a lie about Krogstad's not having been to see her, he does not take the matter seriously: *"(Threatens with his finger)* My little bird must never do that again! A song-bird must sing clear and true! No false notes! *(Puts arm around her)* Isn't that the way it should be? Of course it is! *(Let's her go)* And now we'll say no more about it" (act 1). Torvald now believes that Nora has inherited her father's lack of principle; she has "no religion, no moral code, no sense of duty" (act 3). She embodies everything Torvald abhors in other people and is afraid of in himself.

Torvald can be easily seen as a coward and hypocrite, but the situation is more complicated than that. He had made a show of courage as long as his conduct was unimpeachable, but Nora's behavior has compromised his honor and undermined his belief in his power to control his destiny. Horney observes that for the perfectionistic person the appearance of rectitude may be more important than rectitude itself, and appearances are very important to Torvald. The "matter must be hushed up at any cost" in order to avoid a scandal, and he and Nora must pretend to have a marriage in order to "save appearances" (act 3). Nora's dream was that Torvald would take the responsibility for the forgery on himself, thus showing how much he loved her, but given his own defenses, this is something that Torvald could never do. She is asking him to present his despised image to the world as his true reality. When Torvald says that "one doesn't sacrifice one's honor for love's sake," Nora replies that "millions of women have done so." She is expressing values that belong to her defense system and he values that belong to his.

Krogstad's letter plunges Torvald into a state of psychological crisis. His solution has failed and his "whole world seem[s] to be tumbling about [his] ears" (act 3). He is going to pieces not only because Nora has exposed him to disgrace, but also because his misfortune forces him to realize that he has violated his own principles. His code is that one *should not* sacrifice honor for love, but that is what he did when he was sent to investigate Nora's father and engaged in a cover-up for her sake: "If you hadn't . . . been so kind and helpful—he might have been dismissed" (act 2). Torvald now feels that he is being punished "for shielding" Nora's father (act 3). By failing to live up to his shoulds, he has exposed himself to catastrophe. This generates a sense of helplessness and panic and also a great deal of self-hate, which he externalizes by feeling victimized and blaming his wife. Like Nora, he feels unjustly treated by his mate: "And to think I have you to thank for all this—you whom I've done nothing but pamper and spoil since the day of our marriage" (act 3). As we have seen, Nora is also feeling self-hate, which she externalizes by blaming her father and Torvald.

Torvald's panic subsides when Krogstad withdraws his threat, and he immediately resumes his patronizing behavior. After forgiving Nora, he assures her that she is safe and that he will cherish her as if she were "a little dove" he had "rescued from the claws of some dreadful hawk" (act 3). Despite his craven behavior, Torvald wants to revive the old scenario in which he is Nora's protector, but she no longer believes him. He becomes even more paternalistic than he was before. Nora will become his child as well as his wife, and he will be "both will and conscience" to her.

Torvald's behavior is incredibly inappropriate, and it may seem to some that Ibsen is presenting a caricature of a chauvinistic male. It is understandable, however, in terms of Torvald's psychology. He is a male chauvinist, of course ("I am not a man for nothing"), but there is more to his behavior than that. His description of Nora as his "dearest treasure" is not an exaggeration (act 3). He is an emotionally needy man who, spellbound by Nora, wants to possess her entirely and live in a world of their own. When they are with other people, he romantically pretends that they love each other in secret, and he thinks that Rank's death may be for the best, since now they will be "more than ever dependent on each other." He is proud of Nora's beauty and charm, which bolster his own sense of worth, much as Torvald's success feeds Nora's pride. He has blinded himself to anything faulty in Nora because he does not want to relinquish his idealization of her or to have any flaw in their relationship.

There is an inner conflict in Torvald between his dependency on Nora and his perfectionism. He tries to resolve that conflict by treating her like a helpless, uncomprehending female who was not "able to judge how wrong" her behavior was (act 3). If he continued to condemn Nora, he would lose her. By regarding her as too immature to be held responsible, he is able to forgive her and continue their relationship. He will keep Nora straight, and thus protect himself, by being her will and conscience. He envisions merging with Nora more completely than ever before.

Torvald's fantasy is profoundly oppressive to Nora, who no longer respects his judgment. When he starts regarding her as his little doll again, "whom you would have to guard more carefully than ever, because she was so weak and frail" (act 3), she realizes the degree to which she has been infantilized and demands to be treated like a real person. This does not produce a sudden leap into maturity for Nora, nor could it. She herself is conscious of her inadequacy and uncertainty. She knows that she is not fit to teach her children, that she does not understand society or religion, and that she is bewildered about ethical questions. What she is clear about is that she is not clear. She knows that she is out of touch with herself and the world and that she must get away from Torvald if she is to "learn to face reality." She is aware that she is at the beginning of a long process and that she does not "know what sort of person" she will become.

I have suggested that if Nora continued to grow, there might be a chance for her marriage. That would depend on Torvald as well, but he, too, has begun to change and may have as good a chance as she of arriving at the necessary insights. He does not accept Nora's position that he should have sacrificed honor for love, nor, given his personality, is he ever likely to do so. Nora needs to see the sources of that expectation in her own psychology. Torvald does respond, however, to Nora's indignation at not having been treated as a person. He understands that there is "a great void" between them and asks Nora to believe that he is capable of change. She thinks that he might be when he "no longer [has his] doll to play with" (act 3). Again she is right. The separation is as essential for Torvald as it is for her. Nora appears to be somewhat vindictive when she says that his inability to endure the thought of parting with her is all the more reason why she should go, but perhaps she recognizes that she must be cruel in order to be kind.

The question we are left with at the end of the play is whether Nora and Torvald can change enough so that their "life together might truly be a marriage" (act 3). Unless this happens, says Nora, they will always be strangers. If it were to happen it would be "the most wonderful thing of all," but Nora says that she "no longer *believe[s]* in miracles." Torvald, however, clings to this hope. The last line of the play is his: "The most wonderful thing of all—?" Given the severity of Nora and Torvald's problems and the absence of therapeutic help, it would be a miracle indeed.

Hedda Gabler is above all a study of character; to comprehend the play, we must understand Hedda. It is difficult to establish Ibsen's thematic intentions, but he *shows* with brilliant psychological insight how Hedda's plight as a woman in an extremely restrictive society produces inner conflicts that make her life sterile and lead to her destructive behavior. Hedda is not portrayed sympathetically, like Nora, but psychological analysis reveals that beneath her cold, haughty demeanor she is a suffering human being.

As in *A Doll's House,* the heroine's relationship with a man is the focus of the play. Hedda's most important relationship is not with her husband but with Ejlert Lövborg, whom she had known before her marriage. After the scene is set in act 1, the dramatic action is initiated by Thea Elvsted's visit, which leads to Lövborg's reentry into Hedda's life. Act 2 is focused on Hedda's rivalry with Thea, as she induces Ejlert to take a drink and go to Judge Brack's party. Act 3 shows us her disappointment when Ejlert fails to enact the scenario she had envisaged for him, and it ends with Hedda urging him to kill himself beautifully and burning his manuscript. In act 4, Hedda is driven to suicide when all her solutions collapse after Ejlert's death. If we are to appreciate the subtlety of Ibsen's psychological portrait and make sense of what happens in the play, we must understand Ejlert's role in Hedda's life.

The most widely held view of Hedda's behavior in act 2 is that she is trying to undo Thea's constructive influence on Ejlert, who had been leading a wild bohemian life in the days when he and Hedda were friends. Inspired by Thea, he has stopped drinking, has published a highly acclaimed book, and has written another that is more brilliant still. Envious of Thea, Hedda wishes to exercise a more powerful influence of her own by turning Lövborg back into the man he was when she knew him. She seeks to disrupt Ejlert's relationship with Thea and to replace her as the dominant force in his life. Thea is afraid that Ejlert will be destroyed if he reverts to his old ways, and most people seem to feel that Hedda is trying to undermine him in order to feel that for once in her life she, too, has "the power to shape a human destiny" (act 2).

There is much in this view with which I agree, but I do not think that Hedda induces Lövborg to take a drink and go to Brack's party in order to undermine him. In response to Thea's concern about "what will come of all this," Hedda confidently predicts that "At ten o'clock he will be here, with vine leaves in his hair. Flushed and fearless!" (act 2). She envisions him as a triumphant figure. Hedda is disappointed rather than pleased when she hears from her husband that the drunken Ejlert carelessly dropped his manuscript and learns from Judge Brack that he finally turned up at Mademoiselle Diana's, where he insisted that he had been robbed, raised a row, and was taken away by the police: "So that's what happened! Then, after all, he had no vine leaves in his hair!" (act 4). He is behaving like the Ejlert of old, but that is *not,* evidently, what Hedda had wanted. In order to understand what Hedda was hoping for we must examine her inner conflicts and Ejlert's role in her effort to manage them.

Some of Hedda's conflicts are presented quite vividly in her reminiscence with Ejlert about the old days, when there was a "secret intimacy" between them that "no living soul suspected" (act 2). With General Gabler reading his paper in the same room, Ejlert would describe his "days and nights of passion and frenzy, of drinking and madness" to Hedda. She evoked his confessions by boldly asking "devious questions" that he perfectly understood. Rejecting Lövborg's idea that she was trying to wash away his sins, Hedda explains her motive: "Isn't it quite easy to understand that a young girl, especially if it can be done in secret . . . should be tempted to investigate a forbidden world? A world she's supposed to know nothing about?"

Hedda is a socially prominent woman with a very strong sense of propriety who needs to maintain her dignity at all costs and who cannot bear the thought of doing anything that would diminish her respectability. At the same time, she has powerful sexual and aggressive impulses that she wants to express as men do and that she is bitter at having to deny. She lives in a society that imposes enormous constraints upon a woman of her social class, constraints to which she outwardly conforms but against which she inwardly rebels. Her "secret intimacy" with Ejlert

Lövborg enabled her to escape these constraints vicariously, since he acted out her forbidden impulses and then told her about it. When Ejlert wonders how she could have brought herself "to ask such questions," Hedda insists that she did so "in a devious way," that is, without directly violating decorum (act 2). We see Hedda looking for a similar kind of safe, voyeuristic gratification when she makes oblique references to Judge Brack's affairs and relishes the thought of his stag party, which she wishes she could attend unseen.

Hedda's problem, then, is how to satisfy her "craving for life" (act 2), as Ejlert describes it, without sacrificing her position as a lady. Hedda's need to conform to the rules of propriety is so great that it both alienates her from her real feelings and makes it impossible for her to express the resulting rebellious impulses. It is not a healthy craving for self-actualization but her suppressed neurotic needs that Ejlert Lövborg is acting out. To Hedda, however, he is a man who has "the courage to live his life" as he sees fit (act 3), in a way that she cannot live hers. It is not only his escapades that she vicariously enjoys but also what they symbolize, his freedom from the constraints by which she feels herself to be suffocated.

Ejlert provides a solution to Hedda's problem until he drags their intimacy down to reality by making sexual advances. Hedda is so alarmed by this that she threatens to shoot him, but she is afraid to do so because she has "such a fear of scandal" (act 2). When Lövborg accuses her of being "a coward at heart," she wholeheartedly concurs: "A terrible coward." She confesses that her "greatest cowardice that evening" was in not responding to his advances.

Hedda is caught in a conflict between a desire to act out her rebellious aggression by leading a wild, free, bohemian life, like Lövborg, and an even stronger need to comply with the norms of her society, to be a refined, respectable lady, the proper daughter of an eminent general. To escape the agony of this conflict, she becomes cold, aloof, detached, out of touch with her own emotions and indifferent to other people. She does not believe in love, marries for convenience, and then is terribly oppressed by the boredom of her empty existence. When she returns from a lengthy wedding trip with a husband she cannot bear, she wants a butler, a saddle horse, a new piano, and an active social life partly for reasons of status and partly because she is spoiled, but mostly because she feels desperate and is searching for distractions. She becomes even more frustrated when she learns that they will have to curtail their expenses.

Hedda's plight is vividly depicted in her conversation with Judge Brack at the beginning of act 2. After greeting him with pistol shots and explaining that she is "just killing time" because she doesn't know "what in heaven's name" she is to do with herself "all day long," Hedda complains about the boredom of her wedding trip. She makes it clear that she does not "love" Jörgen ("Ugh! Don't use that revolting word!"), and that she married him because he had a promising career and she "wasn't getting any younger." Hedda is twenty-nine and has a dread of aging. Brack and Hedda then engage in a devious exchange in which Brack proposes an affair and Hedda makes it clear that she would rather continue her tête-à-tête with Jörgen than enter into a triangle that would compromise her respectability. She has no objection to Brack's coming over to amuse her, however.

In response to Hedda's complaint about how "incredibly I shall bore myself here," Brack suggests that she find "some sort of vocation in life," but Hedda cannot imagine a vocation that would attract her. Perhaps she could get Jörgen to go into politics, despite the fact that he is completely unsuited for such a career. Like most of the women in Ibsen's plays—and in his culture, no doubt—Hedda can find an outlet for her expansive tendencies only through identification with or manipulation of a man. There are variations on this theme in *A Doll's House* (as we have seen), *The Master Builder,* and *Rosmersholm.*

Hedda feels that life is "so hideous" because of her "genteel poverty"; but, sensing her detachment, Judge Brack astutely observes that "the fault lies elsewhere," in the fact she has never "really been stirred by anything." He suggests that this may change when she finds herself "faced with what's known in solemn language as a grave responsibility." Hedda angrily replies, "Be quiet! Nothing of that sort will ever happen to me." She is already pregnant, however, and is trying to deny her condition, both to herself and to others. Not only is she confined to a woman's narrow sphere in life, but she can find no satisfaction in what her culture regards as feminine joys. She puts off marriage as long as she can, partly because its restrictions do not appeal to her and partly because the men who attract her are not eligible and the men who are eligible do not attract her. She is appalled by the prospect of mother-hood, again because of her detachment: "That sort of thing doesn't appeal to me, Judge. I'm not fitted for it. No responsibilities for me!" Terribly frustrated herself, she has nothing to give a child, who will further limit her freedom. In rebellion against the feminine role but unable to find any other, she tells Judge Brack that the only thing she is "really fitted for" is "boring myself to death!"

Hedda is in despair about her life. From the beginning of the play, she is full of frustration, irritability, and anger, which she displaces at first onto the self-effacing Aunt Juliane, who lets in too much sunlight, thus revealing Hedda's aging face and filled out figure, and whose hat Jörgen has indecorously left on a drawing room table. When Judge Brack scolds her for tormenting "that nice old lady," Hedda explains that she suddenly gets "impulses like that" and cannot "control them" (act 2). She is not callously amusing herself, but is compulsively discharging some of her pent-up rage, just as she does when she fires off her father's pistols, those symbols of male power.

Constantly looking for something that might interest her, Hedda regards the possible competition for the professorship between Ejlert and Jörgen as an event in which she can take "a sporting interest" (act 1), despite the fact that her husband's professional and financial fortunes are at stake. The arrival of Thea takes her in a new direction, since Thea announces the presence of Ejlert Lövborg, who had once provided Hedda with a way of dealing with her frustrations and inner conflicts. When she learns that Ejlert is in town she has a vague hope that he can somehow be of help to her, and she immediately asks Jörgen to invite him.

Upon Lövborg's arrival, Hedda becomes involved in a competition with Thea for influence over him. Hedda is threatened by Thea and has a powerful need to triumph over her. When they knew each other at school, Hedda used to pull Thea's hair and once said she was "going to burn it all off" (act 1). Ibsen describes Thea's hair as "extremely thick and wavy," while Hedda's is "not especially abundant." Thea's thick hair symbolizes fertility and makes Hedda all the more conscious of the sterility of her own existence, despite her pregnancy. The contrast between the two women is developed throughout the play. Whereas Hedda reveled in Lövborg's debauchery, Thea inspired him to write books, which he describes as their children. Hedda's fear of scandal made her afraid of responding to Ejlert's advances, but Thea leaves her husband in order to follow him to town: "But, Thea, my darling!"—exclaims Hedda—"How did you *dare* do such a thing?" (act 1; my emphasis).

When Thea declares that she will never go back to her husband, Hedda is shocked: "But what will people say about you, Thea?" "They can say," replies Thea, "whatever they like." In pursuit of what is really important to her, Thea ignores public opinion in a way that Hedda cannot. Hedda's envy is exacerbated when Lövborg praises Thea's "tremendous courage" where her "comrade is concerned":

> *Hedda:* God, yes, courage! If one only had that!
> *Lövborg:* What then?
> *Hedda:* Then life might perhaps be endurable, after all . . .
>   (act 2)

Thea is Hedda's nemesis, the woman who demonstrates that it is possible to have a fruitful life if one has the courage to defy convention.

There can be no doubt that Hedda manipulates Lövborg into taking a drink and going to Judge Brack's party in order to disrupt his relationship with Thea and to show that she has more power over him. But she is not yet out to destroy Lövborg, as she is later when she conceals the fact that Jörgen has found his manuscript. At this point in the play she wants Ejlert to enact a scenario she has conceived for him in which he will be a triumphant author who is free of self-doubt and anxiety about himself. She wants "the power to shape a human destiny" in what she regards as a positive way.

Lövborg's refusal to take a drink and go to Brack's party disturbs Hedda because it seems to be motivated by the same kind of fear that has made her life unendurable and filled her with self-contempt. Hedda despises herself for her conformity, her dread of scandal, her cowardice. She taunts Ejlert with not daring to take a drink or go to the party: "Didn't dare! You say I didn't dare!" (act 2). She cannot bear to see him afraid and eggs him on because she wants him to lead the free, uninhibited life that she cannot lead herself. She is caught in a crossfire of conflicting shoulds, since she hates herself for her cowardice but knows that she would hate herself even more for any breach of propriety. She wants Lövborg to rescue her from her impasse by being both rebellious and triumphant, by returning "flushed and fearless," "with vine leaves in his hair." Then he "will have regained confidence in himself. He'll be a free man forever and ever."

Thea may have reclaimed Ejlert, but she has also tamed him, made him fearful of spontaneity, just as Hedda is. She acts boldly on his behalf but is terribly anxious for him. Hedda feels a similar anxiety for herself at the thought of daring behavior, but she wants to believe that Lövborg can act upon his impulses with impunity. She wants to triumph over Thea, to shape a human destiny, and to gain a vicarious fulfillment of her needs to be independent and courageous by having Lövborg owe his freedom and fearlessness to her. Having no hope of becoming what she wants to be herself, she seeks to escape her impotence and self-hate by making Ejlert into a man through whom she can live and with whom she can proudly identify.

Hedda's is an impossible dream. Since Lövborg is an alcoholic, freeing him of his fears and inhibitions is bound to destroy him. When he refuses to join the other men at the punch bowl, Judge Brack says, "Why, surely, cold punch is not poison." "Perhaps not for everyone," Ejlert replies, with the implication that it surely is for him (act 2). Thea is so anxious because she understands Ejlert's vulnerability. Desperate, Hedda blinds herself to his condition and constructs a scenario that will satisfy her contradictory needs but that he cannot possibly fulfill.

When Ejlert has not returned by the next morning Thea is in panic, but, holding onto her dream, Hedda envisions him at Judge Brack's "sitting with vine leaves in his hair, reading his manuscript" (act 3). Tesman comes back with a glowing account of the new work, but finds it "appalling" that Lövborg, "with all his great gifts, should be so utterly incorrigible." "Because he has more daring," Hedda asks, "than any of the rest of you?" This is Hedda's idealized image of Lövborg. It is Ejlert's excessive drinking, however, to which Jörgen is referring, since it has led him carelessly to drop his precious manuscript. Jörgen has found it and leaves it with Hedda when he is summoned to the bedside of the dying Aunt Rina.

Judge Brack's account of the evening shatters Hedda's dream of living through a liberated Lövborg. Having conceived of Lövborg as a kind of romantic hero, an untamed superior being, she is sickened by his sordid fight with Mademoiselle Diana and his arrest. If Hedda had simply wanted to show her power over Lövborg and break up his relationship with Thea by inducing him to revert to bohemian ways, she would have been pleased by his night of drinking and madness.

It is at this point that Hedda turns destructive. Since she has not been able to make Ejlert into the hero of her dreams, she exerts her power in a different way by first concealing and then burning his manuscript. Ashamed to confess that he has lost their "child," Lövborg tells Thea that he has torn the manuscript into a thousand pieces and that he will "do no more work, from now on" (act 3). Thea "despairingly" asks what she will "have to live for," accuses him of "child-murder," and sees "nothing but darkness" before her. Lövborg is also in despair, for he knows "it won't end with last night," and debauchery no longer appeals to him: "she's somehow broken my courage—my defiant spirit." "To think," says Hedda, that that pretty little fool should have influenced a man's destiny."Hedda might have been able to save Lövborg had she revealed that she was in possession of the manuscript, but she allows him to believe it is lost. When he announces that he wants "to make an end of it," Hedda does not try to dissuade him or produce the manuscript but instead gives him a pistol, urges him to use it, and enjoins him to "let it be beautiful." After Ejlert leaves, she burns the manuscript, calling it his and Thea's child.

Hedda's behavior can be explained as a continuation of her rivalry with Thea and of her desire to shape a man's destiny—for ill if not for good; but these are not her only motivations. With the collapse of her dream of triumph for Lövborg, and vicariously for herself, Hedda is confronted once more by her contradictory needs, which she now has no hope of fulfilling. She, too, is in despair, and wishes to make an end of it. She is afraid to commit suicide, however, partly because, as Brack says at the end, "people don't *do* such things!" After Lövborg disappoints her, she develops a new scenario in which he will commit suicide in just the way that she would like to do, and she will glory in this new form of freedom and daring and in her own contribution to it. When Brack announces that Lövborg has shot himself through the heart, Hedda is exultant: "It gives me a sense of freedom to know that an act of deliberate courage is still possible in this world—an act of spontaneous beauty" (act 4). Hedda feels herself to be incapable of such an act, but Lövborg has done it for her, she thinks. Judge Brack destroys her "beautiful illusion" by revealing that Ejlert was accidentally shot in the bowels while demanding his "lost child" in Mademoiselle Diana's boudoir. "How horrible!" exclaims Hedda. "Everything I touch becomes ludicrous and despicable!—It's like a curse!"

Hedda is driven to kill herself by the collapse of all her solutions. She can no longer hope to gain a sense of freedom and to satisfy her suicidal impulses vicariously through Lövborg, and she is put into an impossible position by Judge Brack's effort to blackmail her.

As soon as she returns from her wedding journey, Brack begins pressing for "a triangular friendship" in which he will be her lover (act 2). Hedda welcomes Brack's attentions, but given her fear of scandal, an affair is unthinkable. This is the same Hedda who had drawn a gun on Ejlert Lövborg when he wanted to bring their relationship down to earth. After confessing to Ejlert that she does not love her husband, she hastens to add, "All the same, no unfaithfulness, remember" (act 2). Brack welcomes Lövborg's disgrace after he is arrested at Mademoiselle Diana's because he senses Ejlert as a rival and hopes that Hedda's home will be closed to him, like other "respectable house[s]" (act 3). His aim is to be "cock-of-the-walk," and "for that," he tells Hedda, "I will fight with every weapon I can command." Hedda realizes that he is "a dangerous person" and is "exceedingly glad" that he has "no sort of hold" over her.

Brack gains a hold over Hedda, however, when he recognizes the pistol with which Lövborg was shot. Hedda is now faced with three possibilities, all of which are unbearable. Brack suggests that she can declare the pistol to have been stolen, but she says that "it would be better to die" than to do that (act 4). Brack dismisses her speech: "One *says* such things—but one doesn't *do* them." Why the threat of suicide here? Because lying about having given Lövborg the pistol is an act of cowardice that would exacerbate her self-hate? I have no better explanation. If the police trace the weapon to Hedda, says Brack, she will have to appear in court with Mademoiselle Diana and explain why she gave it to Lövborg: "think of the scandal . . . . of which you are so terrified." If Brack keeps quiet, however, the weapon will not be traced, and Hedda will neither have to lie nor be exposed to scandal. This means, however, that she will be in Judge Brack's power: "Subject to your commands and wishes. No longer free—not free! . . . No, I won't endure the thought. Never!"

Given her psychological needs, Hedda can neither defy Brack nor submit to him. Hedda strikes us as a masterful person who knows how to get what she wants, but the fact is that she is extremely compliant where propriety is concerned. She could not endure the loss of respectability that would result from her defiance of Brack. Confined to the narrow range of activities suitable to a woman of her station, Hedda compensates for her lack of control over her destiny by manipulating the people around her, and especially by seeking to influence the fate of an important man. Being subject to Brack's wishes and commands would render her utterly powerless and would be as unendurable as the consequences of defiance.

Hedda's need for freedom is as compensatory as her craving for power. The product of a highly restrictive environment that has allowed her few choices, she has a suppressed desire to rebel and a longing for liberty. As is typical of detached people, she is hypersensitive to anything that seems to impinge upon her, such as the expectations of others, the march of time, or being touched. She recoils from the gentle embrace of Aunt Juliane: "Please! Oh, please let me go!" (act 1). She cannot bear being pregnant or the responsibilities that parenthood will entail. She pursues a freedom *from* constraint rather than a freedom *to* fulfill herself. She is much too alienated from herself and dominated by her culture to know what she really wants to do with her life. Driven as she is by both social and psychological coercions, Hedda's sense of freedom is an illusion, of course, but it is essential to her to preserve it. Given her phobic reaction to ordinary intrusions, expectations, or constraints, we can imagine her desperation at the prospect of being at Brack's "beck and call from now on" (act 4).

When Hedda says that she "won't endure" the thought of not being free, Brack "half mockingly" replies, "People manage to get used to the inevitable" (act 4). But since Brack threatens Hedda's compulsive needs for respectability, for power, and for freedom, she cannot possibly get used to this situation.

To make matters worse, Jörgen and Thea begin reconstructing Lövborg's manuscript, depriving Hedda of her triumph over Thea and putting her even more into Brack's hands. Like Hedda, Thea has been trying to live through Lövborg. He acknowledges her as the co-creator of his new book, and she follows him to town partly out of anxiety and partly because she wants to be with him when it is published: "I want to see you showered with praise and honors—and, the joy! I want to share that with you too!" (act 3). When Ejlert announces that he has destroyed his manuscript and will do no more work, Thea feels she has nothing to live for. Her reaction to the news of Ejlert's death is remarkable. Instead of being stupefied by shock and grief, she digs his notes out of the pocket of her dress and immediately begins rewriting the book with Jörgen. Ejlert may be dead, but Thea's search for glory is alive. She has gotten from him what Hedda never could and in the process has thwarted Hedda's effort to gain a sense of power by burning the manuscript.

Thea's triumph is all the more complete because she has now begun to influence Jörgen, who says he will devote his life to rewriting Ejlert's book. Thea will move in with Aunt Juliane, and Jörgen will spend his evenings there working with her on the project. When Jörgen asks Brack to keep Hedda company while he is away, Brack readily agrees, anticipating "a very jolly time" (act 4). "That's what you hope," says Hedda from the next room, "Now that you are cock-of-the-walk." Then she shoots herself.

Hedda's suicide is a desperate act of escape—from the collapse of her efforts to fulfill her neurotic needs for respectability, power, and freedom, and from the unresolvable conflict between these needs that had led her to try to live vicariously through Ejlert Lövborg. She is fleeing her self-hate, her boredom, her marriage, her unwanted pregnancy, and the prospective burden of motherhood.

From Hedda's perspective, her suicide is also a triumph, of the sort she thought had been accomplished by Lövborg. Her response to Brack's initial report that Ejlert had shot himself through the heart gives us her view of her own act. "At last," she exclaims, "a deed worth doing!" "I know that Ejlert Lövborg had the courage to live his life as he saw it—and to end it in beauty." He has "made up his own account with life" and done "the one right thing" (act 4). When Hedda learns the truth about Lövborg's death, she realizes that if an act of "deliberate courage" and "spontaneous beauty" is to be performed, she must do it herself. She has not had the courage to live her life as she saw it, but she escapes her self-contempt by defying public opinion and behaving with daring at last. She would be pleased by Brack's comment that "people don't *do* such things." She ends her life beautifully, by her standards at least, with a shot in the temple. She thwarts Judge Brack, who had counted on her cowardice, and punctures her husband's complacency. In the last fleeting moment of her life, she actualizes an idealized image of herself and becomes a person she can respect.

Ibsen has painted a brilliant portrait of a neurotic woman, a product of her restrictive society, who can escape her problems and attain the glory for which she is searching only by killing herself.

As we can see from the preceding discussions, although characters can be identified as displaying one or another of Horney's defensive strategies, they are mixed cases, not to be thought of simply in terms of one personality type. Nora Helmer is strikingly self-effacing through much of the play, but when her predominant solution fails, her aggressive and detached trends emerge, revealing inner conflicts that have been there all along. The domineering, perfectionistic Torvald has dependency needs that make him cling to Nora at the end. Conflicting trends are so evenly balanced in Hedda Gabler that it is difficult to say which is her predominant solution. She is extremely detached, but she is also very compliant in relation to social conventions, and there is so much aggression in Hedda that she is most commonly thought of as manipulative and domineering. All categories are reductive, of course. Horney's are least so when they are used not to classify characters but to reveal their individuality and inner conflicts.

We can also see from our analyses of *A Doll's House* and *Hedda Gabler* that a Horneyan approach enables us to understand motivation and explain behavior even when we have little or no knowledge of a character's childhood. We know most about Nora's history because of her references to her life with her father. We can utilize the information she supplies, but we are not overly dependent upon it, and we do not have to inflate its importance. We know nothing about Torvald's early life and not much about Hedda's. Hedda's problems derive in part from the restrictions that her culture places on a woman of her social class, but we have almost no information about her early experience, and we really cannot say why she responds to her situation in the particular way that she does. Not all women in her position were driven to such sterile, destructive lives. Although we know little about the childhoods of these characters, their personality structures are portrayed in considerable detail, and with the help of Horney's synchronic theory we can analyze them psychologically without having to postulate a history that is not in the text.

A Horneyan approach helps us to understand not only the leading characters of these plays but also the relationships on which they are focused. The interaction between Nora and Torvald becomes intelligible only when we see how their defenses both harmonize and clash. The relationship between Hedda and Ejlert is at the center of the play, and we can appreciate why Ejlert is so important to Hedda only when we recognize how she tries to use him to escape her inner conflicts through the vicarious fulfillment of her needs.

4

The End of the Road

   While Ibsen's plays clearly lend themselves to Horneyan analysis, it may seem that John Barth's *The End of the Road* is a less appropriate choice. Nora, Torvald, and Hedda are mimetically drawn characters in realistic works, but Jake, Joe, and Rennie have been treated by most critics as illustrative figures in a philosophic tale. Although Barth may not have been aiming at psychological realism, his characters are brilliant mimetic portraits nonetheless. This novel is a little masterpiece that I have taught every year for the past several decades and have found to be endlessly elusive and fascinating. Jacob Horner is an excellent example of the detached protagonist common in modern literature, and the bizarre marriage of Joe and Rennie Morgan will remind us of Nora's morbid dependency on Torvald. It will also help us to understand the equally bizarre relationship between patient Griselda and Walter.

   Like Ibsen's, Barth's characters are presented with almost no prior history and would be difficult to analyze with a theory that explains the present in terms of the past. But they display the kinds of defenses and inner conflicts that Horney describes and are intelligible in terms of her structural approach. The plot of the novel evolves from the interaction of the characters' defensive strategies, which both draw them together and cause them to clash. Although there are triangles in Ibsen, his great psychological dramas tend to be focused on a dyadic relationship—between Nora and Torvald, Hedda and Ejlert, Solness and Hilde, Rosmer and Rebekka West. The situation is more complicated in *The End of the Road,* since the Jake-Rennie-Joe triangle is at the heart of the book. There are three relationships to be considered—Jake and Joe, Jake and Rennie, and Rennie and Joe—each of which is complex in itself and must be understood in relation to the other two.

   Since this is the text with which readers are least likely to be familiar, I shall tell more of the story than when I discuss other works. The novel's narrator and central character, Jake Horner, is a Masters candidate in English at Johns Hopkins who becomes psychologically paralyzed in a Baltimore railroad station on his twenty-eighth birthday and is rescued by a black man, known as the Doctor, who prescribes various therapies to treat his condition. Two years later, on the Doctor's advice, Jake takes a job teaching prescriptive grammar at Wicomico State College, where he becomes friendly with Joe Morgan, who is working on a Ph.D. in History at Hopkins, and with Rennie, his wife. It is Jake's relationship with Joe that precipitates the action.

Jake Horner is a descendant of Dostoevsky's underground man and other paralyzed intellectuals in literature, such as Hamlet, Diogenes Teufelsdröckh in Carlyle's *Sartor Resartus,* Conrad's Martin Decoud *(Nostromo)* and Axel Heyst *(Victory),* Harry Haller in Hesse's *Steppenwolf,* and Sartre's Antoine Roquentin in *Nausea.* Saul Bellow's Moses Herzog follows him within the next decade. One of the most striking similarities between Jake and the underground man is that both see their paralysis as the result of superior intelligence and a heightened awareness of the human condition. The underground man attributes his inertia to the fundamental laws of over-acute consciousness and contrasts himself with the dull, strong-nerved, normal men who are able to act because they fail to perceive that there is no foundation on which to base their choices. Jake Horner attributes his paralysis to "the malady *cosmoposis*": when we fix our gaze on "ultimacy," we see that there is "no reason to do anything" (ch. 6). He contrasts himself with the "short-sighted animals" around him in the railway station who hurry "across the concourse toward immediate destinations" while he sits "immobile on the bench."

Both Jake and the underground man are paralyzed, it seems to me, not by the intellectual insight and philosophic problems to which they attribute their difficulties, but by psychological conflicts and self-alienation (see Paris 1974). In Karen Horney's terms, they are predominantly detached individuals who have powerful aggressive and self-effacing tendencies they cannot suppress and that pull them in opposite directions. In order to defend themselves against inner turmoil, they distance themselves from their feelings and withdraw from the external world. They inadvertently become involved with others—the underground man with Liza and Jake with Joe and Rennie—who engage their emotions and activate their conflicts. Traumatized by their involvement, they become even more detached.

Jake writes *The End of the Road* at the Doctor's Remobilization Farm about two years after the events he describes. The book is an elaborate rationale for his sterile, defensive way of life. Unlike the short-sighted animals around him, Jake sees human beings from a cosmic perspective: they are insignificant creatures living in an indifferent universe, and their values are entirely arbitrary. Not only are the heavens empty, but there is no essential human nature. The Doctor and Jake reject the old humanistic view of man as having a stable self that can generate values and be the measure of all things. There is nothing inside of us that gives direction to our lives; our ego consists only of masks. We must create our identity through our actions, but since we have no essence to begin with, we must choose without a basis for choice. With neither an external nor an internal authority to guide us, it is no wonder that we are inconsistent or paralyzed.

The greatest threat to Jake's rationale is Joe Morgan, who also starts from the premise that nothing has ultimate value but who believes that each person has a set of "psychological givens," an essential nature, that generates values which are "subjective absolutes" (ch. 4). Joe's project is to live coherently, in a way that is consistent with his values, but he does not expect others to approve his decisions since they will be operating from their own psychological givens. From Jake's point of view, the flaw in Joe's position is that it "implies a self, and where one feels a plurality of selves," as does Jake, "one is subject to the same conflict on an intensely intramural level" that Joe posits "between individual points of view": "each of one's several selves [claims] the same irrefutable validity for its special point of view that, in Joe's system, individuals ... may claim" (ch. 10).

Jake acknowledges that he has always lacked a strong sense of personal unity, but he concludes from this not that he has psychological difficulties but that "the individual is not individual after all" (ch. 10). His entire philosophic position is an effort to disown his personal problems by generalizing them. From a Horneyan perspective, Jake is alienated from his real self, the source of authentic values, and he experiences his tendencies to move toward, against, and away from people as separate selves that dominate him by turns and between which he has no basis for choosing. The Doctor's view of the ego as an assemblage of masks reinforces Jake's rationalizations and makes him more comfortable with his neurosis; but the Doctor's therapies cannot help Jake to resolve his problems, since they do not address his self-alienation but merely provide him with techniques for making decisions while remaining detached.

Jake is triumphant in the novels's contest of ideas. His version of human nature proves to be more accurate than Joe's. Joe is as full of contradictions as Jake claims everybody is. He is deluded about Rennie, about himself, and about their relationship, and his intellectual approach to life is inadequate. But Jake is not shown to have a better approach. From a Horneyan point of view, Joe and Jake offer only a choice of neurotic solutions, each of which generates an inadequate view of human nature. Alienated from himself and full of inner conflicts, Jake is bound to deny the existence of a stable, authentic identity. Because he, too, is inwardly divided, Joe is a poor exemplar of his position that each person has a set of psychological givens in terms of which it is possible to live coherently.

In contrast to the two positions spelled out in the novel, Horneyan and Third Force psychology posit an essential human nature that generates a community of values. All human beings have the same basic psychological needs but differ in the ways they pursue them and in their self-actualizing activities. Everyone also has a real self, which is a stable source of direction and value, although most people are in some degree alienated from it. What we see in *The End of the Road* is a clash of neurotic positions, each of which offers itself as the truth about human nature and the human condition.

From a psychological point of view, the main action of the novel is the breakdown of Jake's detachment as he moves against Joe and toward Rennie and its reestablishment in a more extreme form at the end. Jake admires Joe and is drawn to him because he is free of Jake's "least fortunate traits," such as insecurity, "indecision," and "almost complete inconsistency" (ch. 3). Jake envies Joe and wishes he could be like him, but he needs to defeat him in order to ward off self-hate. He is so threatened because if Joe has a unified self in terms of which he can live coherently, then something is terribly wrong with Jake. If Joe also lacks personal unity but does not realize it, then his project is hopeless and he is a fool. Jake's need to undermine Joe is incompatible with his detachment, however, and activates his inner conflicts.

Jake is alarmed by Joe at their first encounter, during his interview for a position at Wicomico State. Joe is "so bright, busy, and obviously on his way up" that Jake realizes "at once that the invidious comparisons to oneself that he could not for the life of him help inviting would prevent one's ever being really tranquil about the fact of his existence" (ch. 2). Jake hits Joe "where he live[s]" by poking fun at his being a scoutmaster: inspiring a student, he says, is like "making fire with flint and steel." Unlike the timorous Jake who had circled the drive several times because people were lounging on the front steps, Joe strides "cleanly across the lawn" when they part: "Apparently Joe Morgan was the sort who heads directly for his destination, implying by his example that paths should be laid where people walk, instead of walking where the paths happen to be laid." We can see how Jake feels about this by his reaction to a student who challenges prescriptive grammar by arguing that grammar books just describe how people talk: "A Joe Morgan type, this lad: paths should be laid where people walk. I hated his guts" (ch. 10). Jake sets out "to rescue prescriptive grammar from the clutches of my impudent Mr. Blakesley, and, if possible, to crucify him in the process."

After they become friends, Jake attacks Joe indirectly, through Rennie. Joe and Rennie have an unusual relationship, the rules for which have been laid down by Joe. They are to do everything "on the same level, understanding it in the same way, for the same purpose, nobody making allowances for anybody else" (ch. 5). What one takes seriously, "both ought to be able to take seriously," with their relationship first on the list. They are to make "heavy demands" on themselves and each other, and "they always [have] to be the same demands." Since Joe can defend his ideas whereas Rennie cannot, Rennie throws out all her opinions and completely erases herself, "right down to nothing, so [she] can start over." Rennie is Galatea to Joe's Pygmalion; she tries desperately to be what he wants and would "rather be a lousy Joe Morgan than a first-rate Rennie MacMahon." For reasons to be examined later, Joe wishes to expose Rennie to the influence of Jake, and he encourages them to go riding together while he works on his dissertation. It is during one of their rides that Jake begins to ridicule Joe and to subvert the Morgans' relationship.

Jake begins by calling Joe "funny as hell" for hating pity and "silly" for getting upset at politeness (ch. 5). When Rennie becomes troubled and defensive, Jake presses the attack: "For that matter, what could be sillier than this whole aim of living coherently?" This is really hitting Joe and Rennie where they live, and Rennie is "aghast." "And boy oh boy," Jake continues, "what could *possibly* be sillier than his notion that two people in the same house can live that way!" Jake compares Rennie's expression at this to "that of the Athenians on the morning they discovered that Alcibiades had gelded every marble god in town." Joe is Rennie's god and Jake has tried to emasculate him. Jake claims that his purpose "was not to make a point, but to observe Rennie" and insists that he said "these things without genuine malice, only as a sort of tease"; but it is clear that even two years later he is hiding the truth from himself. Jake is an unreliable narrator who reveals himself so fully that we can see through his self-deceptions.

Rennie tells Jake the history of her relationship with Joe as a way of defending it and of justifying her lack of a separate identity. The relationship begins, as many morbid dependencies do, with a blow to the pride of the self-effacing partner (Horney 1950, 245). Joe and Rennie meet when he is pursuing an M.A. at Columbia and she is working in New York. After some casual dating, Joe tells her that he will not be taking her out anymore: "He said he thought I could probably be wonderful, but that I was shallow as hell as I was, and he didn't expect me to change just for his sake. . . . He wasn't interested in me as I was, so that was that" (ch. 5). Terribly hurt, Rennie returns to her apartment, where she and her roommate are having a party, but she now sees everything through Joe's eyes. She feels that her friends are "just ordinary people," that "everything they said was silly," and that she herself is a "complete blank." Assuming that Joe is "gone for good," she feels "so awful and useless" that she doesn't "give a damn what happen[s] to her."

Once Joe has crushed Rennie's pride, only his approval can alleviate her self-hate. Drunk and in despair, she goes to his apartment, where he expresses interest in a permanent relationship along the lines described above. Rennie assents to his conditions and strives to fulfill his expectations. Joe has told her not only that she is shallow as hell but also that she could probably be wonderful, and Rennie looks to him to transform her from her despised into her idealized image of herself. She glorifies Joe and becomes his devoted worshipper. According to her, he "thinks as straight as an arrow about everything," and "even when he makes a mistake, his reasons for doing what he did are clearer and sharper than anybody else's" (ch. 5).

Given what he wants in a marriage, Joe seems to have made a big mistake in choosing Rennie. He says that they will stay together as long as each can "respect everything about the other, absolutely everything," but Rennie is not capable of becoming a person Joe can respect. Jake observes that he treats her with condescension, and Rennie is afraid that she will never "really get to be what Joe wants" (ch. 5). How could the straight-thinking Joe have made such a poor choice? He says that he was attracted to Rennie because "she was the most *self-sufficient* girl I'd ever met. . . . She was popular enough, but she didn't seem to need popularity or even friendship at all" (ch. 8; emphasis in original). Rennie's account of herself is quite different. She says that she "lived in a complete fog" until the day Joe told her she was shallow: "I was popular and all that, but I swear it was just like I was asleep all through school and college. I wasn't really interested in anything, I never thought about anything, I never even particularly wanted to *do* anything" (ch. 5). In discussing self-alienation, Horney observes that there are many neurotics "who live as if they were in a fog. Nothing is clear to them. Not only their own thoughts and feelings but also other people" (1950, 156). Has Joe interpreted Rennie's indifference, her remoteness from self and others, as self-sufficiency? "If I thought about myself at all," she tells Jake, "I guess I lived on my potentialities, because I never felt dissatisfied with myself" (ch. 5). Once Joe's blow to her pride brings her insecurities to the surface, Rennie becomes a morbidly dependent woman who cannot satisfy Joe's need for a self-sufficient partner.

In order to comprehend Joe's mistake, we must understand his character structure and recognize exactly what he wants from Rennie. A perfectionist, Joe has high standards of which he is extremely proud and that he imposes on others. He has no friends because he refuses to make allowances for other people. He wants them "to be sharp and clear all the time," to live coherently, and to be worthy of respect. These are the demands he makes on himself and on Rennie. Following Joe's lead, Rennie scraps all her friends because "you had to make all kinds of allowances for them; you couldn't take them as seriously as all that" (ch. 5). Joe enjoys his position of lofty superiority, but it leaves him feeling alone and unappreciated. He craves recognition from another person, but if that recognition is to have any meaning, it must come from someone whom he respects himself. Because of the intensity of this need, he misperceives Rennie as someone who can become the partner he desires.

Joe makes his marriage the center of his life, with the remolding of

Rennie his primary project, more important to him than "career or ambition or anything else" (ch. 5). His explanation of his subjective ethic is prompted by Jake's observation that Joe regards Rennie and himself taking each other seriously "as an absolute." Joe acknowledges that his ethic depends upon there being an "*ultimate* end" (emphasis in original) that gives everything else "its relative value" and that "this ultimate end is rationally unjustifiable if there aren't any absolute values." He explains that ultimate ends can "never be *logically* defensible; they'd be in the nature of psychological *givens,* different for most people" (emphasis in original). These psychological givens spring from the individual's essential nature and are "the subjective equivalent of an absolute." As an example, Joe observes that if marital fidelity were one of his givens, his "relationship would have lost its *raison d'être*" if Rennie committed adultery, and he'd probably "walk out flat, if I didn't actually shoot her or shoot myself" (ch. 4). Joe denies that he is describing his own "psychological make-up," but he is a man with remarkably little self-knowledge, and he has inadvertently revealed to Jake the importance of Rennie's fidelity and how he can be undermined.

Joe posits a relativistic universe in which there are subjective absolutes and in which "the most a man can ever do is be right from his point of view." His philosophy rationalizes his sense of being absolutely right while differing from everyone else, just as Jake's rationalizes his confusion and inner conflict. Joe's highest conscious value is acting coherently, in "ways that he can explain, if he wants to." By this standard he is superior to everyone else, but people with other psychological make-ups will have other values. Joe seems to be at peace with this situation and takes pride in his ability to sustain "a cheerful nihilism": "When you say good-by to objective values, you really have to flex your muscles and keep your eyes open, because you're on your own" (ch. 4).

The essential nature Joe posits is unique to the individual, leaving each person alone in the universe. The problem is that Joe cannot stand being on his own. He needs someone else to share his perspective. This leads him to behave in ways that are incompatible with his own beliefs. He declares that each person has different psychological givens and that we cannot expect anyone else to agree with us but can only be right from our own point of view. What he is looking for in Rennie, however, is someone who will understand things just as he does, will respect everything about him, and will make the same demands, both on herself and on him, that he makes on himself.

It seems at first that Joe is looking for a clone and that he has found a person who is willing to become one. He tells Rennie that until she gets "into the habit of articulating very clearly all the time . . . most of the reasonable sounding ideas" will be his, and they will "just try to forget about" hers (ch. 5). Rennie has no difficulty with this, once she becomes aware of her own lack of selfhood and is flooded with self-contempt. She can easily give up her identity, since she does not feel that she has one, and she hopes to escape her feeling of nothingness by merging with Joe and participating in his substantiality.

Joe does not want a clone, however, or a mindless devotee. He wants someone who, once she is trained, will *independently and spontaneously* think exactly as he does. He is drawn to Rennie because he senses her malleability, which he wants to think is combined with an unusual self-sufficiency. This combination would make her an ideal candidate for the kind of relationship he envisions, but after a number of years of marriage (their sons are aged three and four), things have not worked out as he had hoped. Rennie has tried desperately to become like Joe, but she is only a weak imitation: "I'll always be uncertain," she wails, "and he'll always be able to explain his positions better than I can" (ch. 5). She does not even consider having positions of her own. She appreciates Joe, to be sure, but she is so slavish that her recognition is hardly worth having. She was supposed to come to life after he had molded her and to be an autonomous person who happened to be just like himself. Her respect would then be of value, and they could work at leading a coherent life.

We can now understand why Joe throws Rennie and Jake together. He knows he has brainwashed Rennie and fears that she will not become autonomous as long as she is under his influence. He sees Jake as having "a first-rate mind that is totally different from his" (ch. 5) and hopes that exposing Rennie to him will make her think for herself. Perhaps then she will enable him to escape his isolation and reconcile his conflicting psychological needs for consensual validation and unique superiority. Joe's objectives have been unrealistic all along; Rennie was bound to disappoint him because no human being could possess the contradictory qualities for which he was looking. He correctly assessed her malleability and found part of what he sought, but her self-sufficiency and strength were figments of his imagination. Unable to give up his dream, he still misperceives her, exposing her to a situation she cannot handle.

"What scares me," she tells Jake, "is that anybody could grant all of Joe's premises—our premises . . . and *then* laugh at us" (emphasis in original). Jake astutely replies, "Maybe that's what Joe was after." "It could be," says Rennie, "but if it was he overestimated me! I can't take it."

Rennie's experience with Jake is a repetition of her experience with Joe; he injures her pride and makes her feel like "a complete zero." She has defended herself against her sense of inner emptiness by investing her pride in Joe and their relationship, but Jake threatens this by suggesting that Joe and their marriage are silly, and Rennie becomes frightened when she begins to wonder if Jake is stronger than Joe. She reassures herself by concluding that Jake is unreal because of his inconsistency: "I think you don't exist at all. There's too many of you. . . . You cancel yourself out. You're more like somebody in a dream. You're not strong and you're not weak. You're nothing" (ch. 5). Joe is "the same man today he was yesterday, all the way through. He's genuine! That's the difference." "Joe's real enough to handle you," proclaims Rennie. "He's real enough for both of us." "Nothing plus one is one," says Jake, "agreeably." "That's right," replies Rennie. She can live with her own sense of nothingness as long as she believes in Joe and participates in his strength.

Concluding that Jake is unreal alleviates Rennie's anxiety, but it is extremely threatening to Jake. When she says that Jake is "nothing" and that he doesn't "exist," she is articulating his deepest fears about himself, the very fears Joe had aroused and that had made Jake mock him in the first place. Jake responds by inviting Rennie to spy on Joe one evening when they return home. Rennie insists that Joe is "just reading" and that Jake doesn't "know Joe at all": "*Real* people aren't any different when they're alone. No masks. What you see of them is authentic." "Horseshit," replies Jake. "Nobody's authentic. Let's look" (ch. 5). Authenticity is the crucial issue for Jake. If Joe is authentic, then Jake is defective, but if nobody is authentic, Jake need not despise himself. His lack of identity is just a manifestation of human nature and the human condition, about which Joe has deluded himself. When Jake and Rennie look in at the window, they see Joe cavorting about the room in an absurd manner and then "masturbating and picking his nose at the same time." Rennie's image of Joe is shattered.

Jake continues his aggression by cuckolding Joe while he is out of town (Jake's namesake is Jack Horner in Wycherly's *The Country Wife*). He claims that "the whole business was without significance" (ch. 7), but he is clearly deceiving himself. The next day he becomes engrossed in reading several volumes of plays and gives the matter no further thought: "It was insignificant, unimportant, and, as far as I was concerned, inconsequential." Jake is protesting too much. He is frightened at having acted out his vindictive feelings and is trying to deny the significance of his behavior and to reestablish his detachment. He also needs to repress the desire for an emotional connection with Rennie that had partly motivated him. He admits to having been curious to learn not only what Rennie was like in bed, "but also what the intimate relationship (I do not mean sexual relationship) would be like which I presumed would be established by our intercourse."

Jake's detachment quickly breaks down when Rennie calls to say that she must see him. Assuming that what is "in the offing [is] a polishing of the crown of horns we'd already placed on Joe's brow," he experiences "a sudden, marvelous sensation of guilt" while driving to the Morgans (ch. 7). The sensation is marvelous because Jake feels bored and empty most of the time, and the guilt makes him feel alive. His reaction is so intense that he stops being an observer and is caught up in the experience: "What, for God's sake, had I done? . . . I was anguished, as never before in my life. What is more, my anguish was pretty much unselfconscious: I was not aware of watching Jacob Horner suffer anguish."

Jake is now in the grip of his inner conflicts. When his self-effacing side is uppermost, he is appalled by the "enormity of the injury" he has done Joe and hates himself for having betrayed "the only man he can think of as a friend" (ch. 7). His detached side makes him hate himself for being afraid of Joe's "disappointment," "disapproval," and "disgust," "which ordinarily would not bother me." Rennie asks to see him because she, too, is overwhelmed with guilt ("I couldn't have hurt him like that") and wants to confess to Joe. Jake is afraid of what will happen if she does and despises himself for his cowardice.

Jake has violated the shoulds of all his solutions and is tortured by guilt and self-contempt. He has always escaped painful emotions through detachment, but his usual methods do not work: "It was useless to try to read or sleep: there was no slipping into someone else's world or otherwise escaping my own, which had me by the throat" (ch. 7). He feels such "loathing" for himself that he begins to think of suicide: "I envied all dead things—the fat earthworms that lay squashed upon the wet sidewalks, the animals whose fried bodies I chewed at mealtimes, people decomposing in muddy cemeteries." Jake's "self-revulsion" abates when Joe asks him, "why in the name of Christ did you fuck Rennie?" Having to deal with Joe shifts his attention away from his guilt to defending himself and "salvaging [his] self-respect" (ch. 8).

Once life grabs Jake by the throat, his self-effacing tendencies emerge rather powerfully. In addition to punishing himself for his betrayal of Joe, he begins to have "tender, lovelike feelings" toward Rennie (ch. 9). When she says that she might love him, along with hating his "God-damned guts," he is "flattered beyond measure": "I responded easily and inordinately to any evidence of affection from people whom I admired or respected in any way." His use of the word "inordinately" suggests at once an intense craving for affection and a dread of being overpowered by it. Jake is enthralled not just by the possibility of Rennie's love but also by her expressions of hatred. In the scene referred to above, Rennie begins by telling Jake that she still despises him. "Thrilled . . . from head to foot," he becomes "acutely interested in her" and proposes that "we didn't just copulate; we made love." When Rennie reacts to this with "abhorrence," Jake grows "very excited." Rennie's revulsion and Joe's masterfulness bring out Jake's submissiveness and intensify his attachments. The same dynamics occur in his relationship with the Doctor. Jake describes himself as "thrilled" again when Joe tells him that he has put his Colt .45 on the shelf of the living-room closet in case he or Rennie want to use it on themselves or anyone else: "Perhaps it was Joe Morgan, after all, that I loved" (ch. 10). There is an emotionally hungry side of Jake that longs to be loved and a masochistic side that longs to be mastered.

Jake's self-effacing tendencies are in conflict with his detachment. In an effort to understand what has happened, Joe insists that Rennie continue to see Jake, and when Jake says that he might be in love with her, Joe raises the possibility of "a permanent sexual relationship" between them, "a triangle without conflicts or secrecy" (ch. 10). Jake finds that at the very mention of a permanent relationship, he begins "to grow tired of the idea of Rennie." At this possible threat to his freedom, his detachment reasserts itself. Jake's conflicting tendencies are sometimes so evenly balanced that he holds contradictory attitudes simultaneously, as when he feels "both guilty and nonchalant about the Morgan affair" (ch. 9).

Jake can no longer feel nonchalant when Rennie becomes pregnant and, not knowing who the father is, says that she will shoot herself if she cannot obtain an abortion. His affection and sense of responsibility drive him to an uncharacteristic frenzy of activity, as he tries to prevent her suicide. Finally, the Doctor agrees to perform an abortion if Jake will give him all his money and come to live at his new Remobilization Farm in Pennsylvania.

After he arranges the abortion, Jake experiences "a reaction" against his "whole commitment." He wants the adventure to teach him that he is

> not so consistently the same person (not so sufficiently "real," to use Rennie's term) that I could involve myself seriously in the lives of others without doing damage all around, not least to my own tranquillity; that my irrational flashes of conscience and cruelty, of compassion and cynicism—in short, my inability to play the same role long enough—could give me as well as others pain. (Ch. 12)

The conflicting sides of Jake are all represented in this passage. His detached side is cynical and longs for tranquillity, his self-effacing side is conscientious and compassionate, and his aggressive side is cruel. Jake has had a bad scare. His oscillations have led him to experience guilt, anguish, and a longing for death and have led Rennie to the brink of suicide. He feels that, given his inconsistency, it is extremely dangerous for him to become involved with others. He tells himself that he does not "consistently need or want friends" and that if he is to have them "at all [he] must remain uninvolved—[he] must leave them alone," which is a strange way of having friends. He wants to feel so severely chastened that he will never relinquish his detachment and become involved with other people again.

Jake is anxious because even now he does not feel single-minded: "My feelings were mixed: relief, ridiculousness, embarrassment, anger, injured pride, maudlin affection for the Morgans, disgust with them and myself, and a host of other things, including indifference to the whole business" (ch. 12). Indifference is what Jake wants to feel, but it is clear that he is still in the grip of his conflicts, and in order to escape his anxiety, he contemplates leaving Wicomico: "In a new town, with new friends, even under a new name—perhaps one could *pretend* enough unity to be a person and live in the world."

Jake's affair with Rennie has destroyed Joe Morgan's solution as well as his own. Because of his misreading of Rennie, Joe's effort to make his marriage work as he had envisioned seems to have resulted in its destruction. He claims to be glad the affair happened "because it uncovered real problems [he] didn't know existed," and now he will be able to get to the bottom of them (ch. 8). Joe takes pride in dealing with reality, despite the fact that he is out of touch with it, but the reality revealed by Rennie's affair is one he cannot accept. According to Joe's version of Rennie and Rennie's version of herself, the affair could not have happened. Since it did happen, they must correct their version of Rennie, "and right now we can't see how any version that allows for what happened would also allow for the kind of relationship we thought we had." With the loss of his illusions about his marriage, Joe is left with no way of satisfying his contradictory needs for Rennie to be an independent person who thinks exactly as he does.

To cope with his crisis, Joe has recourse to his habitual modes of behavior: he will try to think straight, to face "the facts squarely," to be sharp and clear all the time. He still aims at living coherently. He has, as Jake says, "the delusion that intelligence will solve all problems" (ch. 9). To identify the problem that has to be solved, he feels that he must "know just what happened" and why (ch. 8). He becomes obsessed with the pursuit of this knowledge, regarding it as "a life-and-death business." Rennie says that Joe is "thinking more clearly and intensely" than ever, and she once again regards him as a god, but Jake feels that "he's just insane, a monomaniac." Since one of Joe's axioms is that our behavior always reflects our most strongly held values, he argues that Rennie believes it is all right to make love to other men, or at least to Jake, whether she wants to admit it to herself or not. If they are to know where they stand, she must act on her "real beliefs" (Joe makes no provision for ambivalence) and continue to have sexual relations with Jake. Jake correctly points out (to the reader, though not to Rennie) that Joe's position is "entirely illogical," since Rennie's single adultery at most "implied that she'd been willing to do it just once" (ch. 9). Joe is not thinking straight and is still not facing the facts.

But he is "behaving pretty consistently with his position," and, as

Jake observes, "that knowledge can be comforting even in cases where the position leads to defeat or disaster" (ch. 10). Rennie, however, no longer has "a position to act consistently with," and, unlike Jake's, her personality seems "to require a position in order to preserve itself." Rennie does not want to have sex with Jake, but she feels that she would be letting Joe down if she did not. If she refused to comply, moreover, he might walk out flat or kill "himself or all of us" (ch. 9). Joe's has been a reign of terror from the beginning, since he has used physical violence, or the threat of it, and psychological intimidation. Rennie had been full of rage that she had turned against herself, feeling a failure and taking the blame for everything, until her disillusionment with Joe led her to act out her aggression by committing adultery with Jake. Her guilt makes her all the more desperate for Joe's approval and disposed to be compliant, but pleasing him seems more impossible than ever. Under terrible psychological stress, Rennie tells Jake that she is "desperate" and is "going crazy" (ch. 10).

What saves the Morgans, oddly enough, is Rennie's becoming pregnant. When Rennie says that she'll do whatever Joe wants, he shouts, "Think for yourself, or I don't want anything to do with you!" (ch. 10). Rennie declares that she doesn't want the baby and won't put it up for adoption: "All right," says Joe, "there's the pistol. Shoot yourself." "I will if you want me to, Joe." When Jake suggests abortion as an alternative, Rennie makes up her mind: "I'm going to get an abortion or shoot myself, Joe. I've decided." Joe points out the difficulty of finding an abortionist, Rennie makes a dash for the gun, and Jake prevents her from reaching it. "You people are insane!" he exclaims. "Do you want her to blow her damned head off?" "I want her to think for herself," replies Joe. He tells Jake that he would kill him for "taking something as important as this out of the realm of choice." Jake begins frantically searching for an abortionist in an effort to save Rennie's life, but the Morgans are calm after this. They are waiting for Jake to fail, and then Rennie will commit suicide.

The Morgans are calm, I believe, because at last their impossible dream is coming true. Joe has been insisting that Rennie continue to see Jake because "she's got to decide once and for all what she really feels about you and me and herself" (ch. 10). When Rennie "decides" that she will either get an abortion or shoot herself, she finally becomes what Joe has wanted her to be, an autonomous person whose choices validate him. The fact that she does not want the baby because it might possibly be Jake's signifies her choice of Joe. She would rather die than have a child that might not be his. Ignoring the psychological pressure to which he has subjected her, Joe can believe that she is thinking for herself. He had earlier explained to Jake that what he and Rennie "want of each other isn't possible unless we assume that we're free agents—*pretend* we are even when we suspect we aren't" (ch. 8). He uses the plural pronoun, but it is his needs, not Rennie's, that he is describing. Like God in *Paradise Lost*, Joe demands obedience, submission, and worship and is punitive if they are not forthcoming, but they do not contribute to his glory unless he believes them to be given freely. The God-Satan-Everyman analogy is explicit in *The End of the Road*, with Jake in the role of Satan making it possible for Rennie to be a "free agent."

At the beginning of the novel, Rennie despaired of ever becoming what Joe wanted, but she has finally succeeded. Like Nora and Hedda, Rennie feels that she can escape her problems and attain the glory she seeks through an heroic act of self-destruction. To go on living is to experience more failure and self-hate, but to die is to actualize her idealized image so that it cannot be taken away from her. Joe clearly seems to desire Rennie's death. He threatens to kill Jake if he interferes with Rennie's free choice, makes no effort to provide an alternative to suicide, and keeps suggesting that her only option is to shoot herself. He, too, must be aware that if this crisis passes, Rennie will revert to her slavish ways.

Thus the Morgans are not overjoyed when Jake announces that he has arranged an abortion:

> "Will you be ready at nine?" I asked her.
> "I'll be ready."
> "You'll want to come too, won't you?" I asked Joe.
> "I don't know," he said dully. "I'll decide later."
> It was as though I'd spoiled something. (Ch. 12)

Indeed, Jake has spoiled everything. When he calls for Rennie, she and Joe are just finishing dinner, and she dies from aspirating her vomit after the Doctor administers ether. "She must have eaten a big meal before she came out here," observes the Doctor. "She should've known better." Is Rennie a suicide after all?

Joe is not crushed by Rennie's death. Tears pour down his face, "but he neither sobbed nor made any kind of noise" (ch. 12). When he calls

Jake later to ask what he thinks about things, his voice is "bright" and "clear." Rennie's apparent free choice of him has given Joe the confirmation he has sought, and her death, undergone for his sake, preserves his sense that his solution has worked. He is once again living in a world of his own, one that is no longer vulnerable to the intrusions of reality.

Although Jake is triumphant in the contest of ideas, it is Joe rather than Jake who is intact at the end. When Joe asks him what he thinks about things, Jake replies, "God, Joe—I don't know where to start or what to do!" "Tears ran in a cold flood down my face and neck, onto my chest, and I shook all over with violent chills" (ch. 12). Contrast this with Joe's reaction to Rennie's death. Jake had not meant to keep his promise to the Doctor, but he is driven by his distress to become a resident of the Remobilization Farm, permanently perhaps, like the Doctor's other patients, the old men in the dormitory.

Once he had arranged the abortion, Jake reacted against his commitment, wanted to be chastened, and considered adopting a new identity and trying to "*pretend* enough unity to be a person and live in the world." After Rennie's death, this is no longer a possibility: " 'We've come too far,' " I said to Laocoön. 'Who can live any longer in the world?' " (ch. 12). At the end of the novel, Jake is once again weatherless, devoid of emotion. Having retreated from his feelings, he secures his tranquillity by retreating from the world and submitting himself to the Doctor's authority. At the Remobilization Farm he will no longer be at risk of becoming involved with others, thus activating his conflicts and incurring self-hate. He so distrusts himself that he has chosen a kind of living death. The last line of the novel suggests that his case is "Terminal."So, of course, does the title—*The End of the Road*.[1]

Like Dostoevsky's underground man, however, Jake protects his pride by turning his neurotic condition into a source of superiority (see Paris 1974). The underground man admits to being an antihero but comforts himself with the thought that "we are all cripples, every one of us, more or less." He is better than the others because he has "carried to an extreme what you have not dared to carry halfway, and what's more, you have taken your cowardice for good sense, and have found comfort in deceiving yourselves" (pt. 2, ch. 10). Jake also feels more perceptive than his fellows. He is paralyzed at the end because his limbs are "bound like Laocoön's—by the serpents Knowledge and Imagination, which, grown great in the fullness of time, no longer tempt but annihilate" (ch. 10). Jake cannot live in the world because he has "come too far"; he is more highly evolved than the others, more gifted—and cursed—with knowledge and imagination. Those who can live in the world are short-sighted creatures with simple-minded beliefs who do not perceive the bewildering complexity of life. As is frequent in the detached solution, both Jake and the underground man console themselves for the empti-ness of their existence by taking pride in their ability to see through everyone else's illusions, but they are blind to their own self-deceptions.

When we look at them closely, Barth's characters, too, are amenable to motivational analysis, especially from a Horneyan perspective. Our sense of what is mimetic depends in part upon the breadth of our understanding; often characters seem unrealistic simply because we do not comprehend their motivations and personalities. Both psychoana-lytic theory and literature enlarge our sense of what is human. Jake, Joe, and Rennie behave in extreme ways, but so do many characters in great works of fiction.

5

"The Clerk's Tale"

Among the most extreme characters in literature are Walter and Griselda in Chaucer's "The Clerk's Tale." Griselda is the archetypal submissive, long-suffering wife, and Walter goes to absurd lengths to test her. Not all mimetic characters are realized in the same degree of detail. We are provided with varying amounts of information about such things as early history, family relationships, conscious and unconscious motives. Of the characters I shall discuss, Pip and Jane Eyre are the most fully rendered. The least fully drawn are Walter and Griselda, whose behavior is so bizarre that it is usually thought to have only illustrative significance, about which there is much disagreement. However, some critics have seen that Chaucer provides enough mimetic detail to invite motivational analysis, and I find these characters to be amenable to a Horneyan approach. When we see Walter and Griselda in the context of our discussions of Torvald and Nora, Joe and Rennie, they become recognizably human and not just embodiments of medieval ideas about womanhood, marriage, and the relation between God and his subjects. Indeed, it is because these characters are mimetic as well as illustrative that their emblematic functions are so difficult to define.

Although "The Clerk's Tale" is commonly thought of as the story of patient Griselda, Walter is also important, and we must understand him if we are to grasp the dynamics of their strange relationship. Why does Walter, marquis of Saluzzo, the highest born man in Lombardy, choose to marry Griselda, daughter of the poorest of his liege men? And why, after the marriage, does he take Griselda's children away from her, leading her to believe that he has ordered them to be murdered, and then pretend to cast her off in order to wed a high-born woman? He says he did these things "For no malice, nor for no cruelty, / But for t'assay in thee thy womanhood" (1075–76),[1] but this seems feeble, and the allegorical interpretations of his behavior are problematic. Walter's testing of Griselda is compared to God's testing of "what He wrought" (1152), but Walter is hardly comparable to God, since he is described by the Clerk as obsessive and cruel. Griselda may be the ideal obedient subject, displaying a Job-like submission, but it is difficult to define Walter's emblematic significance.

The initial descriptions of Walter indicate that he is a very detached person. He does not consider the future, lets serious cares slide, follows his present inclinations, and spends his days hawking and hunting. He cannot be prevailed on to marry. A popular but heedless ruler, he wants nothing to infringe on his freedom or to burden him with responsibility. His aversion to wedlock is disturbing to his people, since if he dies without issue they will be ruled by a strange successor, and they send a deputation urging him to marry. Knowing his temperament, the leader assures him that wedlock is a "blissfull yoke / Of sovereignty, not of service" (113–14). Walter replies that he has rejoiced in his "liberty, / That seldom time is found in marriage; / Where I was free, I must be in servage" (145–47). For someone as sensitive to constraint as Walter, marriage is extremely threatening.

He agrees to marry, however, if the people will accept his conditions. They offer to find him a wife "Born of the gentlest and of the most / Of all this land" (131–32), but Walter insists that he will make his own choice. If he is to forgo his liberty for their sake, he must wed where he wishes. They must not grumble or strive against his decision and must give all honor to his wife, no matter who she is. Walter is not only insisting on his freedom to choose but is also laying the groundwork for his choice of Griselda. He argues that goodness comes from God rather than from noble birth and puts his "trust in God's bounty" (159), giving an aura of piety to his decision. Walter seems to know immediately that the only way he can tolerate marriage is to wed a woman far beneath him. If he married the kind of woman his people have in mind, he would have to consider her wishes and be careful of offending her family.

Walter feels obliged to perform his duties when pressed but does not wish to give up his freedom. He hopes that choosing Griselda will enable him to satisfy his conflicting needs. She is at the bottom of the class hierarchy, while he is at the top. Janicula, his poorest vassal, is reverently obeyed by his daughter, who, as a female, is even lower on the social ladder. If Griselda exalts her father by her dutiful submission, what might not Walter expect from her? She is a model of feminine virtue, an embodiment of her society's teachings about the subordination of

women. Walter proposes a bargain to Griselda: he will marry her and
raise her to the heights if she is

> . . . ready with good heart
> To all my lust [wishes]; and that I freely may
> As me best thinketh, do you laugh or smart,
> And never you to grudge it, night nor day.
>
> (351–54)

I believe that Walter is more concerned with freedom than with domination, which is but a means to his end. Griselda's submission insures that
he can still follow his whims.

Griselda readily accepts Walter's conditions, promising "never willingly"
to disobey "in work nor thought" (362–63). She is as eager to submerge
herself in Walter as he is for her to do so. Marriage to Walter is the
culmination of her search for glory. The lowest of the low, she transcends
her humble position by loving virtue and cultivating moral perfection.
For a woman in her society this means, above all, reverent obedience to
male authority. As Janicula's "pearl" of a daughter she gains a reputation for goodness, seriousness, and sagacity, and this, combined with her
beauty, catches Walter's attention. His proposal of marriage is the reward of her virtue. To her, his conditions are light because she is prac-
ticed in womanly self-effacement. Indeed, they are welcome because she
wishes to merge with him as a way of participating in his glory. She feels
vastly inferior to Walter, telling him that she is unworthy of so much
honor, but she eliminates the distance between them by erasing herself
completely and accepting his will as her own. Like Nora and Rennie, she
seeks to escape her sense of inferiority and gratify her repressed expansive desires by becoming one with a powerful male. By abandoning
herself to Walter she can satisfy her conflicting needs to be both humble
and great.

According to the terms of their bargain, Griselda's submission binds
Walter to her: "when I say 'Yea,' ne say not 'Nay,' / Neither by word
nor frowning countenance? / Swear this, and here I swear our alliance"
(355–57). His testing enables her to solidify her claim to him by showing
that no matter what he asks she will be agreeable. When he announces
that he must take away her daughter, she is "not a-moved" (498) and
"not agrieved" (500): "My child and I, with hearty obeisance, / Be yours

all, and you may save or spill / Your own thing; worketh after your will"
(502–4). We can interpret this allegorically as meaning that God has the
right to do what he likes with his creatures or historically as Griselda's
acceptance of her culture's patriarchal view of marriage, but these sentiments are also in keeping with Griselda's character. If Walter treats her
as chattel, to spare or kill as he pleases, he is acknowledging her as his
wife. She possesses him by being possessed.

A scene in Hardy's *Tess of the d'Urbervilles* may help us to understand this triumph through submission. Having rejected Tess on their
wedding night after she confesses her affair with Alec d'Urberville, Angel
Clare carries her toward a river while sleep-walking, and Tess thinks
that he may be about to drown her: "So easefully had she delivered her
whole being up to him that it pleased her to think he was regarding her
as his absolute possession, to dispose of as he should choose. It was
consoling . . . to feel that he really recognized her now as his wife Tess,
and did not cast her off, even if in that recognition he went so far as to
arrogate to himself the right of harming her" (ch. 37; see Paris 1976a).
Angel's regarding her as his absolute possession, whom he has the right
to harm, means that he recognizes her as his wife, and Walter's behavior
has a similar meaning for Griselda. Both women feel vastly inferior to
the men they adore and are ready to sacrifice everything, even life itself,
to the glory of being united with them. There is something similar in the
readiness of Nora and Rennie to die for Torvald and Joe.

While Griselda's behavior can be interpreted allegorically, it also
clashes with an allegorical reading if we look at it closely. Griselda
proclaims that there is nothing she desires to have "Ne dread to lose,
save only" Walter (507), who is "her very worldly suffisance" (759). She
values Walter above God or her own soul and is ready to sacrifice her
child in order to keep him. She tells her infant daughter, "this night shall
thou dien for my sake" (560). These sentiments are not commensurate
with the Clerk's idealization of Griselda, or with most thematic readings,
but they make sense psychologically. Griselda is living for the worldly
glory that Walter represents, her need of which is so intense, because of
her base position perhaps, that she will sacrifice anything to hold onto
it. Like Rennie and Tess, she cannot criticize her husband's cruelty
because that would diminish the man on whom her glory depends. Since
she believes that Walter cannot abandon her as long as she honors their
bargain, her submission gives her a sense of control over him and her
destiny.

One of Walter's conditions is that whether he offers "laugh or smart," she must be "ready with good heart" and never show "a frowning countenance" (351, 353, 356). Griselda swears never to disobey in deed "or thought" (363), thus promising to make her innermost life conform to his desires. She so succeeds that they seem to have between them "but one will" (716). One of the things that has troubled readers about Griselda and made her seem unrealistic is that she does not have the emotions that would be natural in response to the loss of her children and Walter's casting her off. A psychological explanation would be that the emotions are there but deeply repressed, since expressing or even feeling them would invalidate Griselda's bargain and cost her that which is dearer than life. In Horneyan terms, she has an idealized image of herself, imbibed from her culture and refined by Walter's demands, that generates tyrannical shoulds. She must be unmoved and unaggrieved no matter what is inflicted upon her, or she will forfeit her claims, lose her glory, and experience unbearable self-hate. She says she would rather die than disobey in deed or thought though she is "loath to die" (364).

In later episodes Griselda seems remarkably free of anguish when she is tested, but not at first. She does not weep or lament when Walter's villainous looking agent comes to take away her daughter, but she begs to kiss the child before it dies, takes it into her lap, lulls it, commends its soul to Christ, and bids it a farewell that would have rent the heart of a mother or nurse. She quickly controls her emotions, however, and Walter finds her "As glad, as humble, as busy in service, / And eke [also] in love as she was wont to be" (603–4). The emotion Griselda displays when she loses her daughter suggests the feelings she represses more fully when her son is taken away and when Walter divorces her. She seems unreal, to be sure, but it may be the unreality of a person who behaves in a rigidly neurotic way and is not in touch with herself.

Although we see indications of anguish when Griselda is first tested, there is no display of anger with Walter, since to blame him would not only violate her shoulds but would damage her image of him, which she must preserve at all costs. In *King Lear* we do not see Cordelia's anger at her father's injustice because to display resentment would violate her idealized image, but her vindictive feelings are present in the play and are acted out by Goneril and Regan. She can forgive Lear so easily because her sisters have punished him terribly for his mistake (see Paris 1991a). Walter is not punished for his cruel behavior, but he is repeatedly condemned. The resentment that Griselda cannot allow herself to feel is expressed by others. Before the first test, the Clerk describes Walter as obsessed by his need to test Griselda's constancy and declares that it is "evil" "To assay a wife that it is no need, / And putten her in anguish and in dread" (460–62). Before the second test, he again asserts that Griselda was tempted needlessly and observes that "wedded men ne knowen no measure, / When that they find a patient creäture" (622–23). Walter's subjects are appalled by the seeming murders of his children, and their love turns to hate. The third test is deplored not only by the Clerk but also by Walter's subjects and by Janicula, who feels confirmed in his expectation that once the marquis had satisfied his desires he would feel disgraced by his low alliance and abrogate it.

Griselda's resentment does in fact surface when Walter casts her off, but in an indirect way that enables her to preserve her idealized image. She seizes on his statement that she can take again the dowry she brought with her, pointing out that it was only her wretched clothes that were worth nothing and would be difficult to find. "O good God!" she exclaims, "how gentle and how kind / You *seeméd* by your speech and your visage / The day that makéd was our marriage!" (852–54; my emphasis). She continues in a similar vein, testifying to the truth of the statement that "Love is not old as when that it is new" (857). She may be excusing Walter by saying that men are like that, but there is reproach in her words. Afraid that she has violated her shoulds by complaining about her husband, she quickly reaffirms her self-sacrificial devotion, saying that she would never repent having given Walter her heart whatever the adversity, even if it were death. She resumes her attack, however, by asking if he really means to do "so dishonest [shameless] a thing" as to send her home naked, letting "the womb in which your children lay" be "seen all bare" (876–79). It is unlikely that this is what Walter had in mind, but he has provided Griselda with a pretext for characterizing him as infamous and reminding him of the children. This scene reveals some of Griselda's buried emotion.

Before we look further at Griselda's response to her ordeals, let us consider Walter's motivations. We have examined his reasons for choosing Griselda, but why his "mervellous desire his wife t'assay" (454)? It seems that after his marriage he needs to be reassured that he has not been tethered, that he can still do as he pleases. Griselda has given him no cause for complaint, but he cannot be sure of her submission unless he offers her woe. Like many detached people, Walter compulsively needs to prove that he is free. The Clerk is aware that he is being driven by emotions over which he has no control:

> But there been folk of such condition
> That when they have a certain purpose take,
> They can not stint of their intention,
> But, *right as they were bounden to a stake,*
> They will not of that first purpose slake.
>
> (701–5; my emphasis)

Walter has strong reasons for taking away the children, quite apart from his desire to assure himself of his liberty. He had tried to resolve the conflict between his need to comply with the wishes of his people for a successor and his need to retain his freedom by marrying a woman who would give way to him in everything. He is profoundly uncomfortable, however, at having allied himself with someone so poor and low. His discomfort is evident in the lies he tells Griselda when he removes the children. Griselda has performed splendidly in her lofty position, charming the people, gaining fame for her virtue, and advancing the public good. His subjects hold Walter to be "a prudent man" because he has seen "that under low degree / Was often virtue hid" (425–27). But Walter tells Griselda that his nobles regard it as "great shame and woe / For to be subjects and be in servage / To thee, than born art of a small village" (481–83). He says that he is being forced by the will of the people to take away her daughter, presumably because the child of such a lowly mother should not occupy such a high social position. Walter may have invented this lie so as not to appear cruel ("And yet, God wot, this is full loath to me"—491), but it also expresses his sentiments.

With the birth of his daughter, Walter becomes acutely conscious of the disparity between himself and Griselda and the ambiguous status of their child. He is still resentful of the pressure put on him to marry, which is one reason why he presents himself as a victim of coercion, but he is also ashamed at having degraded his family and failed in his duty to his subjects by siring a child of such base descent on the mother's side. He shows his independence of the people by apparently killing the child, thus frustrating their desire for him to have offspring, but at the same time he satisfies his social conscience by sending the child to his sister, who will bring her up as a lady. Griselda is socially accomplished despite having been "born and fed in rudeness" (397), but Walter may be afraid that she will instill her lowly spirit in his child. He wants his wife to be a doormat but not his daughter.

Walter tells a similar set of lies when he removes their son: "My people sickly bear our marrïage; / And namely [especially] since my son y-born is" (625–26). In reality the people have rejoiced at the birth of the child, thanking and praising God. According to Walter, however, there are murmurings that when his reign is done "Then shall the blood of Janicle succeed / And be our lord" (632–33). He presents himself as being harried by opinions that are being secretly advanced in his dominions: "For to mine ears comes the voice so smart / That it well nigh destroyèd has my heart" (629–30). I think that Walter *is* profoundly disturbed by these opinions, which are not his subjects' but his own. He secretly sends his son to his sister's noble household, where he will receive a princely education. His preoccupation with issues of class may be an even more powerful motive for his behavior than his need to assay Griselda.

In his final test, the casting off of Griselda, Walter again explains his behavior as forced upon him by his people. He did not marry her for "lineage" or "riches" (795) but for her goodness, truth, and obedience. His subjects, however, "me constraineth for to take / Another wife" (800–801). Walter complains that "in great lordship . . . / There is great servitude in sundry wise" (797–98) and that he "may not do as every plowman may" (799)."This is true, of course. His position has accustomed him to indulge every whim, but it also imposes responsibilities by which he feels oppressed. He experiences his inner compulsion to do his duty as servitude and coercion, leading his lies to take the particular form that they do.

Walter's pretence of divorcing Griselda and betrothing a highborn lady is designed less as a final test of Griselda's patience than as a vindication of his children and himself. His daughter is deemed fit to be his wife, the people agreeing that "fairer fruit between them should fall, / And more pleasant for her high lineage" (990–91). This tribute to his daughter is also, ironically, a tribute to his wife. Walter's son is likewise approved by the populace. The taint of being Janicula's descendants has been removed from the children, and they can rightfully occupy their exalted positions henceforth. They are no longer half-breeds, so to speak, but full-fledged members of the nobility. The daughter marries a wealthy lord and the son succeeds to the inheritance. The danger of the daughter's being too much like her mother has been averted. As Griselda herself warns, the girl has been "fostered in her nourishing / More tenderly" (1040–41) and must not be goaded and tried as she has been. The vindication of the children vindicates Walter's choice of Griselda, and, no longer tormented by guilt and fear of condemnation, he can own her proudly at last. His people had given her the honor he had demanded, despite her low birth, but he had been unable to do so himself. Only now does Walter relieve Janicula of his poverty and invite him to live at the court.

Griselda responds to the loss of her son as she had to the loss of her daughter, except that she suppresses her anguish completely and is even more self-abasing. Not only does she assure Walter that it does not grieve her "at all / Though that my daughter and my son be slain / At your commandment" (647–49), but she says that if she had known his will before he told it her, she would have done it "withouten negligence" (661)—presumably meaning that she would have killed them herself. "For," she continues, "wist I that my death would do you ease, / Right gladly would I dien, you to please" (664–65). Viola makes a similar statement in *Twelfth Night* when Duke Orsino threatens to kill her (disguised as Cesario) in order to spite Olivia: "And I, most jocund, apt, and willingly, / To do you rest a thousand deaths would die" (5.1.127–28). Like Tess, Griselda and Viola conceive of death at the hands of the beloved as an ecstatic experience of union through submission, of possession by being possessed. "Death," says Griselda, "may not make no comparison / Unto your love" (666–67). As long as she has Walter's love she escapes her sense of unworthiness, participates in his grandeur, and feels that her idealized image of herself is being confirmed. This is more important to her than mere existence.

When Walter tells Griselda that, with the consent of the Pope, he is taking another wife, he violates their bargain, but Griselda's self-effacing defense can accommodate even this. Her humility has been her claim to moral grandeur, and she takes refuge in it when Walter discards her. Her "poverty" makes no comparison with his "magnificence" (815–16); she was not worthy to be his chambermaid, much less his wife. She never thought of herself as "mistress" of his house but rather as an "humble servant" to his "worthiness" (823–24). He has not treated her badly because she has no rights. Walter's behavior confirms the sense of inferiority that Griselda has never shaken off, and this makes it easier for her to reconcile herself to her fate. His treatment of her as unworthy has a value to Griselda, for, as Horney observes, a morbidly dependent person "craves to surrender . . . body and soul," but can do so only if her pride is broken, if she "feels, or is, degraded" (1950, 246).

Griselda does not give up her search for glory. She continues to live up to her idealized image of herself, which she can do independently of Walter, and she continues to glorify him, saying that she will always think of him "Aboven every worldly crëature" (826). We may wonder why she idealizes the man who has treated her so cruelly, especially when she has lost him, but her behavior makes psychological sense. By reminding her of her lowliness, Walter reinforces his elevation above her, inducing her to venerate him all the more. She continues to exalt him because she can still be proud, in her self-effacing way, of *having been* Walter's wife. Her glory is in the past, but it is glory nevertheless. She thanks her God and Walter "That you so long of your benignity, / Have holden me in honor and nobley [regard], / Where as I was not worthy for to be" (827–29). She attributes the honor she enjoyed to Walter's benignity rather than to her own deserts, thus preserving her humility, but her pride shows through nonetheless. She will remain faithful to him as a way of affirming both her virtue and his exalted status: "God shield such a lord's wife to take / Another man to husband or to make [mate]" (839–40). By remaining loyal, she will maintain her sense of still being Walter's possession.

Thus she comes "with humble heart and glad visage" (949) when Walter asks her to help entertain his bride, for this gives her an opportunity to define her new role. She will endeavor "to serve and please" him in her own "degree" (969), for no matter what, she will never stop loving him best. I am reminded of Desdemona's statement that even if Othello shakes her off "to beggarly divorcement," she will always "love him dearly": "Unkindness may do much; / And his unkindness may defeat my life, / But never taint my love" (*Othello* 4, 2). Like Desdemona, Griselda is determined to hold onto her idealized image of her husband and of herself as the perfect wife. She achieves independence of Walter and fortune because she will always worship and love him, even when he causes her grief. She has found an impregnable defense, one similar to that offered by a religion that preaches unconditional submission to the will of God. If we love God no matter what, life will always have meaning and we will share in his high magnificence.

Although Desdemona's self-effacing defense leads to her death (see

Paris 1991a), Griselda's is successful because Walter has always intended to honor their bargain (he does not really mean to divorce her and marry his daughter), and he is compelled by her submission. Her children are restored, untainted by her low birth, and she and Walter live on in "high prosperity" and "concord" (1128–29). Griselda finally receives the confirmation of her worth to the pursuit of which she has devoted her life. Were she to die this moment it would be nothing, she tells her husband, "Since I stand in your love and in your grace" (1091). Her search for glory has now truly succeeded. The Clerk had said that Walter's trials could only produce evil, but they have a very positive result. Walter's neurotic needs are fulfilled in the ways we have seen, and so are Griselda's. She attains the glory not only of winning Walter's love and favor but also of outshining all other wives, since she was tested most. The Clerk praises her humility, comparing her to Job and citing her as an example of how we should "Receiven all in gree [patience] that God us sent" (1151).

One of the difficulties in analyzing "The Clerk's Tale" is that there is ample evidence to support contradictory readings. The tale has been interpreted both as an allegory about the virtue of obedience to God or his human representatives and as an ironic commentary on such allegories. There is a great deal of rhetoric glorifying Griselda, and it is supported by the action. Her submissive behavior is highly rewarded, whereas she would have lost everything had she complained. Yet the Clerk says that it would be "inportable" [insupportable, unendurable] for wives to "Follow Griseld as in humility" (1143–44), and the Envoy has so confused readers that some contend that it ironically praises Griselda while others argue that it mocks her. Critics cannot agree whether the tale is saying that women should or should not be like Griselda. To my mind, what emerges from "The Clerk's Tale" as a whole is ambivalence toward Griselda's extreme self-effacement. She exemplifies her culture's teaching about ideal womanhood and patient submission to authority, but she and Walter are two sick people in a pathological relationship, and Chaucer seems to be aware of this.

6

The Merchant of Venice

Western literature is full of self-effacing women, although few so extreme as Griselda; but, as Horney observed, "self-effacement has nothing to do with femininity nor aggressive arrogance with masculinity. Both are exquisitely neurotic phenomena" (1950, 247). Horney is talking about essential femininity and masculinity, of course, which have yet to be defined, as opposed to culturally constructed gender identities. Our culture favors submissiveness in women and aggressiveness in men, but even so there are still plenty of dominant women and self-effacing males, both in life and in literature. In Shakespeare, for example, Margaret and Eleanor in the *Henry VI* plays, Tamora in *Titus Andronicus,* Elinor and Constance in *King John,* Goneril and Regan in *King Lear,* Lady Macbeth in *Macbeth,* and Volumnia in *Coriolanus* are ruthless, power-hungry women; and there are others who are domineering in their personal relationships. Beginning with the well-meaning but feeble Henry VI, there is also a rich array of self-effacing men, the most fully developed of whom are the poet of the sonnets, Antonio in *The Merchant of Venice,* Hamlet, Duke Vincentio in *Measure for Measure,* Antony in *Antony and Cleopatra,* Timon in *Timon of Athens,* and Prospero in *The Tempest* (see Paris 1991a, 1991b). I shall elaborate here on my brief treatment of Antonio in *Bargains with Fate* and also on his relationship with Shylock.

Criticism of *The Merchant of Venice* has given remarkably little attention to Antonio, despite the fact that he is the title character and his relationships with Bassanio and Shylock are at the center of the play. In addition to being the chief protagonist in the action, Antonio exemplifies the values celebrated by the play. He is presented as loyal, generous, unselfish, merciful, the noblest man "that draws breath in Italy" (3.2.294).[1] A psychological analysis of his relationship with Bassanio shows that much of his "noble" behavior is compulsively self-sacrificial and that a contradictory side of his personality emerges in his treatment of Shylock. His defenses and inner conflicts are reflected in the drama as a whole and are similar in many ways to those of the Shakespeare I infer from the play.

Like most comedies, *The Merchant of Venice* deals with the desire of lovers for union, the forces that block that desire, and the removal of those forces. Critics usually see Antonio as a blocking force in the Portia-Bassanio story, but I shall argue that the central love relationship is between Antonio and Bassanio, that the chief obstacle is Bassanio's marriage to Portia, and that the play concludes happily for Antonio when he becomes part of the Portia-Bassanio relationship. Actually, the play has an intricate plot that resolves the conflict between love and friendship in a way that includes everyone. First Portia obstructs the Antonio-Bassanio relationship, then Antonio obstructs the Bassanio-Portia relationship, then all blocking forces are removed and a permanent triangle is established.

The opening lines of the play introduce a psychological mystery. Antonio knows "not why" he is "so sad" and rejects the explanations of his friends that he is worried about his merchandise, that he is in love, or that he has too much regard for worldly prosperity. The most common explanation offered by critics is that he is a continent, perhaps unconscious, homosexual who is melancholy because Bassanio wants to woo Portia. I find Karen Horney's description of morbid dependency to be useful in understanding this character. As has often been noted, Bassanio is similar to the friend of the sonnets in his higher social status, his narcissism, and his shallowness; and Antonio is similar to the poet in his self-sacrificial devotion. Whether Antonio has a sexual attachment to Bassanio or not, he is clearly the self-effacing partner in the relationship. Like the protagonists of the tragedies, Antonio is in a state of psychological crisis at the beginning of the play. He "only loves the world" for Bassanio (2.9.50) and is threatened with the loss of his friend.

Antonio cannot admit, or perhaps even feel, the true cause of his sadness because this would violate his taboos against selfishness and make him feel unworthy of love. Instead of resenting Bassanio's interest in Portia, he goes to the opposite extreme and does everything he can to facilitate that which is making him miserable. When Bassanio asks for a loan to finance his courtship, Antonio assures him that his "purse," his "person," his "extremest means" (1.1.38) are at his disposal, despite the fact that Bassanio is heavily indebted to him already and admits to improvidence. Bassanio does him "more wrong," he protests, in questioning his "uttermost / Than if [he] had made waste of all [he has]" (1.1.155–57). Antonio's fortunes are at sea, but he authorizes Bassanio to rack his credit "to the uttermost" in order to furnish himself "to fair Portia" (1.1.181–82). Although he despises Shylock and does not believe in either lending or borrowing at interest, he will ignore both his prejudices and his principles for the sake of his friend. The more he sacrifices in order to help Bassanio leave him, the nobler his love. He even risks a pound of his flesh in order to secure the loan.

Antonio is sad, then, because he is losing the person who has given meaning to his life, but he has powerful taboos against acknowledging this directly, either to Bassanio or to himself. Somewhat like Hamlet, he makes his complaint indirectly, through his suffering. Just as Hamlet arouses the concern of Claudius and Gertrude by his mournful demeanor, so Antonio arouses the concern of Solanio and Salerio, who try to figure out why he is sad, and of Gratiano, who finds him "marvellously chang'd" (1.1.76). Bassanio seems impervious to Antonio's state, however, and begins immediately to ask him for money, which Antonio is eager to give. Antonio wants recognition of his generosity, but Bassanio seems to take his sacrifices for granted, as Antonio says he should, and Antonio cannot assert his claims.

The dynamics of this frustrating situation are made evident in Salerio's description of the parting of Antonio and Bassanio:

> Bassanio told him he would make some speed
> Of his return; he answered, "Do not do so.
> Slubber not business for my sake, Bassanio,
> But stay the very riping of the time;
> And for the Jew's bond which he hath of me,
> Let it not enter in your mind of love.
> Be merry, and employ your chiefest thoughts
> To courtship, and such fair ostents of love
> As shall conveniently become you there."
> And even there, his eye being big with tears,
> Turning his face, he put his hand behind him,
> And with affection wondrous sensible
> He wrung Bassanio's hand; and so they parted.
>
> (2.8.37–49)

Although Solario tells this story to show that "A kinder gentleman treads not the earth" (2.8.35), there is a good deal more than kindness at work here. Bassanio's promise of a speedy return seems like a response to Antonio's distress; but Antonio cannot allow his friend to hurry on his account, for that would diminish his nobility and give him less basis for his claims. In telling Bassanio not to worry about the Jew's bond, Antonio is reminding him of it and presenting himself as happy to run this risk for his friend. He displays his grief at his friend's departure but makes a show of hiding it. Antonio wants Bassanio to see how unhappy he is so that he will appreciate his sacrifice, but he also wants him to believe that he does not want him to see it so that he will appear to be nobly unselfish.

At first the other members of Antonio's entourage respond to his "nobility" far more than does Bassanio, who seems completely self-involved. Although Antonio's loss of fortune after pledging a pound of flesh to Shylock seems like a disaster, it enables him to get what he wants. He has sought all along to bind Bassanio to him through indebtedness, and he welcomes this opportunity to suffer for his friend and demonstrate his love. He wants to possess Bassanio in the only way he can, by winning his eternal gratitude for this last and most glorious sacrifice. When Antonio is in danger of losing his life, Bassanio finally pays the tribute for which he longs:

> The dearest friend to me, the kindest man,
> The best-condition'd and unwearied spirit
> In doing courtesies, and one in whom
> The ancient Roman honour more appears
> Than any that draws breath in Italy.
>
> (3.2.290–94)

The fact that the rhetoric of the play as a whole confirms this extravagant praise indicates Shakespeare's admiration of Antonio's self-effacing behavior, which resembles that of the poet of the sonnets toward the friend (Lewis 1985; Paris 1991a).

At this point, Antonio becomes a blocking force in the Bassanio-Portia story, since Bassanio leaves his bride in an effort to save his friend. He does so with Portia's blessing, before the marriage is consummated: "For never shall you lie by Portia's side / With an unquiet soul" (3.2.303–4). Portia accords Antonio great importance as her husband's "dear friend" (3.2.289) and says, in effect, that Antonio must be saved if their love is to thrive. In the courtroom scene, therefore, she is seeking to save not only Antonio but also her marriage.

For his part, Antonio has little wish to be saved. He seems to have no interest in fulfilling his needs for intimacy through a heterosexual relationship, but his devotion to Bassanio connects him to the world. When this is taken away, he describes himself as "a tainted wether of the flock, / Meetest for death. The weakest kind of fruit / Drops earliest to the ground, and so let me" (4.1.114–16). "Wether" is usually glossed as "castrated ram." Because of his sense of defectiveness, Antonio feels there to be no place for him in the human community. He presents his breast to Shylock's knife and "beseech[es] the court / To give judgment" (4.1.241–42).

Antonio does not simply want to die, however; he wants to do so in the presence of his friend: "Pray God Bassanio come / To see me pay his debt, and then I care not!" (3.3.35–36). He writes to Bassanio saying that "all debts are clear'd" between them "if I might but see you at my death. Notwithstanding, use your pleasure. If your love do not persuade you to come, let not my letter" (3.2.316–19). This strange message contains both a bribe—the forgiveness of debts—and an appeal for love. Antonio has been trying to buy Bassanio's love all along, but he has needed to feel that Bassanio loves him for himself. Now he both offers Bassanio a financial inducement to witness his death and structures his message in such a way that he can interpret his presence as a free expression of love. His bargain has been that if he makes great sacrifices for his friend, Bassanio will love him in return. Nora, Rennie, and Griselda have similar bargains and, like Antonio, are ready to die for their love. So far, Antonio has lived up to his end of the bargain, but Bassanio has not reciprocated.

Bassanio responds to his letter exactly as Antonio desires. He leaves Portia, rushes to Venice, and professes readiness to do anything for his friend: "The Jew shall have my flesh, blood, bones, and all, / Ere thou shalt lose for me one drop of blood" (4.1.112–13). Antonio says he is ready to die and urges Bassanio "to live still, and write mine epitaph" (4.1.18). By saddling his friend with a debt of gratitude that even Portia's money cannot repay, Antonio will assure himself of a hallowed place in his memory.

In his farewell speech to his friend, Antonio reminds him of his debt— "Grieve not that I am fall'n to this for you" (4.1.264)—and also tells him how it can be paid:

> Commend me to your honourable wife;
> Tell her the process of Antonio's end;

> Say how I lov'd you, speak me fair in death;
> And when the tale is told, bid her be judge
> Whether Bassanio had not once a love.
>
> (4.1.271–75)

After Antonio gives his life for his friend, even Portia will have to acknowledge the superiority of his love. Because of the lengths to which he is willing to go for Bassanio, Antonio feels that he deserves to be first in his friend's affections, and his bargain finally works when Bassanio honors this claim:

> Antonio, I am married to a wife
> Which is as dear to me as life itself;
> But life itself, my wife, and all the world
> Are not with me esteem'd above thy life.
> I would lose all, ay, sacrifice them all
> Here to this devil, to deliver you.
>
> (4.1.280–85)

Antonio cannot wish for more than this, since his friend is expressing a readiness to do his uttermost similar to what he himself has been expressing all along. His extreme gesture has been reciprocated. Bassanio is prepared to sacrifice not only his life but Portia as well. Nothing is more important to him than Antonio.

After he is freed as a result of Portia's legal maneuver, Antonio seeks a reaffirmation of his primacy. When Bassanio insists that Portia (disguised as the lawyer Balthasar) accept "some remembrance" (4.1.420), she asks for the ring that she gave Bassanio as a token of her love (3.2.171–85), motivated, perhaps, by her own need for reassurance. Bassanio refuses, explaining that the ring was given him by his wife, who made him vow that he "should neither sell nor give nor lose it" (4.1.441); but after Balthasar leaves, Antonio persuades Bassanio to change his mind: "Let his deservings, and my love withal, / Be valued 'gainst your wife's commandement" (4.1.448–49).

In act 4, Antonio defeats Portia twice in the competition for first place in Bassanio's affections, but she remains as an obstacle to their relationship. Indeed, many critics see Portia as triumphant in act 5, while Antonio is left a sad and lonely figure. Although it is true that Portia's claims are reestablished, it is also true that Antonio secures a place in Bassanio's world that restores his enjoyment of life. When Portia castigates Bassanio for giving away her ring, Antonio becomes uncomfortable at having provoked the tension between husband and wife. Neither he nor Portia can bear for Bassanio to be unhappy, and both are too self-effacing to cut off a rival or refuse to share Bassanio's affection. When the news arrives that Antonio has forfeited his bond, Portia offers enough gold to "pay the petty debt twenty times over" and tells Bassanio to "bring [his] true friend" back with him (3.3.305–6). When Antonio blames himself for the quarrel over the ring, Portia tries to reassure him: "Sir, grieve not you. You are welcome notwithstanding" (5.1.239). Some feel this to be merely a formal gesture, but I think that Portia genuinely wants to include her husband's true friend.

The reconciliation is brought about by the joint action of Portia and Antonio. Having broken his oath once, Bassanio has difficulty convincing his wife that he will not do so again, and Antonio comes to his rescue:

> Antonio: I once did lend my body for his wealth,
>   Which, but for him that had your husband's ring,
>   Had quite miscarried. I dare be bound again,
>   My soul upon the forfeit, that your lord
>   Will never more break faith advisedly.
> Portia: Then you shall be his surety. Give him this,
>   And bid him keep it better than the other.
> Antonio: Here, Lord Bassanio. Swear to keep this ring.
>
>   (5.1.249–56)

Just as he had made Bassanio's courtship possible by risking his body, Antonio now cements the marriage by risking his soul. He is once again doing his "uttermost," employing his "extremest means," to further the happiness of his friend. Since his soul is far more valuable than his body, his gesture is all the nobler. Portia's acceptance of that gesture ends her quarrel with Bassanio and gives Antonio a position of great importance in the marriage, since it is not only the ring but also Antonio's bond that joins husband and wife. Portia has never wished to defeat Antonio, for she does not believe that her marriage can thrive unless her husband is faithful to his friend.

At the beginning of the play Antonio tells Gratiano that the world is "A stage, where every man must play a part, / And mine a sad one" (1.1.78–79). His part is sad because he can neither marry nor form a permanent relationship with Bassanio, but he is remarkably fortunate in his friend's wife and becomes part of the family at the end. His problem has been resolved as well as it possibly could be. There is a falling off from the triumphs of act 4, but no one is ever treated as well as when he is facing death. Antonio has had his proof of Bassanio's love. When Antonio learns of the safety of his ships, he responds enthusiastically: "Sweet lady, you have given me life and living" (5.1.286). This is in marked contrast to his demeanor in act 1, when his wealth gave him no pleasure. He can enjoy the restoration of his fortune because his psychological crisis has been resolved.

Antonio is, like Shylock, a character whose psychological complexity tends to subvert his functions in the play. Shylock is rendered too vividly as a wronged and suffering human being to be simply a symbol of vindictiveness and greed or the stock villain whose discomfiture is a source of delight, while Antonio is too manipulative and self-destructive to be the ideal friend and gentleman that the rhetoric presents. The play's glorification of him is undermined also by his conduct to Shylock, which some find to be inconsistent with the rest of his character. Antonio is driven by two intense emotions—love of Bassanio and hatred of Shylock—both of which evoke a kindred response. Much attention has been given to Shylock's side of the relationship but little to Antonio's. An understanding of the interaction between these two characters illuminates them both.

Antonio's behavior toward Shylock is depicted mostly through Shylock's complaints when Antonio's request for a loan frees him to express his resentment. "Many a time and oft" Antonio has berated him about his "moneys and [his] usances" (1.3.101–3). He has called him "misbeliever, cutthroat dog," has "spet upon [his] Jewish gaberdine," has "foot[ed him] as you spurn a stranger cur / Over your threshold," and has "void[ed his] rheum upon [his] beard" (1.3.106–14). When Shylock asks if "for these courtesies" (1.3.123) he is expected to lend money, Antonio replies: "I am as like to call thee so again, / To spet on thee again, to spurn thee too" (1.3.125–26). He urges Shylock to lend the money not as to a friend but as to an "enemy, / Who if he break, thou mayst with better face / Exact the penalty" (1.3.130–32). In view of his need to sacrifice for Bassanio, we can understand why Antonio invites Shylock's harshness, but as Shylock says, he called him "dog before [he had] a cause" (3.3.6), and we must ask why "good Antonio" (2.8.25) treats Shylock with such unprovoked cruelty in the first place.

The answer, I think, is that Antonio and Shylock are opposite psychological types, each of whom represents what the other despises and fears in himself. Antonio and Shylock have more in common than Antonio likes to admit, since both are engaged in the pursuit of wealth through their investments. Antonio, however, sees himself not as acquisitive, but as a generous man who places his fortune at the disposal of his friends. He lends money recklessly, without interest, and seems ready to forgive debts, as with Bassanio. Shylock embodies values that Antonio consciously abhors and from which he distances himself through his over-generous behavior and his abuse of Shylock. He scorns Shylock because seeing another act out his own forbidden impulses threatens to stir up those impulses in himself and to activate the self-hate he would feel if he allowed himself to behave as the other is doing. His moral indignation reinforces his idealized image of himself as an uncompetitive, generous man who would never behave like Shylock.

We can infer a hidden aggressive side of Antonio from his overreaction to Shylock, and we can see it directly in his abusive behavior. This noblest of men spurns, kicks, and spits upon Shylock and "rails" at him in the Rialto (1.3.43): "He hath disgrac'd me, and hind'red me half a million; laugh'd at my losses, mock'd at my gains, scorned my nation, thwarted my bargains, cooled my friends, heated mine enemies" (3.1.47–50). "His reason," says Shylock, is that "I am a Jew" (3.1.50–51). Antonio does not scorn Shylock simply because he is a Jew, but his being a Jew frees Antonio to act out his aggression. Shylock's appeal to a common humanity ("If you prick us, do not we bleed?"—3.1.56) is very much to the point, even though it is part of his justification for revenge. Because Shylock is a Jew, Antonio does not regard him as a fellow human. He behaves toward him much as the equally "noble" Prospero behaves toward the supposedly subhuman Caliban (Paris 1991a).

Antonio abhors Shylock, then, because Shylock's arrogant-vindictive value system (Greenberg 1985) clashes with Antonio's self-effacing one and arouses his need to reinforce his repressions. He feels free to treat Shylock with scorn because he does not see him as part of his moral community. Since no one blames him for baiting a Jew, his idealized image is not at risk and he is not constrained by his Christian values. Shylock becomes a scapegoat, moreover, on whom Antonio can innocently discharge the rage that he feels toward his Christian brethren. Antonio is so frustrated by Bassanio's behavior that he is in despair about his life, but he cannot express resentment toward his friend.

Instead, he bends over backward to be "the ultimate of helpfulness, generosity, considerateness, understanding, sympathy, love, and sacrifice" (Horney 1950, 220). He manages his anger partly by turning it against himself and feeling depressed, even suicidal, and partly by displacing it onto Shylock, whom he eventually destroys.

Given the insulting way he has been treated, it is no wonder that Shylock hates Antonio. There are practical reasons as well, since Antonio's generosity deprives him of customers, delivers debtors "from his forfeitures" (3.3.22), and brings "the rate of usance" down in Venice (1.3.40). A less evident but equally powerful motive for Shylock's animosity is that he is psychologically threatened by Antonio, even more, perhaps, than Antonio is threatened by him. Antonio represents an opposite set of values by which Shylock stands condemned. His constant railing against Shylock's business practices threatens to rouse Shylock's self-effacing tendencies and expose him to self-condemnation. Shylock's elaborate justification of charging interest—through the story of Jacob and Laban (1.3.66–85)—indicates inner conflicts, and he defends himself, like Antonio, by scorning the character and behavior of his adversary. Antonio is a fool who does not understand the ways of the world; in his "low simplicity" he "lends out money gratis" (1.3.38–39). Shylock gets Antonio to agree to his "merry bond" (1.3.168) by imitating his self-effacing behavior: "I would be friends with you and have your love, / . . . Supply your present wants, and take no doit / Of usance for my moneys" (1.3.133–36). Since Antonio himself uses money to buy love, he is taken in by Shylock: "The Hebrew will turn Christian: he grows kind" (1.3.173). Not having Antonio's blind spot, Bassanio is more skeptical.

Shylock shows no mercy to Antonio in part because he needs to demonstrate that his way is right. He needs to show how Antonio's self-effacing behavior has led to his downfall, much as Iago must destroy Othello, Cassio, and Desdemona in order to justify himself (Paris 1991a). Shylock cannot show mercy, moreover, without hating himself for behaving like those whom he scorns: "I'll not be made a soft and dull-ey'd fool, / To shake the head, relent, and sigh, and yield / To Christian intercessors" (3.3.14–16). If Shylock allowed his self-effacing side to emerge, he would be caught in a cross-fire of conflicting shoulds. His arrogant-vindictive side would despise his foolish softness, and his self-effacing side would condemn his entire way of life. It is not only his hatred of Antonio but his dread of self-contempt that makes him so intransigent. In seeking to cut out Antonio's heart, Shylock is trying to cut out the last of his own self-effacing tendencies.

Shylock loses our sympathy when he insists on his bond, despite Bassanio's offers of money and Portia's plea for mercy. He justifies his behavior by a perfectionistic, Old Testament appeal to the law. When Portia asks how he can expect mercy if he renders none, Shylock replies that he does not need mercy because he has done no wrong. The conflict is not only between mercy and revenge, but also between mercy and justice; and here, as in *Measure for Measure* and elsewhere, Shakespeare favors self-effacing values over perfectionistic ones (Paris 1991a). Mercy must season justice because "in the course of justice, none of us / Should see salvation" (4.1.197–98). Shylock is found to be deficient in both mercy and justice and can be savagely punished as a result.

The Merchant of Venice dramatizes the threat of the arrogant-vindictive person by which Shakespeare seems to have been haunted and glorifies the self-effacing Antonio, who has much in common with the Shakespeare we infer from his writings (see Paris 1991a). The play is about greedy, vindictive characters and unselfish, forgiving ones, and about which set of characters is going to prevail. Bassanio wins Portia because he chooses the lead casket, which stands for sacrifice, while his competitors choose silver and gold. It looks as though Antonio will be destroyed as a result of his generosity, but Shylock is undone by his vindictiveness instead. In a last-minute reversal, Antonio is rescued and experiences enormous triumphs—economic, moral, and emotional. This is a wish-fulfillment fantasy in which the self-effacing strategy works.

The various defensive strategies are related to each other as they were, I suspect, in Shakespeare's personality. The arrogant-vindictive solution is disowned and punished, and the self-effacing and perfectionistic solutions are favored, with the former being superior to the latter. There is much aggression, however, in the characters and in the author. Shylock's vindictiveness is condemned, but it is also made understandable as a reaction to having been wronged. Antonio's aggression comes out in his behavior toward Shylock, where it can be expressed without violating his self-effacing shoulds. As I have tried to show in *Bargains with Fate*, the Shakespeare we can infer from the plays is a predominantly self-effacing person who is constantly looking for ways to express his sadistic and vindictive impulses without violating his stronger need to be noble and loving (Paris 1991a). His solution is to create situations that permit disguised or justified aggression and innocent revenge, as he does for Antonio.

The play as a whole supports Antonio's behavior. Because Shylock has refused to be merciful, Antonio and others can treat him with great cruelty at the end. Their vindictiveness is concealed by the fact that Shylock seems to have deserved his fate, that it is less severe than the law allows, and that it is being meted out in the name of mercy. Portia encourages Shylock's insistence on his bond by giving him the impression that the law is on his side, and after she springs the trap, she refuses to allow him to relinquish his claim. According to the law, Shylock's wealth is forfeit and his life is at the mercy of the Duke, but his life and half his wealth are spared when he accedes to Antonio's demand that he convert to Christianity. He says he is "content" (4.1.392), but he leaves the stage a broken man: "I pray you give me leave to go from hence. / I am not well" (4.1.393–94). "If a Jew wrong a Christian," Shylock had asked, "what is his humility? Revenge" (3.1.59–60). Despite Portia's glorification of mercy and the appearance of generous treatment, the play bears out Shylock's observation. Shakespeare's rhetoric conceals this from us because, like his characters, he is at once celebrating self-effacing values and enjoying disguised and justified aggression.

7

Antigone

The conflict between Creon and Antigone is usually considered in thematic terms, as a contest between the claims of the state and those of family, religion, and conscience. Creon prohibits the burial of Polyneices because, in his view, enemies of the state are wicked and should not receive honors that belong to its friends. Antigone believes that she has a duty to bury her brother which takes precedence over the dictates of a ruler. The play vindicates Antigone and teaches Creon the error of his ways, but too late to prevent a tragic outcome.

The play is not just about thematic issues, however. In addition to being illustrative, Creon and Antigone are also mimetic characters whose behavior can be understood in motivational terms. Creon's forbidding the burial of Polyneices has psychological sources, as does Antigone's ready embrace of her martyrdom. Creon and Antigone have complementary needs. He provokes her defiance in order to establish his authority, while she welcomes his edict because it allows her to escape her despair and achieve a glorious end.

Creon deserves as much attention as Antigone, for he precipitates the action and is undone by his mistakes, like the typical tragic hero. He has all and loses everything. From a thematic point of view he illustrates certain failings a ruler should avoid, and from a psychological perspective his neurotic behavior brings about the destruction of all the major characters.

We must distinguish between Creon's philosophy of government, which receives some support from the chorus, and his edict concerning Polyneices, which is criticized throughout the play. Creon argues that since the welfare of the individual requires order in the state, the ruler should have absolute power: "The man the state has put in place must have / obedient hearing to his least command / when it is right, and even when it's not"[1] (665–67). Only those who accept this can be trusted.

The greatest wrong is disobedience, which "ruins cities," "tears down our homes," and "breaks the battle-front in panic-rout" (673–74).

Creon's edict forbidding the burial of Polyneices does not necessarily follow from the value he places on order and obedience, but is justified on the grounds that the wicked and the good should not "draw equal shares" (520). Only those who are "well-minded to the state" should have "honor" in "death and life" (209–10). Eteocles, who died defending Thebes, deserves "all holy rites we give the noble dead" (198), but Polyneices should be left "disgraced, / a dinner for the birds and for the dogs" (206–7). Antigone contends that Creon's conception of justice does not correspond to that of the gods, who prescribe "equal law for all the dead" (519). The rhetoric of the play clearly supports Antigone. Since Creon's edict is out of keeping with the prevailing religious beliefs, we must ask why he issues such a divisive command.

Thematically, Creon is presented as being guilty of hubris, since he, "a mortal man," tries to "over-run / the gods' unwritten and unfailing laws" (454–55). These are Antigone's words, but they are echoed by Haemon ("You tred down the gods' due"—745) and by Tiresias ("You rob the nether gods of what is theirs"—1074). The final chorus drives the point home: "The gods must have their due. / Great words by men of pride / bring greater blows upon them" (1349–51). Filled with the pride of being king, Creon exceeds his authority, trying to rule where he should obey.

This view of his behavior is supported by mimetic detail. When he is named ruler of Thebes on the death of the sons of Oedipus, Creon becomes obsessed with power and command. He himself says that we "cannot learn of any man the soul, / the mind, and the intent until he shows / his practice of the government and law" (175–77). His practice of government reveals a grandiosity that may never have emerged had he not become king. He makes the state supreme in the lives of its citizens and himself supreme in the state. He wants to be unquestioningly obeyed and will not take advice, even from Tiresias. When the latter calls him tyrant, he haughtily replies, "Do you realize you are talking to a king?" (1058). Haemon warns him that "No city is the property of a single man," but Creon insists that "custom gives possession to the ruler" (737–38). Intoxicated by the loftiness of his position, Creon fails to recognize his human fallibility and the limits of his authority. Hungry for glory, he makes irrational claims.

A closer look at Creon reveals, however, that accompanying his grandiosity is an insecurity about his ability to govern. We do not know exactly why Creon is insecure. He has just ascended the throne (in this version of the story) and may fear that he will not be deemed a worthy successor to Laius and Oedipus—Antigone reminds the citizens that she is the "last of your royal line" (941). He may have doubts about his capacity to fulfill the responsibilities of his office and to exercise regal authority. Or he may be insecure because he is pursuing an impossible dream of glory and fears that his illusory grandeur will be punctured by reality. Creon seems caught in a vicious circle in which his grandiosity and insecurity heighten each other, it being impossible to say which comes first. Whatever the reason for Creon's insecurity, his irrational behavior throughout the play indicates that he expects opposition, fears his own weakness, and needs to assert himself forcefully as a way of gaining reassurance. Although he insists on absolute power, he is afraid that others will not accede to his demands, and he feels extremely vulnerable.

Creon's edict concerning Polyneices seems devised as a test of his subjects' loyalty and obedience. His council (the chorus) has been chosen from people who had been "constant" (165) to Laius and Oedipus, and Creon wants them to show their constancy to him by assenting to his controversial decision. Intimidated, they give him what he wants by saying that he "can make such rulings as [he] will / about the living and about the dead" (213–14). However, when they hear that the corpse has been buried, they wonder if this action is not "possibly a god's" (279). Creon reacts with rage, calling them "insane" (281), because this response questions his edict and shows that they really feel it to have been wrong. He is convinced that the deed has been done by those who "growled against" his command but "hid the fact that they were rearing back, / not rightly in the yoke, no way my friends" (291–93). In Creon's mind, people are either friends or enemies, good or wicked, obedient or rebellious, and his edict may be intended in part to sort them out. In order to determine who is "rightly in the yoke," it is necessary to impose it. He confirms his own anxieties by provoking disobedience and then tries to quiet them by exercising his power.

Creon's behavior throughout the play is that of an emotionally unstable man who fears external opposition and internal weakness. In his desperate need to assure himself and others of his potency, he reacts defensively in every situation and makes a series of terrible mistakes.

After he recognizes his errors, Creon says that "it was a god" who drove him "to wild / strange ways" (1271–73), and the chorus observes that the " 'bad becomes the good / to him a god would doom' " (621–22). From a modern perspective, it is not the gods but Creon's fears and compulsions that doom him.

When the guard arrives with word that Polyneices has been buried, Creon immediately jumps to the conclusion that his enemies have bribed the sentinels to disobey his order, thus assimilating the event into his paranoid scenario. He accuses the guard of having sold his "mind for money" (322) and shows his power by threatening him with a terrible fate. This is not an isolated incident. Just before the guard arrived, he had warned the chorus "not to take sides with any who disobey" his edict (219), risking their lives for "hope of profit" (222). He later accuses Tiresias of pleading "a shameful case . . . in hope of profit" (1047). Creon is prone to believe that people are conspiring against him, and he defends himself against feelings of personal inadequacy by attributing their behavior to greed. His complaint against Tiresias is absurd, but he can ignore the seer's criticisms by calling him "money-mad" (1055). When Antigone is brought back a captive, Creon dismisses her charge that he has pridefully ignored the law of the gods and accuses her and Ismene of being "secret plotters" (494) against the throne.

Creon is compulsively driven to condemn Antigone to death, an act that will destroy his family and his reign. He must prove that he places the state above bonds of kinship, as he has required others to do, and fears that he will lose face if he does not carry out his threat to execute anyone who disobeys his edict. His need to punish Antigone's "insolence" (480) is all the greater because she is a woman: "I am no man and she the man instead / if she can have this conquest without pain" (485–86). Creon has a profound fear of being perceived as weak. He has an idealized image of himself as a masterful leader who can easily "bring raging horses back to terms" (478) and a despised image of himself as an impotent man who is not respected and cannot impose his rule. To allow Antigone to get the better of him would expose him to unbearable self-hate: "No woman rules me while I live" (526). To be ruled by Antigone is to be weaker even than a female.

The long speech to Haemon (639–80) in which Creon presents the most impressive arguments for his philosophy of government ends on a similar note of personal anxiety and defensiveness:

I must guard the men who yield to order,
not let myself be beaten by a woman.
Better, if it must happen, that a man
should overset me.
I won't be called weaker than womankind.

(675–80)

Haemon responds by defending Antigone's behavior ("Isn't her real desert a golden prize? — 699) and warning his father not to be rigid, but Creon's pride will not allow him to be counseled by a youth, and given his fear of being weaker than a woman, nothing Haemon can say could change his father's mind. When Haemon tells him that he is treading "down the gods' due," Creon calls him "weaker than a woman" (745–46), and when he describes his father as mad, Creon calls him a "woman's slave" (756). He orders Antigone to be brought out so that she may die in Haemon's "sight, close at her bridegroom's side" (760), but Haemon storms off, telling Creon that he will never see his face again. Creon is so obsessed with his need to maintain his idealized image that he is ready to sacrifice his son.

Creon encounters a series of challenges to his wrong-headedness, first from Antigone, then from Haemon, and finally from Tiresias. Each challenge offers him an opportunity to recant and save himself, but instead he becomes more determined to carry out his will. Thematically he is presented as a rigid ruler who will not listen to counsel: "You wish to speak," says Haemon, "but never wish to hear" (757). Mimetically Sophocles shows that Creon's fears and compulsions prevent him from heeding what anyone else has to say.

Creon dismisses Antigone's words because she is his enemy and Haemon's because he is his son, but Tiresias is a seer whose counsel he should respect. He tells Creon that he has made mistakes, confirmed by many bad omens, but that "he's no fool / nor yet unfortunate, who gives up his stiffness / and cures the trouble he has fallen in" (1025–27). If Creon will "yield to the dead" (1029), there is still time to save the situation, but instead he accuses Tiresias of greed and wickedness. He vows never to "cover up that corpse. / Not if the very eagles tear their food / from him, and leave it at the throne of Zeus" (1040–41). Creon submits after Tiresias predicts the "horrors" that "lie in wait" for him (1075), but even then only with great difficulty, for "To yield is dreadful" (1095).

Yielding is so dreadful to Creon because it means giving up his claims and becoming his despised self. In his effort to defend himself against the fears of inadequacy that have haunted him, he has externalized his self-hate (hating others instead and feeling hated by them), has arrogated to himself powers that were not rightfully his, and has insisted on his absolute rightness in the face of all opposition. In this tragedy, as in life, defenses ironically bring about the very things that are feared. When Creon finally yields, it is too late. Antigone has hanged herself, Haemon kills himself after trying to murder his father, and Creon is flooded with self-condemnation: "O crimes of my wicked heart, / harshness bringing death. / You see the killer, you see the kin he killed" (1261–63). After his wife commits suicide, cursing him "as the killer of her children" (1307), Creon asks to be taken "out of the sight of men. / I who am nothing more than nothing now" (1321). His aspiration to be all has led him to be nothing; his efforts to ward off self-doubt have plunged him into self-hate. He feels that his "life is warped past cure" (1342) and wishes that someone would kill him.

Creon's story has an education pattern in which he learns that "it's best to hold the laws / of old tradition to the end of life" (1113–14) and that "to reject good counsel is a crime" (1244). The pattern is tragic in that he achieves wisdom too late to save him from the consequences of his errors. Antigone's story has a tragic *vindication* pattern in which even Creon comes to recognize that she was right, but too late to prevent her destruction. At the beginning of the play, Antigone is alone in her determination to bury Polyneices. The chorus would approve her act, she says, "did fear not mute them" (505). As the play progresses Antigone's virtue is increasingly recognized and celebrated. Ismene regrets not having joined her, Haemon calls her action "glorious" (695), the townspeople feel that she really deserves "a golden prize" (699), Tiresias supports her position, and the chorus celebrates her as godlike. Whereas Creon begins as everything and ends as nothing, Antigone is apotheosized.

We had to ask why Creon issued an edict that was so out of keeping with prevailing religious beliefs. Since Antigone's behavior accords with those beliefs, it may seem unnecessary to look for other motives, but there is something "wild" and "strange" about Antigone as well as about Creon. When Ismene says that although she is afraid to assist in the act of burial she will keep it hidden, Antigone becomes enraged and urges her sister to "denounce" her: "I shall hate you more / if silent, not proclaiming this to all" (86–87). She does not simply want to bury Polyneices; she wants to be put to death in the process. Life seems a burden from which she is eager to escape:

> If I die
> before my time, I say it is a gain.
> Who lives in sorrows many as are mine
> how shall he not be glad to gain his death?
> And so for me to meet this fate, no grief.
>
> (461–65)

The question we have to ask about Antigone is not why she "dare[s] the crime of piety" (75) but why she feels that "For me, the doer, death is best" (72).

At the end of the play, Creon feels that his "life is warped past cure" (1342); this seems to be Antigone's condition from the beginning. In her very first speech, she dwells on the suffering sprung from her father: "There's nothing grievous, nothing free from doom, / not shameful, not dishonored, I've not seen" (4–5). She feels that she cannot escape "the doom that haunts . . . the royal house of Thebes" (860–61), a sentiment echoed by the chorus: "No generation can free the next. / One of the gods will strike. There is no escape" (594–95). Her sorrows include the past sufferings of her family, which have weighed heavily on her as Oedipus's caretaker, and also the sufferings to come, unknown but inescapable. Her life is bound to turn out unhappily.

Antigone feels not only doomed but dishonored, tainted by the guilt of her parents and her status as the offspring of their incestuous marriage:

> My mother's marriage-bed.
> Destruction where she lay with her husband-son,
> my father. These were my parents and I their child.
>
> (862–64)

At the end of *Oedipus the King,* Oedipus grieves for the plight of his daughters:

> I weep when I think of the bitterness
> there will be in your lives, how you must live
> before the world. At what assemblages

of citizens will you make one? to what
gay company will you go and not come home
in tears instead of sharing in the holiday?
And when you're ripe for marriage, who will he be,
the man who'll risk to take such infamy
as shall cling to my children, to bring hurt
on them and those that marry with them? What
curse is not there? "Your father killed his father
and sowed seed where he had sprung himself
and begot you out of the womb that held him."
These insults you will hear. Then who will marry you?
No one, my children; clearly you are doomed
to waste away in barrenness unmarried.[2]

(1486–1502)

This is a later play, to be sure, but in *Antigone* Sophocles seems to have conceived of his heroine as having the feelings about herself that would have been induced by the life experiences Oedipus describes. Despite her betrothal to Haemon, about which Creon is unenthusiastic, Antigone appears to feel unmarriageable, doomed "to die unwed" (869). She may feel that infamy clings to her, as Oedipus's speech suggests, and that she would be a source of contamination to her husband and children.

Antigone resembles Shakespeare's Antonio, who calls himself "a tainted wether of the flock, / Meetest for death" (*Merchant of Venice*, 4.1.114–15). Her tainted origin and the curse upon her house separate her from others, whose life she cannot share. Antonio escapes his isolation when he is taken into the Bassanio-Portia relationship, but nothing can restore Antigone to the human community. When Creon condemns her to be shut up in a tomb with just enough food to sustain her, Antigone laments, "Alive to the place of corpses, an alien still, / never at home with the living nor with the dead" (850–51). Because of her sense of immitigable alienation Antigone feels that her "life died long ago" and that this has made her "fit to help the dead" (559–60).

Antigone anticipates being more at home with the dead than she has been with the living. She feels entirely alone on earth, but when she dies she will go to her "own people" (893), to whom she will "come as a dear friend," since she has "dressed them for the grave" (900–901). There is no one alive with whom she feels a sense of community, but in death she will be with her kind once more, with those who have shared her doom. She has devoted herself to the service of her family, and life seems to have no meaning for her outside of this activity. The burial of Polyneices is her final service, after which she no longer desires to live.

It is striking that Antigone regards herself as alone despite the existence of Ismene. When she contemplates going to her own people, she describes herself as "last of them all" (895), and she asks the leaders of Thebes to pity the suffering of the "last of your royal line" (941). She seems to have forgotten her sister completely. At the beginning of the play, she speaks to Ismene of the suffering of "us survivors" (3) and asks her to assist in the burial of Polyneices. When the fearful Ismene tells her that she is "wrong from the start, to chase what cannot be" (92), Antigone turns upon her with savage contempt: "If that's your saying, I shall hate you first, / and next the dead will hate you in all justice" (93–94). After Antigone is caught, Ismene wants to share her sister's fate, but Antigone will not allow it: "You did not / wish for a part, nor did I give you one" (538–39). Ismene begs her not to "fence me out from honor" (544), but Antigone is unrelenting, leaving her sister to feel as isolated and empty as she: "What life is there for me to live without her?" (566).

In order to understand Antigone's behavior toward Ismene, we must delve more deeply into her psychology. Antigone seeks to compensate for her sense of contamination by pursuing a course of absolute rectitude. Creon's edict forbidding the burial of Polyneices gives her an opportunity to prove herself, to live up to her standard of moral perfection, no matter the cost. After telling Ismene that anyone who defies the edict "will die by public stoning in the town," she says "you soon will show / if you are noble, or fallen from your descent" (36–38). Afraid of crossing royal power, Ismene says that they must submit to "these orders, or any that may be worse" (64), asking forgiveness from those beneath the earth. Such a course is unthinkable to Antigone, who feels toward Ismene the contempt she would feel toward herself should she thus fall from her noble descent and be a "traitor" to her brother (46).

Whereas Ismene sees herself as a weak, helpless woman who has no choice but to capitulate, Antigone seeks to master her fate by maintaining her virtue. She can do nothing about the taint she has inherited from her family, but she can gain recognition from her fellow Thebans, the dead, and the gods for her righteousness. Creon insists on obedience to his commands even if they are wrong, but Antigone would be overwhelmed with self-hate if she acceded to this demand. The price of defiance is death, but she has no wish to live, and for her there could be no greater suffering than "dying with a lack of grace" (97). By burying

Polyneices she avoids self-hate and actualizes her idealized image: "what greater glory could I find / than giving my own brother funeral" (502–3). She is so unrelenting toward Ismene in part because she does not want to share her glory: "Death and the dead, they know whose act it was" (542). Ismene is afraid of temporal power, but Antigone pleases "those whom I most should please" (89), those whose recognition will be eternal.

Antigone is enacting a scenario similar to that which Sophocles later gave to her father in *Oedipus at Colonus*. She is transformed from a creature who is tainted and doomed into a transcendentally glorious being. She achieves her transformation partly through her virtue and partly, like Oedipus, through the magnitude of her suffering. Creon's edict makes it possible for her to achieve a grand fate despite, indeed because of, the curse on her house. The fact that she is being punished for her virtue, "because I respected the right" (943), heightens the injustice of her fate and makes it all the more poignant. She refuses to be reconciled with her sister in part because she wishes to cling to her sense of abandonment, which increases her suffering. She portrays herself as not only the last of them all but "ill-fated past the rest" (895). The more she suffers, the greater her distinction.

Creon mocks Antigone for singing the "dirge" for her own death "ahead of time" (881–82), but his remark is not entirely inappropriate, since Antigone is histrionically self-pitying. Although she welcomes death, she bewails the fact that she is descending "before my course is run" (896). Some critics feel that the "death-devoted maiden" of the first part of the play shows herself to be attached to life after all. She laments again and again that there will be "no marriage bed" or "marriage-song" for her and "since no wedding, so no child to rear" (917–18). Are we to see this as genuine grief that she will be deprived of marriage and motherhood, or as an effort to embellish her image as a martyr? I lean toward the latter interpretation. My reading of Antigone is that she felt herself to be cut off from marriage and motherhood by the taint that attaches to her as the child of Oedipus and Jocasta. As she says, her life died long ago. She can achieve meaning through death, however, and the greater her suffering, the more grandeur is attached to her end. Thus she repeatedly laments that she has "No friend to bewail my fate" (881). What about Haemon, Ismene, and the chorus? Haemon says that "the whole town is grieving for this girl, / unjustly doomed" (693–94). Antigone glories in her fate and seeks to portray it as more terrible than that of anyone else in her spectacularly ill-fated family: "Look what I suffer" (942).

The chorus empathizes with Antigone's suffering and even more with her self-glorification. She will go "in fame to the vault of the dead" (816). When Antigone compares herself to Niobe, saying that "My own putting to sleep a god has planned like hers" (831), the chorus assents: "Yet even in death you will have your fame, / to have gone like a god to your fate" (834–36). The play strikes down the arrogant Creon, whose pride must be crushed, but Antigone's bargain with fate succeeds: she lives up to her shoulds and the world honors her claims. She does not receive justice on earth, but the play affirms the higher justice in which she believes.

From a Horneyan perspective, Creon and Antigone are both destructively engaged in a search for glory. Creon's fate is typical of the hero in Greek tragedy who arouses the enmity of the gods by seeking more mastery than is granted to human beings. As the chorus observes, "any greatness in human life brings doom" (613). Antigone also seeks to master her fate, but through rectitude rather than power. A rebel in relation to Creon, she is submissive to the gods and scrupulously performs her religious and familial duties. She is not caught between the demands of temporal and eternal authority, like Ismene and the chorus, because she is ready to die. Although submissive to the gods, Antigone is not self-effacing. She takes pride in her righteousness, despises the timidity of others, and overtly engages in self-exaltation. Although those who pursue glory are usually destroyed in Greek tragedy, Antigone succeeds because she plays by the rules of the gods. While condemning the over-stepping Creon, the play endorses Antigone's perfectionistic solution.

Creon and Antigone are not as fully drawn as most of the other characters discussed here, but they have a mimetic dimension that contributes to the richness and dramatic intensity of the play, which would be a much lesser work if they were merely illustrative figures. Although their attitudes and behaviors are products of a culture very different from our own, there are some enduring features of human psychology beneath all the differences. We have seen Creon's combination of insecurity, grandiosity, and the assertion of arbitrary authority in dictatorial leaders through the ages and in such literary figures as Captain Queeg of *The Caine Mutiny*. Antigone's sense that her life died long ago has specific sources in her culture, but her hopelessness, alienation, and despair are familiar emotions, as is her longing for vindication. Her combination of suicidal impulses with a search for glory is one we have already seen a number of times in this study, and her strategy of coping with a feeling of worthlessness through absolute rectitude is one we shall see again.

PART III

Character, Plot, Rhetoric, and Narrative Technique

8

Great Expectations

Perhaps the major division among critics of *Great Expectations* is between those who see it as a novel of growth and education and those who feel that Pip at the end is far from having attained wisdom or maturity. Whereas most critics regard Pip the narrator as a wise and trustworthy guide, some argue that he remains a severely damaged person whose interpretations and judgments are unreliable. These conflicting readings are in part the product of different perspectives, but they are also sponsored by tensions between rhetoric and mimesis within the novel itself.

Great Expectations has a comic education pattern in which the protagonist errs as a result of his faults, suffers as a result of his errors, grows as a result of his suffering, and prospers as a result of his growth. Pip interprets his earlier behavior from the perspective he has arrived at by the end, which seems to be that of the novel as a whole. In thematic terms, this is a story of fall and redemption in which Pip is good at first, catches the disease of snobbery from Estella and Miss Havisham, sins against his friends while he is infected, is cured by the collapse of his hopes, and becomes good again at the end. The guilty Pip is a social climber who places undue value on wealth and position. The story of his expectations is pervaded by unnatural relationships in which people use or abuse others out of ambition, greed, and vindictiveness. The story of Pip's education emphasizes such values as love, unselfishness, gratitude, humility, and the acceptance of one's natural place in the order of things. Earning one's living through honest labor is contrasted with living off others, and the warmth of hearth and home is contrasted with the coldness of ambition. Joe and Biddy embody the values that Pip betrays and to which he returns at the end, while the remote and heartless Estella symbolizes the perversity of Pip's impossible dream.

Although sanctioned by plot and rhetoric, this reading is not supported by the mimetic portrayal of Pip. The entire novel comes to us in the words of Pip the narrator, but we must distinguish between his detailed portrayal of his experience, which is relatively trustworthy, and his often questionable explanations and judgments of his own and others' behavior. Pip sees his transformation from a loving child into an ambitious snob to be the product of inferiority feelings induced by Estella's contempt. When we look at the mimesis, Pip's problems do not seem to result from contamination by Estella and Miss Havisham but from maltreatment by his sister and the resulting emotional harm. Pip sees himself as having arrived at maturity and wisdom, but, as I interpret it, the mimesis shows that when his expectations collapse, he regresses to a childish dependency. The "educated" Pip is a troubled human being whose view of things is distorted by his compulsions and blind spots. He thinks he has renounced his project of becoming "uncommon," but as he narrates his story he is still engaged in defending an idealized conception of himself.

As the title suggests, *Great Expectations* is about a search for glory. Pip's dream of greatness is initiated by his first visit to Satis House and shattered by the return of Magwitch. According to Pip, his need to be "uncommon" comes into being when Estella treats him with scorn. She is indignant at being asked to play cards with "a common labouring-boy" and despises the cards "for having been won" of him (ch. 8). "Her contempt for me was so strong that it became infectious, and I caught it." He becomes obsessed with his "coarse hands" and "common boots," which now seem "vulgar appendages," and wishes that "Joe had been rather more genteelly brought up" so that he "should have been so too." He becomes increasingly "dissatisfied" with "home" and "trade" (ch. 15), longs to be a gentleman, and dreams that Miss Havisham will make his fortune one day. When he confides his discontent to Biddy, he asks, "what would it signify to me, being coarse and common, if nobody had told me so!" (ch. 17).

Great Expectations begins as a psychological novel about an abused child, but it turns into a novel of social criticism as the behavior resulting from Pip's emotional problems is attributed to his experience at Satis House. Pip believes that his sense of social inferiority is the source of his self-contempt, but his feelings of inferiority do not begin when he encounters Estella, nor are they intensified by her scorn. Instead, her contempt gives him a way of coping with the profound sense of worthlessness he has carried through childhood and of explaining it in a manner that is comforting to himself. Pip's interpretation of the "great changes" that occur on that "memorable day" (ch. 9) obscures the significance of his earlier formative experiences.

The conditions of Pip's childhood are such as to generate intense feelings of worthlessness, anxiety, and guilt. His "first most vivid and broad impression of the identity of things" is that he is a helpless orphan who lives in a threatening world (ch. 1). His sense of the precariousness of existence is epitomized by the graves of his five little brothers and is intensified by Magwitch, who threatens to cut his throat if he does not stop crying and to eat his heart and liver if he does not bring him supplies. Pip's encounter with Magwitch is so significant because it epitomizes, in an extreme way, his everyday experience.

Magwitch's question of whether Pip is "to be let to live" is one that reverberates through his childhood, which is filled with a "sense of helplessness and danger" akin to that which the convict inspires (ch. 1). Pip is dependent for his existence on an "all powerful" sister who resents having to care for him and wishes him dead. She tells him that if it were not for her he would "have been to the churchyard long ago, and stayed there," that she does not know why she brought him up, and that she would "never do it again" (ch. 2). "Possessed by [the] idea that a mortifying and penitential character ought to be imparted to [Pip's] diet" (ch. 8), she seems literally to have deprived him of nutriment. He is undersized for his age. Magwitch threatens to cut Pip's throat and roast his heart and liver, and those at the Christmas dinner seem to have similar fantasies. Pip is admonished to be grateful for not having been born a "Squeaker," since if he had, he would not be at the feast except to be eaten, and Pumblechook follows with a vivid account of how Dunstable the butcher "would have shed [Pip's] blood" with his penknife if he had been a pig (ch. 4). This reawakens his sister's desire for his death, and she enters "on a fearful catalogue" of all the "illnesses," "sleeplessness," and "injuries" of which he "had been guilty" and "all the times she had wished [him] in [his] grave, and [he] had contumaciously refused to go there."

Pip is made to feel guilty not only for being so much "trouble" but also for his lack of gratitude. He is not grateful for his ill-treatment, of course, but is full of suppressed rage. During his sister's recital of his "misdemeanors," Wopsle's Roman nose so aggravates Pip that he "should have liked to pull it until he howled" (ch. 4). Another reason

Pip is regarded as ungrateful is that he is not perceived as having any rights, any fair claim to care and attention, so that the pitifully little he does receive seems more than he deserves. His sister feels victimized by having to take care of him and describes herself as his "slave" (ch. 7). She vents her rage at feeling trapped by treating him with a "capricious and violent coercion" (ch. 8), all the while reproaching him for his ingratitude.

It is impossible to determine the reliability of Pip's account of his sister, which may be exaggerated, but it is clear that he feels blamed for being alive: "I think my sister must have had some general idea that I was a young offender whom an Accoucheur Policeman had taken up (on my birthday) and delivered over to her, to be dealt with according to the outraged majesty of the law" (ch. 4). Not only is he born sinful, but he is sinful for having been born. His very existence is a violation of "the dictates of reason, religion, and morality," and his sister seems to regard it as her job to punish him. Since his offense is being alive, the only way he can remove his guilt is by going to his grave.

Pip grows up feeling that every manifestation of his existence compounds his ontological guilt and that others regard him as destined to end up in prison or on the gallows. When Joe says that the firing of the great guns means that there's another convict off, Pip asks for an explanation: "While Mrs. Joe sat with her head bending over her needlework, I put my mouth into the forms of saying to Joe, 'What's a convict?' Joe put *his* mouth into the forms of returning such a highly elaborate answer, that I could make out nothing of it but the single word, 'Pip' " (ch. 2). The equation of "Pip" with "convict" is not what Joe intends, but it is confirmed by his sister's reaction when Pip continues his queries: "I didn't bring you up by hand to badger people's lives out. . . . People are put in the Hulks because they murder, and because they rob, and forge, and do all sorts of bad; and they always begin by asking questions."

It is impossible to say whether others entertain a similar scenario for Pip, as he feels they do. He may be externalizing the self-image he has derived from his sister and interpreting their behavior accordingly. Or her friends may take their attitude toward Pip from Mrs. Joe. Or both things may be occurring simultaneously. Pip feels that Mrs. Hubble contemplates him "with a mournful presentiment that [he] should come to no good" (ch. 4) and that Pumblechook pushes him over to the Town Hall to sign his indentures "exactly as if [he] had that moment picked a pocket or fired a rick" (ch. 13). He reports that while his indentures are being attested, Pumblechook holds him "as if we had looked in on our way to the scaffold, to have those little preliminaries disposed of"; and that at the celebratory dinner, Pumblechook takes fiendish delight in his being "liable to imprisonment" if he engages in "vagaries which the form of [his] indentures appeared to contemplate as next to inevitable." When acting the part of George Barnwell, Pip feels that others identify him with the murderer (ch. 15).

In light of all this, Pip's ambivalent response to Magwitch is quite understandable. Despite the fact that he is terrified of Magwitch, who threatens him with evisceration, he thinks of him as "my fugitive friend" and hopes he will not be caught (ch. 5). Magwitch is just such an abused, despised, guilty creature as Pip, with an equally tenuous hold on existence. In the churchyard, the shivering, hungry, battered Pip empathizes with the shivering, hungry, battered convict. Since Magwitch is treated by society as Pip feels himself to be treated by everyone but Joe, Pip readily imagines himself in Magwitch's situation. He sees in Magwitch an actualization of the image of himself as a criminal that has long been part of his identity, and he pities the man who already is what he feels destined to become. Magwitch is a symbol of Pip's fate: he acts out the aggression that everyone senses in Pip and suffers the inevitable punishment. It is no wonder that Pip thinks of his contact with Magwitch as his "companionship with the fugitive" (ch. 19) and feels that he would be "treacherous" if he betrayed him (ch. 5). Magwitch senses Pip's empathy and is grateful to him as the only compassionate presence in an otherwise hostile world, much as Pip is grateful to Joe.

Magwitch's demand that he steal a file and "wittles" throws Pip into a conflict between his "mortal terror" of Magwitch and his dread of his terrible sister. He pities Magwitch, but in order to relieve his suffering he must commit an act that will confirm his identity as a "young offender" destined to end up in jail. He dreams that he is drifting down the river toward the Hulks and a "ghostly pirate" calls out from "the gibbet-station, that [he] had better come ashore and be hanged at once" (ch. 2). As he makes his way to the marshes after the theft, the wooden finger post seems "like a phantom devoting [him] to the Hulks" (ch. 3), and he feels that everything is accusing him.

Some critics attribute Pip's sense of criminality to his theft, but the theft only exacerbates the feelings of worthlessness, anxiety, and guilt that led to his identification with Magwitch in the first place. Before he visits Miss Havisham, Pip has no way of coping with these feelings. He tries compliance and detachment, but these strategies do not work, and he is afraid to act out his aggression.

Pip is a submissive child who tries to be good, but he cannot win his sister's love and approval. He is more successful in moving toward Joe, but Joe cannot protect him. Although Joe sympathizes with Pip at the Christmas dinner, his "station and influence were something feebler (if possible) when there was company" (ch. 4), and he just keeps spooning gravy into Pip's plate. A fellow victim of abuse, Joe has never learned to cope with his own situation constructively, and all he can offer Pip is a rationale for accepting ill-treatment. He does not "rise" against his wife because his father abused his mother, and he is so afraid of becoming like him that he minimizes his own suffering, represses his resentment, and allows himself to be bullied. He feels guilty about Pip and wishes that he could "take it all" on himself, but even the daily spectacle of Pip's suffering cannot induce self-assertion (ch. 7). The fact that Pip accepts Joe's explanation of his impotence and begins to look up to him "in [his] heart" indicates Pip's own deep rooted compliance.

Detachment works no better than compliance as a defensive strategy for Pip, since his tormentors will not allow him to remove himself from their power. He says he would not have minded being crowded in at the Christmas dinner table and given the least desirable food if people would only have left him alone, but instead he is "smartingly touched up" by their "moral goads" (ch. 4). Pip feels so incessantly impinged on his sister and her cohorts that he develops phobic reactions to being touched or confined by his clothing. He complains bitterly about having his hair rumpled and poked in his eyes and describes himself as having been "severely mauled" by Wopsle when he goes to him for instruction (ch. 15). Pip *is* severely mauled by his sister, who wears Tickler "smooth by collision with [his] tickled frame" (ch. 2), and he is hypersensitive, as a result, to anyone else's laying hands on him. His sister's capricious and violent coercion makes him prone to feel oppressed by anything confining, such as his indentures or his dress clothing. He says that the "tailor had orders to make [his suits] like a kind of Reformatory, and on no account to let [him] have the free use of [his] limbs" (ch. 4). He feels painfully "trussed up" when he is dressed to visit Miss Havisham. Pip's recurring thoughts of imprisonment are a product not only of his sense of criminality but also of his claustrophobic feeling that he is already unbearably confined.

Detachment fails for Pip not only because people will not leave him alone but also because he cannot entirely stifle his needs and desires. His sister does not want to be bothered with him and becomes outraged when he requires attention. Short of dying, the only way Pip can avoid guilt and punishment is to be completely undemanding, but that, of course, is impossible. He needs food, gets sick, asks questions, has accidents, and is full of normal human cravings, all of which are regarded as criminal.

The feelings Pip is under the greatest pressure to repress are, of course, his aggressive ones. He has an immense rage toward his sister that he cannot act out, express, or even allow himself to experience. He is so afraid of his sister that he displaces his fury onto far less threatening objects, such as Wopsle's nose, although even then his assault is only imaginary. "Exasperated" by the kitchen councils in which Pumblechook and his sister engage after his visit to Miss Havisham, Pip indulges in fantasies of retaliation. He wants to "fly at Pumblechook, and pummel him all over" (ch. 12). If his "hands could have taken a linchpin out of his chaise-cart, they would have done it." Pip's rage is murderous. The bullied and battered child has no way of releasing his fury except through these fantasies, and he is profoundly inhibited even in them, since they never include his sister. It is not surprising that he is "disposed to believe" that he "must have had some hand in the attack" (ch. 16) when she is struck down, since his most deeply buried wish has been enacted.

Pip's experience at Miss Havisham's seems at first glance to be simply another instance of the devaluation to which he has been subjected throughout his childhood, but it allows him to develop, for the first time, a set of usable defenses. The fact that Estella despises him for his "coarse hands," "thick boots," and general lack of refinement is actually helpful to Pip, for these deficiencies can be remedied (ch. 10). The "felicitous idea" occurs to him that he can work toward becoming "uncommon" by improving his education. His coarseness is neither an essential part of his identity nor something for which he is responsible. Those who have hitherto abused him are themselves common people who are to blame for his lack of gentility. By virtue of his relationship with Miss Havisham, he has already risen above them. Instead of being a superfluous creature at the bottom of the pecking order, Pip has become the family's hope for social advancement.

When he returns from Miss Havisham's, Pip drives his sister into a frenzy by his lack of response to her questions. The more she shoves his face "against the kitchen wall," the more obstinate he becomes, and the arrival of Pumblechook makes him "vicious in [his] reticence" (ch. 9). When the "bullying old" man persists in "applying the screw," Pip tells a series of outlandish lies. At first he explains his reticence as "a dread of not being understood," but he comes closer to the truth when he says that he feared "Miss Havisham too would not be understood" and that there would be something "coarse and treacherous" in "dragging her as she really was (to say nothing of Miss Estella) before the contemplation of Mrs. Joe." If he is to escape the self-contempt he now associates with his commonness, Pip must protect the glamour of Estella and Miss Havisham and the value of their patronage. He is afraid that Miss Havisham will seem pathetic or ludicrous if he describes her as she is, so he at first withholds information and then paints an exotic picture of life at Satis House.

This "memorable" day makes such "great changes" in Pip because it enables him to imagine an escape from what had seemed a hopeless situation (ch. 9). Pip is now caught between three different conceptions of himself and his destiny. He has been accustomed to think of himself as a young offender who is destined for the Hulks or the gibbet. His visit to Miss Havisham opens up two new possibilities: one that he is a coarse and common laboring boy who will become a "mere blacksmith" and the other that he can become uncommon by acquiring gentility. The great question for Pip is which of these will prove to be his true identity. Each is associated with a particular person—the young offender with Magwitch, the coarse and common laboring boy with Joe, and the gentleman with Estella.

Under the influence of Estella, Pip forms an idealized image of himself and embarks on a search for glory. When she insults him, he becomes morbidly dependent on her approval; he is everything if he can gain it, nothing if he cannot. Pip hopes to restore his pride by adopting the values and meeting the standards of the person who has crushed it. His pride has been crushed before by his sister and her friends, but he cannot become what they want. Estella's position is superior to theirs, and the superficiality of her objections allows Pip to redefine his worthlessness in such a way that he can imagine overcoming it. Perhaps he can gain Estella's approval and rise above his sister and Pumblechook by acquiring a veneer of gentility. His hunger for education, his fantasies of becoming a gentleman, and his compulsive attachment to Estella are all driven by his need to escape self-contempt by actualizing his idealized image.

Pip cannot escape his self-contempt through Estella, however, for he has contradictory needs of her. Estella's power over him lies in his sense of her superiority, which is fed by her superciliousness, condescension, and abuse. Pip identifies with her lofty position and sees both himself and others through her eyes. This at once humiliates him and enables him to scorn those who have always looked down on him. Pip deals with his humiliation by regarding it as provisional; one day Estella will confirm his grandeur by giving him her love. He is always unhappy in her society, but his present unhappiness is a guarantee of future glory, for it is a product of the superiority that makes her acceptance so valuable. Pip needs Estella to love him if his pride is to be restored, but he also needs her to be scornful. Winning her love could not restore his pride, for then she would no longer be above him. He is spellbound by her inaccessibility and can feel that his search for glory has a chance of success only when she is making him miserable.

When he is apprenticed to Joe, Pip feels "as if a thick curtain had fallen on all [life's] interest and romance" (ch. 14). He tries to hold onto his dream by being loyal to Estella's values and refusing to be identified with people she would scorn. This creates a problem in relation to Joe, who has been his only source of support. Since Joe symbolizes his coarse and common self, Pip must dissociate himself from him, but he feels terribly guilty about doing so. His effort to make Joe "less ignorant and common" (ch. 15) so that he will not have to be ashamed of him is frustrated by Joe's apparent ineducability.

Pip also has inner conflicts in relation to his vocation. He knows that his aspirations make him "dissatisfied" (ch. 17), and he contrasts himself unfavorably with "plain contented Joe" (ch. 14). But although he feels guilty about his discontent, it is a defense against despair. To be content with his plain working life is to acquiesce in being the coarse and common boy Estella despises; to be discontent is to refuse to be that Pip and to hold onto his apparently impossible dream. Thus the vehemence of his response when Biddy asks if he is not happier as he is than he would be as a gentleman: "I am not at all happy as I am. I am disgusted with my calling and with my life. . . . understand once for all that I never shall or can be . . . anything but miserable . . . unless I can lead a very different sort of life" (ch. 17). Pip can try to define himself at this point only by refusing the identity that life is forcing upon him. His unhappiness is a means of maintaining his claim that he is meant for higher things.

Pip's aspirations make him feel angry with himself for his folly. He wants to be a gentleman both to spite Estella and to impress her, but he agrees with Biddy that she is "not worth gaining over" and that it "might be better" to care nothing for her words (ch. 17). He feels his attachment to Estella "to be so very mad and misplaced" that it would serve his "face right" if he "knocked it against the pebbles as a punishment for belonging to such an idiot." Pip wishes that Biddy "could put [him] right," but they both know that he will never fall in love with her, for she is "common," and to love her would be to accept the identity he is trying to escape. The fact that he is "good enough" for Biddy makes her love of little value, since only a person who makes him feel inferior can assuage his sense of unworthiness. Pip calls himself "a fool" for preferring the woman in whose presence he is miserable and has "states and seasons" when he is sure that his disaffection to the forge has disappeared and he is "growing up in a fair way to be partners with Joe and to keep company with Biddy." But this prospect is so unacceptable that his wits are invariably scattered by some "remembrance of the Havisham days," and he clings to the hope that, despite her many warnings, Miss Havisham will make his fortune when he completes his apprenticeship.

After the transformation that occurs as a result of his visit to Miss Havisham, Pip's character remains much the same until the return of Magwitch. When Jaggers announces his expectations, Pip feels that his dream of glory is coming true, but he finds that his inner life is not much changed by his new prospects. His expectations neither bring him happiness nor reduce his self-hate. He is still in an all-or-nothing situation in which he must actualize his idealized image if he is to feel worthwhile. Estella's inaccessibility symbolizes the hopelessness of this project, while Pip's persistence in the face of it indicates the desperateness of his need. In order to preserve the possibility of success, he pursues Estella and stays away from Joe, although he continues to feel foolish in relation to the one and guilty toward the other. In his present discomfort he thinks he would have been "happier and better" if he had never seen Miss Havisham (ch. 34), but he still would have suffered from the problems that preceded his search for glory. His sense of himself as an offender is not expunged by his expectations, any more than is his sense of himself as a coarse and common boy. As he tries to rise to the heights, Pip feels like an impostor who is bound to be exposed. This may be why he experiences Jaggers as acting as though he knows things to his "disparagement" (ch. 18). Perhaps Jaggers behaves in this way, given his clientele, but I suspect that Pip is hypersensitive to his manner because he already feels like a criminal and is afraid of being found out.

It is his sense of identification with Magwitch that poses the greatest threat to Pip's self-idealization. The "shame" with which he had often thought of his "companionship with the fugitive" (ch. 19) is intensified after he learns of his expectations. He takes comfort in the thought that it happened long ago, that Magwitch has probably been transported, and that he is "dead to me, and might be veritably dead into the bargain." This is highly ironic in view of the source of his expectations; but even if Miss Havisham had been his benefactor, Magwitch in partic- ular and convicts in general would continue to symbolize a version of his identity that fills Pip with dread.

This is evident from Pip's response to the convicts traveling with him on the coach when he returns to see Estella. When he recognizes one of them as the man through whom Magwitch had sent him two one pound notes, he is afraid that this man will recognize him and expose his secret identity. He not only shrinks from the convicts, as do the other passengers, but he also identifies with them as victims. The way in which everyone "looked at them and kept from them" made them "a most disagreeable and degraded spectacle" (ch. 28), just as he had been when he felt that others looked at him with indignation, abhorrence, and contempt. When the convicts laugh, crack nuts, and spit the shells about in response to rejection, Pip feels that he would have behaved so himself, "if [he] had been in their place and been so despised." He empathizes with them as he had done with Magwitch. But when the convict he has recognized sits behind him and breathes on his hair, his fear of exposure returns. "The sensation," which he feels "all along his spine," "was like being touched in the marrow with some pungent and searching acid." Since his acquaintance with Miss Havisham, the central issue for Pip has been his true identity. He is afraid here that in his essence, his marrow, he is the Pip who has offended the outraged majesty of the law. He fears that contact with these convicts will dissolve his veneer of gentility and reveal him to be "degraded and vile" like them.

Pip's encounter with the convicts precipitates an attack of anxiety. After he alights on the outskirts of town in order to prevent a coincidence that might reveal his name, he is overcome with a "great fear" that is "undefined and vague" (ch. 28). It is "a dread much exceeding the mere apprehension of a painful recognition," and Pip is convinced that it is "the revival for a few minutes of the terror of childhood." In childhood he feared for his life; what he fears now is the destruction of the glorified version of himself that gives life its meaning. His fear is heightened by his impending visit to Estella, which he hopes will confirm his gentility. Seeing his "companionship" with convicts through her eyes is a terrifying experience.

A similar confrontation of his idealized with his despised images of himself occurs when Pip visits Newgate while waiting for Estella's coach. He cannot help thinking "how strange" it is that he should be "encompassed by all this taint of prison and crime," that he should have encountered it in his childhood on the marshes, that "it should have reappeared on two occasions, starting out like a stain that was faded but not gone," and that "it should in this new way pervade [his] fortune and advancement" (ch. 32). Pip does not know the half of it, of course. He is so sensitive to this encompassment with prison and crime because it keeps reminding him of the identity he is trying to escape. He thinks "with absolute abhorrence of the contrast" between Newgate and the "proud and refined" Estella, but the contrast he truly abhors is between Estella and Pip the offender, who is symbolized by the jail. Pip endeavors to disown his sense of being intrinsically at fault by seeing the taint as something outside of himself, but this defense does not entirely succeed. He tries to shake the "prison dust" out of his dress and to exhale "its air from [his] lungs," but he still feels "contaminated" by "the soiling consciousness" of the prison when Estella arrives.

The most dramatic confrontation of Pip's idealized and despised selves occurs when Magwitch returns. In view of what Magwitch means to Pip, it is not surprising that his revelations produce another anxiety attack. Pip's heart beats "like a heavy hammer of disordered action," the room begins "to surge and turn," and he feels that he is "suffocating" (ch. 39). He regards Magwitch with "abhorrence," "repugnance," and "dread," and "recoil[s] from his touch as if he had been a snake." It is striking that although he shrinks from Magwitch when he first reappears, he recognizes "something good in the feeling" of gratitude that has brought him and tries to turn him away gently by citing the difference of their ways. It is only when Magwitch reveals that he is Pip's benefactor and claims him as his son that he seems like a "terrible beast" whose "hand might be stained with blood." He is afraid to be shut up with him in the "wild and solitary night." Pip is in no physical danger, but, profoundly threatened by Magwitch's revelations, he has violent impulses of his own that he experiences as belonging to the convict.

Pip's "abhorrence" of Magwitch increases "every hour" (ch. 40). He tries to disguise Magwitch by changing his clothes, but the better he dresses him, the more evident it becomes that there is "convict in the very grain of the man." This must seem like a repetition of Pip's own failure to hide his identity as an offender by assuming the guise of a gentleman. A "ghost could not have been more terrible" than Magwitch, who symbolizes the version of himself that Pip wants to think is dead but by which he is haunted. He has an impulse to sneak out in the middle of the night in order to enlist for India but is held back, in part at least, by his fear for Magwitch's safety. Since Magwitch has returned to see him at the risk of his life, Pip would regard himself "as his murderer" if he were "taken" (ch. 41). He is all the more protective of Magwitch because he wishes him dead and must avoid the guilt he would feel if his murderous impulses were acted out by another, as they had been toward his sister.

Pip feels trapped by his situation. He cannot continue to accept Magwitch's money without giving up his pretensions to gentility, but he cannot maintain himself as a gentleman without Magwitch's beneficence. His sense of connection with Magwitch exacerbates his self-revulsion, but he cannot abandon his "dreadful burden" (ch. 40) without feeling like a murderer. He is loved by a man he abhors and whose life is dependent upon him. "Was there ever," he exclaims, "such a fate!" (ch. 41). He will try to get Magwitch out of the country so that he can break with him safely, but that leaves him with no imaginable future.

Although Pip feels his "aversion" to be "insurmountable" (ch. 40), his attitude toward Magwitch changes dramatically within a relatively short period of time. When he visits Magwitch at Clara's, he is not "at all clear or comfortable" about breaking with him once they are abroad, and he is surprised at how "heavy and anxious" his "heart" is "at parting from him" (ch. 46). Pip attributes his change to Magwitch's being "softened—indefinably, for I could not have said how"; and Herbert shares his new impression of Magwitch: "Do you know, Handel, he improves?" (ch. 50). I find Pip's explanation of his change to be both inadequate and misleading, and I am suspicious of his use of Herbert to confirm it. It is not Magwitch who has softened but Pip, who tends to project and externalize and to see other people in the light of his needs and fears.

This is not the first time Herbert is used to validate perceptions that are distinctively Pip's. When Jaggers appears at the Three Jolly Bargemen, Pip describes his manner as "expressive of knowing something secret about every one of us that would effectually do for each individual if he chose to disclose it" (ch. 18). This is so clearly expressive of Pip's concern about his own secret that there can be little doubt that his perception of Jaggers is colored by his anxiety. Pip describes Jaggers again and again in ways that reflect his own preoccupations. Jaggers has an "air of bullying suspicion" and throws his finger at Pip "as much as to express that he knew all kinds of things to my disparagement, if he only chose to mention them." This reflects Pip's fear that others suspect his secret and that the things *he* knows to his disparagement will be revealed. Jaggers's masterfulness oppresses him because, by making him feel "at a disadvantage," it reminds him "of that old time when I had been put upon a tombstone" (ch. 36). Pip is particularly aggravated by Jaggers on his twenty-first birthday, and he tells us that Herbert's reactions are exactly the same as his own: "Mr Jaggers made not me alone intensely melancholy, because, after he was gone, Herbert said . . . that he thought he must have committed a felony and forgotten the details of it, he felt so dejected and guilty." This is a reflection of Pip's preoccupations, not Herbert's; there is no reason for Herbert to have this response.

When Pip tells Herbert "the whole of the secret" in order to explain Magwitch's presence, he sees his "own feelings reflected in Herbert's face": "and, not least among them, my repugnance toward the man who had done so much for me" (ch. 41). After Magwitch goes to his own lodgings, Herbert "unconsciously" takes the chair in which he had been sitting, but when he realizes what he has done, he "start[s] out of it, pushe[s] it away, and [takes] another." "He had no occasion to say, after that," explains Pip, "that he had conceived an aversion for my patron."

Again, why should Herbert's feelings be so similar to Pip's when Magwitch does not have the same significance for him?

It is difficult to say what is going on in these episodes. Is Pip imagining Herbert's behavior, which includes words as well as looks and gestures, is he distorting or amplifying it in order to support his version of reality, or is Dickens manipulating Herbert so as to confirm the appropriateness of Pip's responses and his reliability as a reporter? Given the fact that Pip is a profoundly insecure, fearful, self-castigating person, he is bound to overreact to people or events that trigger his anxieties and to give us a highly subjective account of them. Is he really looked at so frequently with scorn, disdain, aversion, indignation, and contempt, or is he imagining or exaggerating the behavior of others because of hypersensitivity or externalized self-hate?

Pip is so melancholy on his twenty-first birthday because "coming of age at all seemed hardly worth while in such a guarded and suspicious world as [Jaggers] made of it" (ch. 36); but, whatever may be the truth about Jaggers, Pip himself is "guarded and suspicious," and understandably so, given his experiences. He always anticipates rejection and punishment and often fears for his life. After his fight with Herbert, he is afraid that the "myrmidons of Justice" may be "lying in ambush" for him at Satis House, or that Miss Havisham might "take personal vengeance" by drawing a pistol and shooting him, or that "a band of mercenaries" might "fall upon me in the brewery, and cuff me until I am no more" (ch. 12). When Orlick uses the expression, "I'm jiggered," Pip has a "belief that if he had jiggered me personally, he would have done it with a sharp and twisted hook" (ch. 17). Orlick is an ominous presence, to be sure, but Pip is prone to experience the world as threatening. While waiting for Herbert at Barnard's on his first day in London, he opens the staircase window and nearly "behead[s himself], for the lines had rotted away, and it came down like the guillotine" (ch. 21).

Pip sees the world with an hallucinatory intensity. He invokes Herbert, and sometimes others, to confirm his version of reality because he may be dimly aware of his tendencies toward distortion and needs to assure himself of his mental balance. He defends himself against self-doubt and self-accusation by convincing himself that he is reacting appropriately to the way things are. He feels guilty about his repugnance toward the man who has done so much for him, but if Herbert feels a similar aversion, it is not he but Magwitch who is to blame. By exaggerating the external world, Pip justifies his extreme response. It is impossible to say whether Herbert actually mirrors Pip's feelings, but Pip's reactions are so intense and idiosyncratic that it seems highly unlikely that Herbert shares them to the extent that Pip reports.

It is quite possible that in addition to being an expression of Pip's needs, Herbert's mirroring of Pip's emotions is a rhetorical device by which Dickens validates Pip's reliability as a narrator. Dickens seems in many ways to collaborate in the confirmation of Pip's sense of reality. He presents Pip as living in an unjust, threatening world to which his reactions are appropriate. Pip must react as he does, given his character, but living in such a world generates anxieties and defenses that make it impossible for him to be the good analyst, observer, and judge that Dickens would have us believe him to be. When, from the implied author's point of view, Pip the actor goes astray, Pip the narrator calls attention to his errors, but there is no rectification of the errors of the narrator, or of the errors of the actor that author and narrator share.

Perhaps the most vivid example of Dickens' confirmation of Pip's sense of the world is his invention of the lime-kiln episode. Pip grows up feeling that he lives in an environment in which people are eager to have his life, and Orlick is one of the many who seem out to get him. Orlick threatens him at one point with a "red-hot bar" and tells him that it is "necessary to make up the fire, once in seven years, with a live boy, and that I might consider myself fuel" (ch. 15). Dickens proves that Pip's sense of being endangered is not a paranoid delusion by having Orlick reveal that he had often thought of killing Pip when he was small (ch. 53) and then actually attempt to do away with him. Many critics have seen that Orlick acts out Pip's murderous wishes toward his sister, although it is misleading to use this as a primary explanation of Pip's guilt. What has not been seen, I think, is that Orlick is also an agent of Mrs. Joe's wish for Pip's death. He threatens to bring about precisely the kind of nonexistence that his sister desired for Pip. By confirming the deepest fears of Pip's childhood, Dickens obscures his psychological problems and makes his anxieties seem reasonable.[1]

Pip's second transformation begins with his shifting attitude toward Magwitch, a complicated phenomenon that he himself but dimly understands. After learning that Magwitch is his benefactor, Pip perceives him (in Herbert's words!) as a "fierce" and "desperate" man and is filled with dread and repugnance (ch. 51). He describes Magwitch to Herbert as "the miserable wretch who terrified" him in his "childhood," but the young Pip had also identified with Magwitch as a fellow sufferer. When Magwitch describes his younger self as "a ragged little creatur" and recounts a history in which he has "been done everything to, pretty well—except hanged," Pip begins to empathize with him again. He feels "great pity" until a "look of affection" revives his abhorrence (ch. 42). The narrator asks how much of his "shrinking" from Magwitch "might be traced to Estella" and compares the state of mind in which he had tried to rid himself "of the stain of prison before meeting her . . . with the state of mind in which [he] now reflected on the abyss between Estella in her pride and beauty, and the returned transport whom [he] harboured" (ch. 43). Once again Pip experiences the contrast between his idealized and despised selves as a contrast between Estella and a symbol of his identity as an "offender." He recoils from an affiliation that would make it impossible for him to transcend that identity.

Magwitch does seem softened to Pip when he sees him at Clara's, but that is the *result* of a change in Pip's attitude rather than its cause. Pip's softer feelings toward Magwitch are liberated by his loss of Estella. When he learns that Magwitch is his benefactor, he realizes that Estella was not destined for him. He cannot accept losing her and shrinks from Magwitch as a way of holding onto his hopes. He visits Miss Havisham not only to seek money for Herbert, but also to declare his love for Estella. "Perfectly unmoved," Estella announces her engagement to Bentley Drummle (ch. 44), and Pip returns to London feeling that they have parted forever. He finds Magwitch softened because a change has occurred in himself. Now that Estella can never be his, he has far less reason to shrink from his benefactor.

When Pip discovers Estella's parentage, his positive feelings toward Magwitch are strongly reinforced. After Herbert informs him that Molly and Magwitch had a child, Pip is "seized with a feverish conviction" that he ought to "hunt the matter down," although he does not know whether he is doing this "for Estella's sake" or because he is "glad to transfer to" Magwitch "some rays of the romantic interest that had so long surrounded her" (ch. 51). He is certainly not doing it for Estella's sake, since, as Jaggers points out, the revelation of her parentage would disgrace her. If Estella is Magwitch's daughter, however, she is no longer far above Pip, and this assuages his sense of inferiority. Pip is unaware of this motive, but he is conscious of his desire to invest Magwitch with romantic interest. With the collapse of his dream of marrying Estella and restoring Satis House, Pip begins to develop a new fantasy in which he will still do "the shining deeds of the young Knight of the romance" (ch. 29) by saving the father of the princess whom he has lost but still adores.

Pip's shifting attitude toward Magwitch is also part of a larger transformation precipitated by the collapse of his dream. When he begins "fully to know how wrecked" he is, the "sharpest and deepest pain of all" is the thought that he had deserted Joe for Magwitch (ch. 39). He had felt compelled to desert Joe in order to have a hope of Estella, and he had managed his guilt by adopting her perspective. When it turns out that he has abandoned Joe for a "convict, guilty of I knew not what crimes," Pip has no defense against his self-hate. He longs for the "comfort" he would derive from Joe's "simplicity and fidelity," but he cannot go back now because of his sense of his "worthless conduct." This is the beginning of a process in which Pip abandons the idealized image he had modeled on Estella and replaces it with one modeled on a glorified version of Joe. In the early stages of the process Pip experiences a great deal of self-hate, but as he begins to behave in ways that meet his new standards, his pride is gradually restored. He embarks on another search for glory in which he becomes the nobly forgiving, faithful Pip who thinks the best of others and little of himself.

When he visits Miss Havisham again to conclude the arrangement for Herbert, Pip's second transformation is well under way. At the sight of his misery when Estella rejected him, Miss Havisham had looked at Pip with "a ghastly stare of pity and remorse" (ch. 44); she now asks if he is "very unhappy" and hopes he can forgive her someday (ch. 49). Instead of punishing her with his suffering as he had done before, Pip replies that he can forgive her immediately: "my life has been a blind and thankless one; and I want forgiveness and direction far too much, to be bitter with you." Pip minimizes the wrongs that have been done to him, turns his criticism inward, and forgives in hopes of being forgiven himself. When Miss Havisham grieves for what she has done, Pip assures her that she has done "very little" to injure him, tells her to "dismiss" him from her "conscience," and dwells on the harm done to Estella and herself. Much like Joe in relation to his father and his wife, Pip denies the importance of his own injuries and thinks only of the suffering of others.

With the collapse of his quest for gentility, Pip begins to see himself from the perspectives of Joe and Biddy, Herbert and Clara, and even

Magwitch, and to despise himself for his snobbery, greed, and ingratitude. He feels "deservedly humbled" (ch. 52) when he thinks of his "miserable errors" (ch. 53) and is full of profound "remorse" (ch. 52). Despite his initial feeling that he can "never, never, never undo what [he] had done" (ch. 39), he tries to combat his despair by correcting his mistakes and proving himself worthy of the people he now idealizes.

Among Pip's miserable errors are the "wretched hankerings after money and gentility that had disturbed [his] boyhood" (ch. 39). Winning Estella was to be the means of confirming his worth, gentility was to be the means of winning Estella, and spending unearned money was the mark of gentility. When he goes to London, he compulsively engages in lavish expenditure because he needs to assure himself of his status. Now, in order to cleanse himself, he has an equally compulsive need to let money slip through his fingers, despite the fact that he is deeply in debt. He rejects Magwitch's benefits at first because of his shrinking from the convict, but he does so later, to the disgust of Wemmick and Jaggers, because he needs to prove that he is no longer a greedy parasite. He asks Miss Havisham to help him complete his arrangements for Herbert but refuses her offer to do something for him. Assisting his friend is so important because he must try to compensate for having led Herbert into expensive habits.

The mistake for which Pip hates himself most is his "thanklessness to Joe" (ch. 52), whom he now sees as a true and noble man who has always stood by him and whom he has repaid by abandonment. He is too ashamed of himself to seek forgiveness, but he tries to repair his self-image by behaving toward Magwitch as he should have behaved toward Joe and as Joe and Magwitch have behaved toward him. Pip has been to Magwitch as Joe has been to Pip in that he is the only person who empathized with Magwitch and showed him compassion, and Magwitch's adoption of Pip is partly motivated by gratitude. It is also motivated by his desire to use Pip as a means to rise above those who have despised him as an "ignorant common fellow": "If I ain't a gentleman, nor yet ain't got no learning, I'm the owner of such" (ch. 39). Magwitch has created Pip to be his instrument of vindictive triumph, much as Miss Havisham has done with Estella. The objectionable aspects of Magwitch's motivation are clear enough to Pip at the outset, but once his defenses begin to shift, they are obscured by his need to idealize others and blame himself. He comes to see Magwitch as "a much better man than [he] had been to Joe," a man "who had felt affectionately, gratefully, and generously towards [him] with great constancy through a series of years" (ch. 54). Pip incorporates Magwitch into his new idealized image, in which affection, gratitude, and constancy are primary values.

Pip feels that he can never redeem himself in relation to Joe, but the fact that Magwitch is in danger provides him with a wonderful opportunity to atone for his errors. Magwitch has risked his life in order to see Pip, and Pip can do no less to ensure his safety. He falls into Orlick's trap because he could never forgive himself if any harm should befall Magwitch through his not responding to the anonymous letter. The failure of the escape gives Pip fresh opportunities to undo his mistakes and confirm his transformation. He is too humble to boast of his self-sacrifice, but he calls attention to the contrast between his former worthless conduct and his present fidelity: "Please God, I will be as true to you as you have been to me!" (ch. 54). He undoes his earlier snobbery in a spectacular way by holding Magwitch's hand during the trial, and he reports that the audience pointed down "most of all at him and me." Instead of feeling ashamed of the connection, Pip glories in this public display of his loyalty. He is absolved of his guilt for once having meant to abandon Magwitch by the words of the dying man: "Thank'ee, dear boy, Thank'ee. God bless you! You've never deserted me, dear boy" (ch. 56).

The return of Magwitch and the loss of Estella bring to an end the search for glory that has been the focus of Pip's life since the day of his momentous visit to Miss Havisham, but he soon embarks on a new search for glory in which his shining deeds have a self-sacrificial character. He suffers painful burns rescuing Miss Havisham, risks his life helping Estella's father, gives up chances of money from Magwitch and Miss Havisham, sacrifices all claim to gentility by standing by Magwitch after his capture, and makes himself ill through his exertions on Magwitch's behalf. His idealized image is no longer modeled on Estella, but on dutiful, loving, forgiving people like Joe, Biddy, Herbert, and Clara, and grateful, constant, generous ones like Magwitch.

When his opportunities for heroic sacrifice come to an end with the death of Magwitch, Pip is left with two unresolved problems: how to effect a reconciliation with Joe and what to do with the rest of his life. His solution is to regress to a childlike dependency. When Joe comes to care for him during his illness, he fancies he is "little Pip again," enjoys being carried about as though he were still a "small helpless creature," and pretends to be weaker than he is so that Joe will continue to treat him like a child (ch. 57). As he becomes stronger, he remains morally dependent on Joe. He does not know if Joe is aware of his "change of fortune" and hesitates to bring up the subject: "I was so doubtful of myself now, and put so much trust in him, that I could not satisfy myself whether I ought to refer to it when he did not." Having made dreadful mistakes when governed by his ambition, Pip wants to avoid further self-hate by submitting himself to Joe. This is not a transitional state but the final stage of Pip's development.

One evidence of this is the narrator's treatment of Joe. The reborn Pip has a powerful need to invest Joe with absolute moral authority, and this leads him to idealize Joe, both in the present and retrospectively: "Exactly what he had been in my eyes then, he was in my eyes still: just as simply faithful, just as simply right" (ch. 57). Pip's first evaluation of Joe is more balanced and accurate: "He was a mild, good-natured, sweet-tempered, easy-going, foolish, dear fellow—a sort of Hercules in strength, and also in weakness" (ch. 2). This is cast in the educated language of the narrator, but it seems to represent the unidealizing perspective of the child. Little Pip is not sure of the meaning of being "brought up by hand," but knowing that his sister lays her "hard and heavy hand" on her husband as well as himself, he supposes that he and Joe "were both brought up by hand." Joe is his "fellow-sufferer" whom he treats "as a larger species of child."

When Pip puts his bread and butter down the leg of his trousers in order to save it for Magwitch, Joe thinks he has bolted it and carries on so that Mrs. Joe becomes furious with both of them. Since he won't answer her questions but keeps addressing himself to Pip, she takes him by the whiskers and knocks his head against the wall: "Now, perhaps you'll mention what's the matter . . . you staring great stuck pig" (ch. 2). Joe looks at her "in a helpless way," takes "a helpless bite," and looks at Pip again. When Joe eventually reveals that Pip has bolted his food (as he thinks), his wife doses him with tar-water also, "because he had a turn." "Judging from myself," observes Pip, "I should say he certainly had a turn afterwards, if he had none before." Tar-water is an emetic.

In the early chapters of the novel, Joe is a comic figure at whose discomfiture we laugh, partly because of the incongruity of a muscular blacksmith being knocked about, scolded, and dosed like a child. He means well but cannot protect Pip because of his inability to assert himself. He offers a great deal of psychological comfort, however, thus earning Pip's gratitude. Pip begins to admire him when he explains why he does not "rise" against his wife and wishes he could take all the abuse on himself (ch. 7). This is the long-suffering, loving, self-sacrificial Joe on whom Pip models himself when his expectations collapse and whom as narrator he celebrates whenever he can.

Once Pip begins to dream of becoming a gentleman, he measures himself against Estella, while as narrator he measures himself against Joe. Joe is the moral norm through most of the book, despite the weakness and folly that had seemed evident to the seven-year-old Pip and presumably to Dickens when he began to write the novel. Joe's mixture of strength and weakness becomes "his combination of strength with gentleness" (ch. 18). "Plain contented Joe" is the source of "any good" that intermixes itself with the apprenticeship of "restless aspiring discontented" Pip. It is because Joe is "faithful" that Pip does not run away and because Joe has "a strong sense of the virtue of industry" that Pip works "with tolerable zeal against the grain." This testimony to the "influence" of "amiable honest-hearted duty-going" Joe (ch. 14) is composed from the perspective of Pip the narrator who needs to prove his mature wisdom by celebrating Joe's virtues and denying any to his earlier self. When Joe refuses all thought of compensation for the loss of his apprentice, Jaggers looks at him "as if he considered him a fool for his disinterestedness," much as he later looks at Pip when he imitates Joe by not taking money from Magwitch and Miss Havisham. The man whom the ambitious Pip "was so ready to leave and so unthankful to" becomes little less than a deity to the "educated" Pip: "O dear good faithful tender Joe, I feel the loving tremble of your hand upon my arm, as solemnly this day as if it had been the rustle of an angel's wing!" (ch. 18).

Pip's need to reestablish his relationship with Joe is only temporarily satisfied by his illness. Since Joe has no way of knowing of his second transformation, he withdraws as Pip becomes stronger, and Pip blames himself, having given Joe "reason to doubt [his] constancy, and to think that in prosperity" he would "cast him off" (ch. 57). Pip responds to Joe's departure by deciding to propose to Biddy, whom he will show "how humbled and repentant" he is. In his imaginary declaration, he addresses Biddy not as a prospective partner with whom he will have an adult relationship, but as a mother who will comfort him and tell him what to do with his life: "if you can receive me like a forgiven child (and indeed I am as sorry, Biddy, and have as much need of a hushing voice and a soothing hand), I hope I am a little worthier of you than I was—not much, but a little." Notice how careful Pip is to preserve his humility while offering himself as improved. It will rest with Biddy to say whether he will "work at the forge with Joe," or try for a "different occupation down in this country," or accept Herbert's invitation to join him in a foreign land. Too distrustful of himself to decide his own course, Pip wants to be directed entirely by people who have always been right, "whose simple faith and clear home-wisdom" he has "proved" (ch. 58).

The discovery that Joe and Biddy have married leaves Pip with no alternative but to move in with Herbert and Clara. His account of the next eleven years is brief, but every detail is important. He lives "frugally," pays his debts, and maintains "a constant correspondence with Biddy and Joe" (ch. 58). He begins as a clerk but eventually becomes a partner in the firm: "We were not in a grand way of business, but we had a good name, and worked for our profits, and did very well." Herbert is so industrious and apt that Pip wonders how he had "conceived that old idea of his inaptitude" until he is "enlightened by the reflection" that the inaptitude "had never been" in Herbert "at all" but had been in himself.

Pip is still trying to undo past mistakes, and his version of reality is still full of distortions and blind spots. His frugality is the opposite of his previous lavish expenditure, he pays his own debts instead of depending on others, and he does not try to become uncommon but is content with a modest success achieved through honest hard work. His models are Joe, who ever does "his duty in his way of life" (ch. 35), and Herbert, who announced at the outset that he had his "own bread to earn" and would not take anything from his father if he had it to give (ch. 21). Pip is out to prove that he is no longer a restless, ambitious parasite but a mature person who takes responsibility for himself and earns his own way in the world.

What Pip leaves out is the fact that he and Herbert have obtained their positions with money supplied by Magwitch and Miss Havisham. He blames himself for his old idea of Herbert's inaptitude in order to idealize his friend and obscure the fact that neither he nor Herbert has truly made it on his own. His original perception of Herbert had been supported by a wealth of detail:

> Every morning, with an air ever new, Herbert went into the City to look about him. I often paid him a visit in the dark back-room in which he consorted with an ink-jar, a hat-peg, a coal-box, a string-box, an almanack, a desk and stool, and a ruler; and I do not remember that I ever saw him do anything else but look about him. If we all did what we undertake to do, as faithfully as Herbert did, we might live in a Republic of the Virtues. (Ch. 34)

Like Joe, Herbert begins as a comic figure. He has "greater expectations" than Pip's (ch. 22) but no idea of how to make a living. He succeeds only because Pip becomes his secret benefactor. When Herbert proudly proclaims that he is "working up towards a partnership," Pip comments, "Poor fellow! He little suspected with whose money" (ch. 41).

In Pip's mind, however, and in the rhetoric of the novel, awareness of the role of Magwitch's money is suppressed, and emphasis is placed on Pip's benevolence and Herbert's "industry and readiness" (ch. 58). The fact that Pip is able to find a place for himself because of his earlier good deed supports a thematic structure that is simultaneously subverted by the fact that neither Herbert nor Pip could have achieved economic independence without the kind of patronage that Pip now feels virtuous for rejecting.

Despite the fact that neither Herbert nor Pip illustrates the theme of earning one's way quite as Dickens seems to intend, they display the virtue of industry once they get their chance; and it might be argued that Pip does achieve the maturity the novel claims for him. "I work pretty hard for a sufficient living," he tells Estella, "and therefore . . . I do well!" (ch. 49). But Pip is not doing well psychologically. He successfully imitates Joe by being plain, contented, hard-working, duty-going Pip, and this enables him to feel better about himself, but he has to pay a high price for this rather limited achievement. There is no evidence that he comes to trust himself any more than he did when he was recovering from his illness, and he seems to have withdrawn from active living and subordinated himself permanently to Herbert and Clara, Joe and Biddy in order to ensure his rectitude. He lives with the one couple, maintains a constant correspondence with the other, and shows no interest in having a life of his own. Herbert and Clara say that he "must marry," but Pip does not think he will: "I have so settled down in their home, that it's not at all likely. I am already quite an old bachelor" (ch. 59). Pip is so afraid of himself that he leads a sterile, embedded existence in order to keep himself straight. His true psychological state is obscured by the novel's celebration of his defenses.

The original ending of *Great Expectations* is quite compatible with my reading of Pip's character. Drummle has died, Estella has remarried, and Pip's interview with her assures him that suffering "had given her a heart to understand what [his] heart used to be." Given Pip's massive resignation—he is once again trying to defend himself against being bad by not wanting very much—and his anxious dependence on his moral exemplars, Pip is likely to have renounced all thought of Estella, as he has the values she represents, and to be frightened by the idea of a relationship with her. I believe him when he tells Biddy, in both versions, that "that poor dream . . . has all gone by" (ch. 59). In the original ending Estella is safely unavailable, and Pip is glad to have seen her because she confirms his belief in moral growth through suffering. He is not frustrated by her remarriage because she is no longer an object of desire. Her suffering has enabled her to understand what he had felt in the past.

This is much more compatible with the mimetic portrayal of Pip than his statement in the revised ending that she has "always held [her] place" in his heart. The fact that she, too, has been "bent and broken . . . into a better shape" would make her less threatening, but so much time has passed and they are both so changed that I do not understand why he wants to marry her. His behavior seems out of keeping with his character. Some critics, indeed, have tried to harmonize the revised ending with the rest of the novel by arguing that Pip sees "no shadow of another parting" from Estella because they will now part forever. I cannot accept that reading, but I can understand the temptation to impose it on the text. The revised ending provides closure at the expense of verisimilitude, while the original ending provides verisimilitude at the expense of closure.

9

Jane Eyre

As we have seen, psychological analysis of realistically drawn characters reveals them to be "creations inside a creation" who are "often engaged in treason against the main scheme of the book" (Forster 1927, 64). In nineteenth-century fiction, such characters tend to subvert two schemes in particular: the education pattern that we find in such novels as *Emma* (Paris 1978b), *Great Expectations,* and *The Mill on the Floss* (Paris 1974), and the vindication pattern that we find in such novels as *Mansfield Park* (Paris 1978b), *Henry Esmond,* and *Jane Eyre.*

In the education pattern, which reflects the archetype of the fortunate fall, the protagonists' flaws lead them to make mistakes that bring suffering to themselves and others, and out of this suffering comes moral and emotional growth. In the vindication pattern, which reflects the Cinderella archetype, deserving protagonists are discriminated against or devalued by parental figures and the surrounding community, but they prove their worth and eventually receive widespread approval and an appropriate social position. These patterns have tragic and comic forms, and some novels contain both education and vindication patterns. In *Middlemarch,* for instance, Lydgate is educated while Dorothea is vindicated; in *The Mayor of Casterbridge,* Elizabeth-Jane is vindicated while Henchard is educated. Although *Jane Eyre* is predominantly a novel of vindication, it also presents Jane as undergoing a process of moral growth.

A Horneyan approach shows the supposedly educated characters to be less mature and the vindicated characters to be less admirable than plot and rhetoric suggest. In novels of vindication, the protagonists are often mimetically portrayed as having extremely harsh childhoods that force them to develop compulsive strategies of defense; but instead of being recognized as destructive, these strategies are celebrated by the rhetoric and, in comic versions of the pattern, validated by the plot. Jane Eyre's emotional problems are presented in vivid detail, but the world of the novel is manipulated so as to obscure the compulsiveness of her behavior, to satisfy her conflicting psychological needs, and to sanction her self-glorifying rhetoric. Like Pip's, her distortions and blind spots are in keeping with her character but sometimes make her account of herself unreliable. A Horneyan approach will help us to see Jane more clearly, to appreciate her motives for telling her story, and to do justice to the brilliance of Brontë's mimetic characterization.

As is typical in novels of vindication, Jane has a miserable childhood. Her mother is disinherited when she marries a poor clergyman, both parents perish of typhus soon after Jane's birth, and Jane is taken in by her uncle Reed, who dies while she is an infant, leaving her to the care of an aunt who resents her as an alien intruder. The destitute child is constantly reminded of her dependent position. Her cousin John tells her that she "ought to beg, and not to live here with gentlemen's children like us" (ch. 1); and Abbot, the lady's-maid, informs her that she is "less than a servant," for she does nothing for her keep (ch. 2). Bessie, the nurse, admonishes her to be good, for she would have to go to the poor house should her aunt turn her out. "My first recollections of existence," says Jane, "included hints of the same kind. This reproach of my dependence had become a vague sing-song in my ear; very painful and crushing." Like Pip, Jane is perceived as having no rights and as being insufficiently grateful for the inadequate care that is so grudgingly bestowed on her.

As a result of these conditions, Jane develops intense feelings of insecurity, vulnerability, and hopelessness. Entirely dependent, she lives with a constant dread of being abandoned by a hostile aunt who perpetually criticizes her, excludes her from family life, and gives her children license to torment her. John Reed bullies and punishes Jane "not two or three times in the week, nor once or twice in the day, but continually: every nerve I had feared him, and every morsel of flesh on my bones shrank when he came near" (ch. 1). Jane is "bewildered by the terror" he inspires because she has "no appeal whatever" against his "menaces" and "inflictions" (ch. 1). Her aunt turns a blind eye, and the servants will not intervene. Although she strives "to fulfill every duty," she is "always suffering, always browbeaten, always accused, for ever condemned" (ch. 2). It seems "useless to try to win any one's favour."

Of all the terrible childhoods in Victorian fiction, Jane's is one of the worst. As despised and rejected as Heathcliff, she is even more isolated, since Heathcliff has Cathy, whereas Jane has no ally at all. Like Pip's sister, Jane's aunt feels burdened by having to care for an orphan, takes out her resentment on the child, and then excuses herself by blaming her victim, whom she sees as irredeemably bad. Tormented by the Reed children as well as their mother, Jane leads "a life of ceaseless reprimand and thankless fagging" (ch. 3). Like Pip, she is made to feel unsafe, unloved, and unworthy by a foster-parent who wishes her dead; but her case is worse than Pip's, for she must live "without one bit of love or kindness" (ch. 4) for the first ten years of her life, whereas Pip has Joe for emotional support.

Jane tries to defend herself by striving to please Mrs. Reed and by escaping into imaginary worlds, but the opening episode shows that neither of these strategies works. Mrs. Reed banishes her because she does not have a "franker, more natural" manner, and John Reed flushes her out of the window seat, where she has taken refuge with a book, in order to harass her (ch. 1). No matter what she does, Jane can neither win acceptance nor escape abuse.

It is part of the vindication pattern for the protagonist to be surrounded by detractors who are shown to be mistaken about her, but when we study the mimetic portrait of Jane we can see that Mrs. Reed's complaints are not without foundation. Jane is not "sociable and childlike" (ch. 1), frank and natural, nor could she be when her mistreatment at the hands of the Reeds has made her angry, insecure, and distrustful. Her aunt's description of her "as a compound of virulent passions, mean spirit, and dangerous duplicity" (ch. 2) is supposed to be seen as profoundly unfair, but it is, in fact, accurate. Although Mrs. Reed fails to understand her own contribution, Jane *is* "a compound of virulent passions," as the opening chapters show, for she is full of rage and resentment. She has a "mean spirit" in the sense that she is too fearful to express her outrage directly and accepts too much abuse. "What a miserable little poltroon had fear, engendered of unjust punishment, made of me in those days!" exclaims the narrator (ch. 4). The charge of duplicity is also understandable. Jane tries to be "useful and pleasant" (ch. 2) in order to avoid being sent away, but she is too full of hostility to play this role successfully, and her pretense is transparent. After Jane explodes, Bessie says that "she never did so before," but Abbot observes that "it was always in her": "She's an underhand little thing: I never saw a girl of her age with so much cover." Before her explosion, Jane is a sullen, brooding, silently accusing child (John Reed calls her "Madam Mope") whose demeanor makes the Reeds defensive.

Mrs. Reed cannot comprehend "how for nine years [Jane] could be patient and quiescent under any treatment, and in the tenth break out all fire and violence" (ch. 21). Although compliance did not work, Jane had clung to it out of a fear of total rejection. When she is subjected to more abuse than she can bear, her pent-up fury erupts, and she finally rebels. The precipitating event is John Reed's attack. Having been told to stay away from the family, Jane retreats to the window seat in the breakfast room with *Bewick's History of British Birds,* draws the curtain, and sits "shrined in double retirement," entering imaginatively into the scenes of desolation pictured in the book (ch. 1). She is not permitted to defend herself by moving away, however, any more than is Pip, for John Reed finds her and hits her with the book, causing her to fall and cut her head. At this point, Jane loses control of herself and bitterly accuses John of being wicked and cruel. Enraged, he assaults her and, for the first time in her life, she fights back: "I received him in frantic sort. I don't very well know what I did with my hands, but he called me 'Rat! rat' and bellowed out aloud." My guess is that Jane struck him in the genitals.

Having allowed her aggression to emerge, Jane expects the worst, and, feeling that she has nothing more to lose, resolves, in her "desperation, to go all lengths" (ch. 2). She resists, "a new thing" for her, as she is dragged off for punishment. In "the mood of the revolted slave," she broods on the injustice of her lot: the Reed children are selfish, spoiled, sadistic, but they are approved, while she, who "dare[s] commit no fault," is "termed naughty and tiresome, sullen and sneaking, from morning to noon, and from noon to night." She resolves to escape this "insupportable oppression" by running away or starving herself to death. Imagining that Mr. Reed's spirit, "harassed by the wrongs of his sister's child," might "revisit the earth to punish the perjured and avenge the oppressed" (ch. 2), she thinks she sees a ghost and becomes terrified. Her screams bring her aunt, who ignores her pleas for another form of punishment, and Jane has a fit when she is shut up in the Red Room once more.

Despite the trauma of this experience, Jane finds that the consequences of her rebellion are predominantly positive. Her hysterical behavior brings about the intervention of the apothecary, Mr. Lloyd, and arouses Bessie's sympathy for the first time. She is to be sent away from Gateshead, to be sure, but to school rather than to the threatened poorhouse. When John Reed attacks, she fights back, and he thinks it better to desist than to confront her "deep ire and desperate revolt," the effects of which he has already felt (ch. 4). The worm has turned; Jane is mean-spirited no more.

Instead of being a passive victim, Jane puts her aunt on the defensive, asking "What would uncle Reed say to you, if he were alive?" (ch. 4). When Mrs. Reed reacts with a look of fear, Jane presses the attack, saying that her dead relatives in heaven see how she treats her. "Shaking from head to foot, thrilled with ungovernable excitement," Jane attacks again after Mrs. Reed tells Brocklehurst that she is a liar. She calls her aunt "bad," "hard-hearted," and "deceitful" and says that when she is grown she will tell people that "the very thought of you makes me sick, and that you treated me with miserable cruelty." The "frightened" Mrs. Reed seeks to placate Jane, whose soul begins "to exult" with a "sense of freedom, of triumph." Whereas compliance has failed, aggressiveness works, a lesson that is reinforced when Bessie praises Jane's new-found boldness and warns that the people she meets at school will dislike her if she fears them.

Jane's experiences at Gateshead establish the agenda for her vindication. She needs to prove she is not mean spirited and duplicitous; hence her boldness, bluntness, and repeated declarations that she is not afraid. She needs to prove she is not bad, worthless, inferior to people like the Reeds; hence her need to be good at all costs, her boasting about the recognition she receives, and her great satisfaction in social and economic advancement. Jane is extremely sensitive about her plainness (Abbot says that "one really cannot care for such a little toad"—ch. 3); hence her critical or condescending attitude toward beauties like Blanche Ingram and Rosamond Oliver and her sense of triumph at being preferred to them by Rochester and St. John.

The world of the novel is so arranged that after Jane leaves Gateshead her feelings of personal, social, and economic inferiority, of friendlessness, isolation, and undesirability, and of weakness, vulnerability, and cowardliness are all reversed. Her value is attested by her intellectual and artistic accomplishments; the friendship of admirable people like Helen Burns, Miss Temple, and the Rivers sisters; the fondness of her pupils; the venerating love of Rochester; and St. John's appreciation of her sterling qualities. She proves herself fearless, truthful, and good in every situation; and her poverty, low status, lack of family, and frustration in love are all removed by manipulations of the plot.

Jane's vindication begins at Lowood, where she reverts to her self-effacing ways. She wants to be "good" so as to make "many friends, to earn respect, and win affection" (ch. 8), and she is well-received until Brocklehurst stigmatizes her as a liar and instructs the girls to shun her. Feeling "crushed and trodden on" once more, Jane "ardently" wishes "to die." When Helen Burns urges her to take comfort in the approval of her own conscience, Jane says that thinking well of herself is not enough if others do not love her: "I would rather die than live—I cannot bear to be solitary and hated." Helen complains that Jane thinks "too much of the love of human beings," but Jane has felt solitary and hated all her life and is desperate for warmth and approval. She tells Helen, "I would willingly submit to have the bone of my arm broken, or to let a bull toss me, or to stand behind a kicking horse, and let it dash its hoof at my chest" in order to "gain some real affection from you, or Miss Temple, or any other whom I truly love." Fortunately, Miss Temple treats Jane fairly, and when she realizes that she will be evaluated on her merit, her energies are liberated, and she proves that Mrs. Reed had misjudged her.

The aggression that had emerged at Gateshead has not disappeared but takes the form of indignation on behalf of Helen Burns, with whom Jane identifies as another abandoned, abused, but truly superior child. When Miss Scatcherd strikes Helen, Jane proclaims that if the teacher struck her, she would take the rod from her hand and "break it under her nose" (ch. 6). But Helen disapproves of Jane's violent impulses. In addition to being self-effacing, like Jane, Helen is also very detached. She gets into trouble because she "cannot *bear* to be subjected to systematic arrangements" and is off in a dream world much of the time. Since Helen is so resigned, she does not feel the degradation, the sense of injustice, and the desires for revenge that Jane experiences on her behalf.

Disappointed by her father, Helen has given up looking for love and justice from human beings and has made her bargain with God, the "mighty universal Parent," who sees "our tortures," recognizes "our innocence," and "waits only the separation of spirit from flesh to crown us with a full reward" (ch. 8). Her vindication will come in the afterlife. She urges Jane to disregard ill-usage, to try to forget Mrs. Reed's "severity, together with the passionate emotions it excited" (ch. 6). Why "should we ever sink overwhelmed with distress, when life is so soon over, and death is so certain an entrance to happiness—to glory?" (ch. 8). Jane is not ready to adopt this perspective; she wants happiness and glory on earth.

Nor is Jane ready for Helen's rejection of the major lesson she had learned at Gateshead, that we should be good to those who are good to us but "strike back again very hard" at those who are cruel and unjust so as to teach them "never to do it again" (ch. 6). Helen says that "heathens and savage tribes hold that doctrine; but Christians and civilized nations disown it." She advocates, instead, the imitation of Christ: "Love your enemies; bless them that curse you; do good to them that hate you and despitefully use you." Jane protests that it is impossible for her to love Mrs. Reed and to bless John and bitterly pours out "the tale of [her] sufferings and resentments."

Although she cannot accept Helen's philosophy, Jane is uneasy about her rage and vindictiveness. The explosions of anger with which the novel begins give her an exhilarating sense of freedom and triumph, but they also fill her with self-hate and anxiety. She is sustained for a while in the Red Room by the energy of rebellion, but then her courage sinks, and in her "habitual mood of humiliation, self-doubt, [and] forlorn depression" she begins to wonder if she is wicked, as everyone says she is (ch. 4). She has just been thinking of starving herself to death, and surely this is a crime. After she tells Mrs. Reed that her mother, father, and uncle know "how you wish me dead," Bessie says that she is "the most wicked and abandoned child ever reared under a roof," and Jane half-believes her, for she has "only bad feelings surging in [her] breast." When she attacks her aunt after Brocklehurst's visit, the taste of vengeance is like "aromatic wine," but the "after-flavour" gives her the "sensation" of having been "poisoned." Feeling her "indignation" to be "fiendish" (ch. 4), she leaves Gateshead with "a sense of outlawry and almost of reprobation" (ch. 21).

In the vindication pattern of the novel, Jane eventually proves that she is superior to the people who devalued her and receives her just deserts. In the education pattern, she is rewarded because she triumphs over her own passionate nature, resists powerful temptations, and succeeds in living up to a lofty moral ideal. Whereas the agenda for her vindication is set at Gateshead, that for her education is established by Helen Burns. Jane cannot immediately follow Helen's injunction to love her enemies, but when she fully and freely forgives Mrs. Reed, who is unrelenting even on her deathbed, she proves to herself that she has spiritually matured (ch. 21). As narrator she displays a Christ-like attitude toward her tormentors: "Yes, Mrs. Reed, to you I owe some fearful pangs of mental suffering. But I ought to forgive you, for you knew not what you did" (ch. 3). Helen shows Jane how she *ought* to deal with her resentment, and Jane incorporates Helen's dictates into her idealized conception of herself.

The author collaborates with Jane not only in bringing about her vindication but also in making it possible for her to live up to her idealized image of herself. If Jane continued to experience her anger, she would fail to exemplify the teachings of Christ and would feel herself to be an uncivilized heathen. But what is she to do with her aggression? Part of it is channeled into the feistiness that Bessie encourages and that charms Rochester, but most of it is acted out for her by others, enabling her to satisfy her vindictive and rebellious impulses without losing her nobility. Jane's enemies are all brought down by the author, Mrs. Reed and John quite horribly, making it easier for her to forgive them; and an alter ego is provided in Rochester, whose fierceness, mysterious sufferings, and volcanic passions reflect the side of Jane she cannot express and that the rhetoric conceals.

Jane must find a way to manage not only her anger but also her craving for life. As long as Miss Temple is there to satisfy her desire for warmth and approval, Jane lives contentedly at Lowood "in allegiance to duty and order"; but as soon as Miss Temple leaves, Jane develops a powerful longing for "Liberty, Excitement, Enjoyment" (ch. 10). Having spent all her vacations at Lowood, she has known only "school-rules, school-duties, school-habits and notions, and voices, and faces." Tiring of her narrow existence in the space of a few hours, Jane remembers that "the real world [is] wide, and that a varied field of hopes and fears, of sensations and excitements, [await] those who [have] courage to go forth into its expanse, to seek real knowledge of life amidst its perils."

Jane never has this courage. Since her cravings are out of harmony with both her lot as a woman and her need to be good, she quickly relinquishes them. Her prayer for liberty seems scattered on the wind, and she frames "a humbler supplication: for change, stimulus" (ch. 10). When that petition, too, seems swept off into space, she asks to be granted "at least a new servitude!" This is what she pursues when she advertises for a situation as a governess. Although she longs for "life and movement," she is pleased by the old-fashioned character of Mrs. Fairfax's response. She had been haunted by a fear that she would get into a "scrape" by acting for herself and wishes "above all things" for the result of her "endeavours to be respectable, proper, *en règle.*"

Once she is settled at Thornfield, Jane's restlessness returns. Adèle and Mrs. Fairfax are "good," but she believes "in the existence of other and more vivid kinds of goodness" that she wishes to behold (ch. 12). She insists that she is longing for more vivid kinds of goodness because she must moralize her desire for experience, which she fears is improper. To justify her discontent she invokes the millions of women who, suffering "too rigid a constraint, too absolute a stagnation" are "in silent revolt against their lot" (ch. 12). This passage is justly celebrated for its feminist sentiments, but we must remember that Jane could never engage in a real revolt against the constraints of her lot because of her need to protect her respectability. She dares not do anything that might prove Mrs. Reed to have been right in calling her wicked. At this point Rochester arrives at Thornfield and Jane's restlessness disappears.

Jane and Rochester have such an intense romantic relationship because they fulfill many of each other's emotional cravings. The relationship is glorified by the rhetoric and is a major part of the vindication pattern, but from a Horneyan perspective the mimesis shows that each party brings into it emotional problems and contradictory needs. The contradictions are magically resolved by manipulations of the plot, but, even so, the relationship Jane celebrates at the end is not as ideal as she claims it to be.

Jane's attraction to Rochester has many components. Insecure about her own charm and appearance, she is set at ease from the first by his rough manner and lack of good looks. She would have shunned anyone displaying "beauty, elegance, gallantry" from a feeling that he could not "have sympathy with anything" in her (ch. 12). Given Jane's tastes, Rochester is not unappealing. She likes his "decisive nose," his choleric nostrils, his "grim mouth, chin, and jaw" (ch. 13). When Mason later appears on the scene, he repels Jane "exceedingly" (ch. 18). He is handsome and amiable-looking, but there is "no firmness in that aquiline nose, and small, cherry mouth," "no thought on the low, even forehead; no command in that blank, brown eye." He is a "sleek gander" to Rochester's "fierce falcon." Rochester is a domineering man whose "dark, irate, and piercing" eyes frighten others but not her (ch. 13). The fact that she is not intimidated proves that she is no longer the miserable little poltroon for whom she has such contempt. Being able to stand up to such a powerful man gives her a feeling of strength.

Whereas Jane has been bored by the decent but unremarkable people at Thornfield, Rochester is a lofty, mysterious being who fascinates her. She "reverence[s]" his "vigorous," "original," "expanded mind" (ch. 23), and he in turn expresses great admiration for her. He tells her that she is "cast in a different mould to the majority" (ch. 14), regards her as a fit person in whom to confide, and assures her that her "unique" mind is not "liable to take infection" from him. To him, she is a princess in the guise of a governess. His tributes feed her pride and counterbalance the devaluation she had experienced at Gateshead. They are all the more gratifying because he is a "proud, sardonic" man who is "harsh to inferiority of every description" and treats others with "severity" (ch. 15). Rochester and Jane form a community of two superior beings who appreciate each other and look down on everyone else. Instead of being excluded from the privileged circle, as she had been at Gateshead, Jane is at the center of things.

Rochester describes Jane as being like a caged bird, a "vivid, restless, resolute captive" that "would soar cloud-high" if it were free (ch. 15). But Jane never soars. Instead, she satisfies her desire for knowledge of real life amidst its perils by living vicariously through Rochester, much as Hedda Gabler lives through Ejlert Lövborg. Rochester has had the kind of exciting life for which Jane longs but of which she is afraid, and he regales her with "glimpses" of the "scenes and ways" of the world— not "its corrupt scenes and wicked ways," she hastens to assure us, "but such as derived their interest from the great scale on which they were acted, the strange novelty by which they were characterised." Concerned for her respectability, Jane is eager to let us know that she was "never startled or troubled by one noxious allusion." She is so "gratified" by following Rochester "in thought through the new regions he disclosed" that her restlessness subsides, the "blanks of existence" are filled, and she gains "flesh and strength."

Jane's assurance that Rochester does not describe corrupt scenes and wicked ways is all the more striking because he has already confessed that he has led a degenerate life and has told her the story of his affair with Cécile Varens, a French opera dancer and the mother of Adèle. Rochester's lurid history is part of his appeal because it allows Jane glimpses of corrupt scenes and wicked ways in which she really is interested, but it also makes her anxious. More puritanical than Hedda, Jane can enjoy Rochester's transgressions only if she can convince herself that he is now reformed: "I believed that his moodiness, his harshness, and his former faults of morality (I say *former* for he now seemed corrected of them) had their source in some cruel cross of fate" (ch. 15).

Jane has reason to know, however, that Rochester has not yet conformed to the established morality. He has presented himself to her as a victim of fate—his sinfulness being due "rather to circumstances" than to his "natural bent"; but he has acknowledged that he "turned desperate" when fate wronged him and that he is desperate still: "since happiness is irrevocably denied me, I have a right to get pleasure out of life: and I *will* get it, cost what it may" (ch. 14). Jane does not know what Rochester has in mind, but his plan is to marry her despite the fact that he already has a wife. He convinces himself that his pursuit of pleasure need not lead to further degeneration if the pleasure is "as sweet and fresh as the wild honey the bee gathers on the moor." Jane's innocence will somehow purify their union. When he decrees that his aims and motives are right, Jane protests that they cannot be "if they require a new statute to legalise them." They do demand a new statute, he replies, because "unheard-of combinations of circumstances demand unheard-of rules." Jane opposes Rochester's situational ethic with an absolute one: "The human and fallible should not arrogate a power with which the divine and perfect alone can be safely entrusted." This conversation occurs shortly before Jane declares that Rochester seems to be free of his former faults.

Rochester's rebelliousness is part of his appeal to Jane. She, too, has felt unjustly treated by family and fate, and she, too, has broken out in angry insurrection against irrational authority. Before Rochester's appearance, she was feeling silently rebellious against her woman's lot and was longing to escape her confinement. As a rich upper-class male, Rochester is able to act out his resentments, and Jane can experience her own forbidden impulses through him.

Jane is excited not only by Rochester's rebellion against the norms of respectability to which she herself is enslaved but also by his aggressive behavior. His fierce, volcanic passions mirror feelings of her own that had emerged at Gateshead but that she has repressed. She delights in the fact that he is "a bold, vindictive, haughty gentleman" (ch. 16). Her vindictiveness and haughtiness must be concealed (although they are evident in her narration), but she can relish such qualities in Rochester. She is critical of him at first, but his "sarcasm" and "harshness" come to seem like "keen condiments in a choice dish." She is attracted to his strange and "sinister" depths and wishes to "look into the abyss" and "explore its secrets" (ch. 18). This is much safer than exploring her own inner depths, which are also strange and sinister, as some of her paintings reveal. It is no wonder Jane feels that she and Rochester are soul mates. Although they are divided by rank and wealth, she has "something in [her] brain and heart, in [her] blood and nerves, that assimilates mentally to him" (ch. 17).

Sensing Jane's affinity to the turbulent side of his nature, Rochester also feels that they are soul mates, and this is part of what draws him to her. He is most powerfully attracted, however, by Jane's rigorous morality, which gives him the hope that she can redeem him. She represents the person he might have been had he not gone astray. He tells her that he has been on the wrong course since the age of twenty-one but that he "might have been as good as you—wiser—almost as stainless. I envy you your peace of mind, your clear conscience, your unpolluted memory" (ch. 14). Jane sees Rochester as he wishes to see himself, as "naturally a man of better tendencies, higher principles, and purer tastes than such as circumstances had developed, education instilled, or destiny encouraged." She thinks there are "excellent materials in him," though "somewhat spoiled and tangled at present" (ch. 15), and he sees in her purity and rectitude the promise of regeneration. She wants to reform him, and he longs to be reformed.

After living with Bertha for four years, Rochester is filled with despair, but he determines to seek renewal by returning to Europe. He spends ten years searching for "a good and intelligent woman" whom he can love, but he finds no one in all of his travels he would wish to marry if he were free (ch. 27). Made reckless by disappointment, he tries "dissipation—never debauchery: that I hated, and hate." The distinction may seem elusive, but in Rochester's mind "debauchery" is associated with Bertha, whom he loathes: "Any enjoyment that bordered on riot seemed to approach me to her and her vices, and I eschewed it." If he felt that he had become promiscuous like Bertha, he would be overwhelmed with self-hate, so he contents himself with one mistress at a time. Beginning "to regard the notion of an intellectual, faithful, loving woman as a mere dream," he returns to Thornfield and finds what he has been looking for in Jane. He thinks her "good, gifted, lovely"; she is his "better self," his "good angel" (ch. 23). In Horneyan terms, Rochester perceives Bertha and Jane as embodiments of his despised and idealized selves. He dreads becoming like Bertha and aspires to emulate Jane.

Rochester's search for renewal through the love of a good woman is doomed by its contradictions. Frustrated by his plight, he has convinced himself that his bond to Bertha is "a mere conventional impediment," that it is "absolutely rational" that he should be "free to love and be loved," and that he can and should marry again (ch. 20). His "original intention" is not "to deceive" but to explain his situation to a woman who is "willing and able to understand the case" (ch. 27). Any woman who accepted his bigamous proposal would lose her value for him, however, since she would no longer be on a higher moral plane. He conceals the truth from Jane not only because he fears her refusal but also because, having found in her the qualities he has been seeking, "without soil and without taint" (ch. 20), he needs to preserve her innocence. Even if he had succeeded in his deception, he would not have been regenerated, since he would have increased his sinfulness by wronging Jane. Despite his dismissal of "custom" and "mere human law" (ch. 27), Rochester has not freed himself of the values of his culture. It is because he is burdened by guilt that Jane's purity and rectitude are so important to him. He cannot possibly cleanse his conscience by compromising her.

Rochester has conflicting needs of Jane. He wants her to be a liberated woman who is capable of understanding his case, of overleaping the obstacles of custom, convention, and mere human law in the name of a rational morality. He senses the caged spirit that wishes to escape its constraints, and he celebrates her as a "savage, beautiful creature," a "wild, free thing," "resolute" and "indomitable" (ch. 27). At the same time, he needs her to be his good angel without soil or taint. Once his marriage to Bertha is revealed, he tries to persuade Jane to remain with him, but, as she well understands, if she succeeds his former mistresses, he will one day regard her "with the same feeling which now in his mind desecrate[s] their memory."

Rochester has misread Jane, of course, as have the critics who see her as a feminist heroine. She longs for greater freedom and a wider range of activity, but she is afraid to pursue her desires. Jane's will and energy, resoluteness and indomitability are all on the side of propriety. Far from being a free spirit who rebels against the constrictions of her feminine lot, she is a compulsively conventional woman who must live her life according to rule.

At first Jane and Rochester seem to complement each other perfectly, since the repressed side of each is dominant in the other. Rochester is a rebel against society and religion who is troubled by conscience, while Jane is a super-conscientious woman with repressed rebellious impulses. He looks to her for reformation, while she satisfies through him the bold, vindictive, haughty side of her nature. But the match is not really perfect since they have contradictory needs of each other that reflect their own inner conflicts. Rochester wants a wild, free thing who is absolutely virtuous, while Jane desires a worldly adventurer who will not threaten her innocence. He is looking for a pure mistress, and she wants him to be a reformed sinner so that she can gratify her forbidden impulses through his past escapades. When Jane learns that Rochester still means to defy the established morality, a conflict arises between them that cannot be resolved.

Jane feels like a criminal for driving the man she adores to despair, but she cannot possibly remain with Rochester, for this would prove that she is bad and undo her efforts at self-vindication. Helen Burns had chastised her for thinking too much of the love of human beings and urged her to live for the approval of her conscience. Jane now proves her moral growth by giving up the man who has fulfilled her romantic dreams in order to do her duty, even though she has no one who cares about her or whom she would offend by living with him. "*I* care for myself," she proclaims (ch. 27). "The more solitary, the more friendless, the more unsustained I am, the more I will respect myself. I will keep the law given by God; sanctioned by man." She had told Helen that thinking well of herself was not enough if others did not love her, but now she embraces Helen's scenario. Jane is to Rochester as Helen had been to her. She urges the impulsive, vehement man to "trust in God" and "believe in heaven." When he complains that she is condemning him "to live wretched, and to die accursed," she advises him "to live sinless" and "die tranquil."

By leaving Rochester, Jane proves that she is not the bad person the Reeds said she was and actualizes the idealized image she has modeled on Helen Burns. Like Helen, she feels invulnerable in her self-regard as long as she remains true to her principles. Now she is ready to risk her life not to win love but to preserve her virtue. When she finds herself solitary, rebuffed, and in danger of starving, she does not regret her decision or murmur against her fate. Helen had said that "if we were dying in pain and shame, angels see our tortures, recognise our innocence" (ch. 8). Jane feels surrounded by the divine presence. Since she has lived sinless, she hopes for a tranquil death and is confident "that neither earth should perish, nor one of the souls it treasured" (ch. 28). She utters a prayer of thanksgiving and puts herself in the hands of Providence.

For the first three-quarters of the novel, Jane lives in a relatively realistic world, but after she leaves Thornfield the novel takes on a fairy tale quality as the action seems increasingly contrived. Jane is mimetically drawn to the end, but the world in which she lives seems manipulated for the purpose of rewarding her virtue, glorifying her character, and satisfying her conflicting psychological needs.

With Jane's departure from Thornfield, the education pattern is complete. Her forgiveness of Mrs. Reed, resistance to the temptations of love, and readiness to die for the sake of conscience all show that she has learned the lessons of Helen Burns. From a psychological point of view, Jane is obeying tyrannical shoulds so as to feed her pride and avoid incurring self-hate. Her bargain, like Helen's, is no longer with human beings but with God, on whom she relies to honor her claims. Since one of her shoulds is that her claims must not be for earthly rewards, she cannot be disappointed by anything that happens to her.

This is not a permanent solution for Jane, however, as it is for Helen Burns, since Jane is not of an otherworldly disposition and is full of appetites. Once the crisis created by the revelation of Rochester's marriage passes, her desires for earthly fulfillment return. She does not experience these desires as conscious claims, however, for that would violate her taboos. She is rewarded for her virtue by the author, the God of this fictional universe, who makes her every wish come true. Jane finds the family she has always longed for in the Rivers and becomes financially independent when she inherits a fortune from her uncle Eyre. The obstacles to the kind of union she desires with Rochester are cleared away by the death of Bertha and his maiming and reformation.

The last quarter of the novel continues Jane's vindication. She wins the love and respect of the Rivers sisters, who are among the handful of people in her world whose esteem is worth having, and she becomes a favorite with her pupils and their parents when she teaches at the village school. She receives an impressive tribute from St. John Rivers, who asks her to be his wife and accompany him to India as a missionary. When Jane protests her unfitness for the task, St. John recounts all the virtues she has displayed in the ten months he has been studying her character. In the village school, she demonstrated that she "could perform well, punctually, uprightly, labour uncongenial to [her] habits and inclinations" (ch. 34). The "resolute readiness" with which she divided her inheritance into four shares, showed her freedom from avarice and respect for abstract justice, as well as a soul that revels "in the flame and excitement of sacrifice." In studying Hindustani at his request, she displayed "tractability," "untiring assiduity," and an "unshaken temper." She is "docile, diligent, disinterested, faithful, constant, and courageous; very gentle, and very heroic" (ch. 34). The despised child of Gateshead could wish for no higher praise. St. John is in love with the wealthy, beautiful, socially accomplished Rosamond Oliver, but it is Jane who has the moral and intellectual qualities he desires. She has triumphed once again over the kind of woman to whom she has felt inferior.

What Jane misses in St. John is "the sweet homage given to beauty, youth, and grace" that she had received from Rochester. "He was fond and proud of me—it is what no man besides will ever be" (ch. 31). Only Rochester can satisfy her need to be loved as a woman, but she seems to have lost him forever. On the verge of acceding to St. John's wishes, Jane is saved by a mysterious summons, as she hears Rochester calling. When she revisits the environs of Thornfield, the innkeeper tells her that Rochester "set store on her past everything" and sought her, after she ran away, "as if she had been the most precious thing he had in the world" (ch. 37). The fact that life seems empty to Rochester without her is another tribute to Jane. When they are reunited at Ferndean, his reception does not disappoint, and after their marriage, Jane overhears a conversation between the servants in which they recognize her fitness to be Rochester's wife despite the fact that she is neither beautiful nor a fine lady, two things about which she has always been insecure. This is the final note in the swelling chorus of praise that accompanies her vindication.

The last quarter of the novel tailors the world to Jane's needs. Although she still has the insecurities, compulsions, and conflicts induced by her childhood, she does not have to outgrow them to avoid their destructive effects. By solving her problems for her, the author encourages us to see Jane as a strong, mature person who achieves an ideal happiness. Jane's psychological problems must be obscured, of course, if we are to accept the self-congratulatory rhetoric that contributes to our sense of her vindication and growth.

While St. John's proposal is a tribute, it is also extremely threatening; for although Jane knows that marriage to him would destroy her, she has difficulty resisting his dominating personality. St. John is a "cold, hard, ambitious man" (ch. 32) who becomes restless after entering the clergy because "the heart of a politician, of a soldier, of a votary of glory, a lover of renown" beats under his curate's surplice (ch. 31). His solution is to seek glory in the service of God as a missionary. He will not be "subject to the defective laws and erring control" of his "feeble fellow-worms" but will be the servant of an "All-perfect," "infallible master" (ch. 34), who will reward him with an "incorruptible crown" (ch. 38). He represses his need for love and channels his energy into his calling, in which he wishes Jane to participate. He wants Jane to be his wife so that she can help him in his missionary work, but she does not share his calling and knows that he does not love her. She feels that he would not protect her or care if she died. Jane refuses to marry St. John, but she offers to accompany him as his assistant, despite her conviction that the climate of India will kill her and that going there is "almost equivalent to committing suicide" (ch. 35). She can fight for a certain kind of emotional integrity (if they did not marry, her thoughts and feelings would still be her own), but not for the freedom to do what she wants or, indeed, for her very life. Why is this so?

Although Jane is ashamed of her childhood pusillanimity and frequently boasts of her fearlessness and ability to stand up for herself, she remains a predominantly compliant person who is looking for approval and conforms to traditional values. Her resoluteness and indomitability tend to be exercised in the name of religion and propriety. She can resist what she regards as immoral but is submissive toward people she admires as her superiors. As we have seen, she models herself on Helen Burns and follows her teachings. She tells us that Rochester exerted "an influence that quite mastered me—that took my feelings from my own power and fettered them in his" (ch. 17). She reverences his mind and likes to serve and obey him "in all that [is] right" (ch. 20). She can assert her independence only when he asks her to do wrong. Jane feels that

Diana Rivers "far excel[s]" her in beauty and "animal spirits" (ch. 30) and explains that "it was my nature to feel pleasure in yielding to authority supported like hers; and to bend, where my conscience and self-respect permitted, to an active will" (ch. 29).

St. John also triggers Jane's compliance. Although she criticizes him for being stern, exacting, and ambitious, she sees him as a great and glorious figure: "his is the ambition of the high master-spirit, which aims to fill a place in the first rank of those . . . who are called, and chosen, and faithful" (ch. 38). St. John gains an influence that takes away Jane's "liberty of mind." This is partly because his perfectionistic standards exacerbate her feelings of inadequacy. Whereas everything she did suited Rochester, she is afraid of not pleasing St. John and is driven to satisfy him. As Diana observes, whatever St. John exacts, Jane forces herself to perform. She finds, however, that "his praise and notice" are more oppressive "than his indifference," since "only serious moods and occupations" are acceptable to him, and she is forced to repress her "vivacity": "I fell under a freezing spell. When he said 'go,' I went! 'come,' I came; 'do this,' I did it. But I did not love my servitude: I wished, many a time, he had continued to neglect me" (ch. 34). She wants more and more to please him but feels that to do so "I must disown half my nature, stifle half my faculties, wrest my tastes from their original bent, force myself to the adoption of pursuits for which I had no natural vocation." Trying to explain her own behavior, Jane points out that never in her life has she "known any medium in my dealings with positive, hard characters, antagonistic to my own, between absolute submission and determined revolt" (ch. 34). She observes the one up to the "very moment of bursting, sometimes with volcanic vehemence, into the other." We have seen Jane driven to rebel against the Reeds and Rochester, but since "present circumstances" do not warrant a "mutiny," she submits to St. John Rivers.

Much as she dislikes her servitude, Jane cannot stand up for herself because she has no self to stand up for. She grew up in an environment that gave her no opportunity to remain in touch with her spontaneous feelings. Instead, she developed neurotic needs and defenses that continue to govern her. Her life is focused on managing her rage, gaining security, and assuaging her feelings of being wicked, unworthy, and unlovable. She is pursuing not self-realization but reassurance; her behavior is governed by external sources of validation, whether they be other people, God, or a set of absolute values. She can rebel against

Rochester when he threatens her need for rectitude, but she has difficulty resisting a righteous man like St. John, especially when the occupation he offers promises "sublime results" (ch. 34).

St. John appeals to Jane's craving for glory and a significant life. Like Helen Burns, he admonishes her not to "cling so tenaciously to ties of the flesh," and he warns that if she refuses to marry him, she will limit herself "for ever to a track of selfish ease and barren obscurity" (ch. 34). What Jane most craves, however, is human warmth, the domestic pleasures of life, to be valued and loved as a person—the things she missed as a child. St. John prizes her abilities "as a soldier would a good weapon," but he has no affection for her. She can summon the force to resist his demand for marriage because it arouses some of her deepest insecurities. Unlike Rochester, St. John is a handsome man who exacerbates her feeling of unattractiveness, and he is in love with the beautiful Rosamond. If they married, she would have to "endure all the forms of love . . . and know that the spirit was quite absent." Marriage to St. John would be a "monstrous" "martyrdom" in which she would continually be made to feel unappealing and unloved, a poor substitute for Rosamond Oliver. Moreover, she fears that as his wife she would have to disown much of her nature. Whereas merging with Rochester would allow her to fulfill her repressed desires, merging with St. John would force her to stifle her feelings.

Because she objects to his conception of marriage and scorns his idea of love, Jane has moral grounds on which to decline St. John's proposal, but she has no such grounds on which to refuse to accompany him as his assistant. Her aversion to the life she would lead and fear of a premature death are not enough to overcome her submissiveness and need for his approval. When St. John withdraws after her refusal to marry him, Jane cannot bear the estrangement and complains that his coldness is killing her. Trying to regain his friendship, she renews her offer to accompany him, although she continues to be afraid that he will destroy her. She tells Diana that he is a "good and great man" who pitilessly forgets "the feelings and claims of little people" (ch. 35). The "insignificant" had best "keep out of his way; lest, in his progress, he should trample them down."Nonetheless, Jane is all but swept away when St. John makes a final effort to persuade her to marry him. Overcome by veneration, she is tempted "to rush down the torrent of his will into the gulf of his existence, and there lose my own": "Religion called—Angels beckoned—God commanded—life rolled together like a scroll—death's gates opening, showed eternity beyond: it seemed, that for safety and bliss there, all here might be sacrificed in a second" (ch. 35). Jane is propelled along this path not only by the influence of St. John but also by that of Helen Burns.

When Dorothea Brooke is about to say "yes to her own doom" because of her compulsive compliance, George Eliot rescues her by killing off Edward Casaubon. Charlotte Brontë saves Jane from a similar fate by an even more intrusive device, the mysterious summons from Rochester. The author's psychological realism having led her heroine to the verge of a self-destructive act, she extricates Jane and preserves the comic structure of the novel by the introduction of a supernatural element. The voice Jane hears is not a psychologically explicable delusion; Rochester actually calls her from Ferndean and she miraculously hears him. His summons gives Jane the strength to break with St. John, who goes off to a glorious but early death, thus confirming Jane's fears for herself should she accompany him.

While Jane remains a mimetic character to the end, the author's manipulations of the action obscure her psychological problems. She does not have to outgrow her compulsive compliance in order to escape the danger posed by St. John but is rescued by the mysterious summons from Rochester. She goes back to Thornfield, but as she approaches the house she realizes that if Rochester is there with his lunatic wife, she "can have nothing to do with him" (ch. 36). She will still be caught between her needs for love and rectitude and will have to leave once again. Happily, Bertha is dead and Rochester is free. Even better, Rochester is helpless, "blind and a cripple." "I love you better now," she tells him, "when I can really be useful to you, than I did in your state of proud independence" (ch. 37). Rochester's dependence gives Jane something significant to do with her life. She will not be limited to the selfish ease and barren obscurity that St. John had said would be her lot if she refused to marry him but will be busy looking after Rochester.

Although Jane enjoys the power Rochester's helplessness gives her, she needs to preserve her sense of him as a formidable person in whom she can lose herself and through whom she can vicariously fulfill her expansive desires. He is a "sightless Samson" who is "dangerous to approach" in his "blind ferocity," a "royal eagle, chained to a perch," who must "entreat a sparrow to become its purveyor" (ch. 37). Jane is content with the role of sparrow—she had described herself as one of the insignificant little people who should keep out of St. John's way—as long as she can continue to see Rochester as a majestic being whom she possesses through her submission. She need not be afraid that *he* will trample her down. Jane needs at once to be great and small, and her merger with Rochester satisfies both requirements.

Jane says that Rochester suits her "to the finest fibre of [her] nature" (ch. 37), and, indeed, he suits her better now than before. We have seen that when Miss Temple leaves Lowood, Jane longs to go forth into the world to seek real knowledge of life amidst its perils but is afraid of doing anything that might expose her to reproach. When she meets Rochester, she finds that she can experience an exciting life vicariously through him while keeping the real thing at a safe distance. She wants him *to have had* an adventurous existence, to be a nearly extinct volcano whose occasional modest eruptions frighten others but not herself. She does not know that he poses a threat to her virtue. After Rochester proposes, Jane is apprehensive about being his wife. She feels inferior because of her lack of "fortune, beauty, [and] connections" (ch. 25). She likes to hear about his travels, but she does not look forward to accompanying him as a fine lady, and she strenuously resists his efforts to adorn her. Her conquest of Rochester at once compensates for and exacerbates her sense of inadequacy. She could not have been happy had they married at this point, even if Rochester had been free.

When Jane marries Rochester at the end, she is no longer poor, she has connections, and, since he is maimed and blind, her looks no longer matter. As he says, "fine clothes and jewels" are "not worth a fillip" now (ch. 37). Jane will not have to encounter the perils of traveling with him as a fine lady. Rochester is as dependent on her as she is on him and just as content to lead a reclusive existence. He no longer poses a threat to her piety and rectitude, since he has been humbled by his misfortunes, which he has accepted as the chastisements of divine justice: "I began to experience remorse, repentance; the wish for reconcilement to my Maker" (ch. 37). His rebellion is now all in the past. He has learned the lessons Jane was trying to teach him, just as she has learned the lessons of Helen Burns. He is rewarded for his new piety when his call for Jane mysteriously reaches her and when he recovers some of his vision.

Jane Eyre has a fairy-tale ending in which Cinderella gets the prince and lives happily ever after. After ten years of marriage, Jane holds herself "supremely blest" (ch. 38), and her happiness is understandable. She has received the love, the validation of her worth, and the social position she deserves in a way that does not activate her conflicts or arouse her insecurities.

That conflicts and insecurities are still there we may infer from Jane's narration. Like Pip, she tells her story in part to celebrate herself, to show how well she turned out and how her virtue has been rewarded. She would not be motivated to do this unless she still felt a need for self-vindication. If Jane were at peace with herself, would she be so self-congratulatory, so persistently boastful, self-justifying, and condescending toward others? She is at pains to repeat all the tributes she has received and to call attention to her talents, virtues, and triumphs. She has a continuing need to repudiate the things said about her at Gateshead and to prove her superiority. The Jane who narrates the novel is not as inwardly serene as she supposes herself to be.

Jane presents her life with Rochester as ideal, and it is certainly the most satisfying she can achieve, given her needs and conflicts. But it does not seem to fulfill her earlier longing for a fuller existence. When Miss Temple leaves Lowood to marry, Jane craves the "varied field of hopes and fears, of sensations and excitements" that awaits those who have "the courage to go forth" into the world. She desires liberty, excitement, and enjoyment but settles for a new servitude in which everything is "respectable, proper, *en règle*" (ch. 10). Restless at Thornfield before the arrival of Rochester, she says that human beings cannot be satisfied with "tranquillity," that they "must have action," and she evokes the image of millions of women "in silent revolt against their lot" (ch. 12). They "need exercise for their faculties" and suffer as men would from "too rigid a constraint, too absolute a stagnation." It is narrow-minded of men "to say that they ought to confine themselves to making puddings and knitting stockings, to playing on the piano and embroidering bags."

Jane exercises her faculties to some extent as a teacher at Morton school, but she is eager to leave that unprestigious position when she receives an inheritance. St. John asks if the "consciousness of having done some real good" has not given her pleasure and proposes that she devote her life to the task of regenerating her race, but Jane replies that she wants to "enjoy [her] own faculties as well as to cultivate those of other people" (ch. 34). Jane seems to be saying that she wants to actualize herself, but when St. John asks what employment she proposes as a substitute for the one she is relinquishing, she replies that she wants "to *clean down* Moor House from chamber to cellar," "to rub it up . . .

till it glitters again," and "to arrange every chair, table, bed, carpet with mathematical precision." She wants to have things "in an absolutely perfect state of readiness" for Diana and Mary when they return. St. John trusts that "when the first flush of vivacity is over," Jane "will look a little higher than domestic endearments and household joys." "The best things the world has!" Jane exclaims. Is there a difference between cleaning down and rubbing up Moor House and the pudding making and stocking knitting to which women should not be confined? What has happened to Jane's revolt against the feminine lot?

There is a disparity, as we have seen, between the rebellious, adventurous, expansive side of Jane and her timid conventionality. While leading a "tranquil, settled," dutiful life as teacher at Morton school, she rushes "into strange dreams at night: dreams many-coloured, agitated, full of the ideal, the stirring, the stormy—dreams where, amidst unusual scenes, charged with adventure, with agitating risk and romantic chance, I still again and again met Mr. Rochester, always at some exciting crisis" (ch. 32). What a contrast between such dreams, full of sensation and excitement, and the life she celebrates as so idyllic at the end. She is living at Ferndean, a damp, "desolate spot" (ch. 36), so "insalubrious" that it cannot be rented (ch. 37). As an act of conscience, Rochester kept Bertha at Thornfield rather than housing her there. She and Rochester "are ever together," with Jane reading to him, conducting him where he wants to go, and "doing for him what he wished to be done" (ch. 38).

Except for the presence of Rochester, Jane is leading the tranquil, confined life full of domestic duties against which she envisions millions of women being in silent revolt. But Rochester makes all the difference, of course. Jane craves freedom from time to time, but it is freedom from constraint rather than freedom to fulfill herself. When she achieves a measure of independence through her inheritance, she does not know what to do with it, other than to clean down Moor house. She has no answer to St. John's question about "what aim, what purpose" she has in life (ch. 34). Like the average woman of her culture, Jane lives for and through a man. Without Rochester, she would become like the old maids of whom Brontë writes with such compassion in *Shirley*.

What separates Jane from the average is the intensity of her relationship with Rochester, the completeness with which she merges with her mate. She holds herself "supremely blest" because "I am my husband's life as fully as he is mine. No woman was ever nearer to her mate than I am: ever more absolutely bone of his bone, and flesh of his flesh" (ch.

38). Whereas love is for most men a thing apart, it is Rochester's whole existence. Because of his disability, Jane is the exclusive object of his attention. For ten years, he and Jane have been talking "all day long," never wearying of each other's company. Jane glories in this existence, but it seems stagnant and confined to me.

The relationship that Jane so romanticizes is, in Horneyan terms, a morbid dependency in which she has no life of her own but lives through Rochester. The relationship is so intense because he needs Jane as much as she needs him; the morbid dependency is mutual. Together, they lead an extremely embedded existence in the damp, womblike world of Ferndean. Jane no longer desires stimulation or the exercise of her faculties—or perhaps she does, since she becomes a writer. But she is writing from a safe retreat, like Jacob Horner and Pip.

10

The Mayor of Casterbridge

Critical discussion of *The Mayor of Casterbridge* has focused on Michael Henchard, a character much admired but little understood. For some he is an epic or tragic hero who evokes comparisons with Achilles, Prometheus, Oedipus, Orestes, Lear, Macbeth, Faust, and such biblical figures as Cain, Samson, and Saul. Those who see him primarily in terms of plot, theme, or archetype either pay little attention to his psychology or discuss him in terms of traditional dichotomies between reason and passion, conscience and impulse, virtue and vice. He is often regarded as a towering figure in the grip of elemental forces who is lacking in emotional complexity. Joseph Warren Beach calls him "the original caveman," "a bull in a china shop," whose "gentlest movement is accompanied by the crash of breaking crockery" (Robinson 1977, 313). A few critics have seen him as a masterful portrait of an imagined human being who undergoes significant changes in the course of the novel, but even they have had difficulty accounting for his ambivalences and inconsistencies. These can be understood in terms of his inner conflicts, which are of the kind that Karen Horney described.

Henchard is such an arresting figure that little attention has been paid to other characters. Although Farfrae is often regarded as second in importance, Elizabeth-Jane is the most fully drawn character next to Henchard. Henchard is the protagonist of a tragic education plot who, unlike Pip, learns his lesson too late. Elizabeth-Jane is the protagonist of a comic vindication plot who, like Jane Eyre, is undervalued at first but wins recognition and love by the end. Hardy celebrates her from the start and offers her as a foil to Henchard.

Like *Great Expectations* and *Jane Eyre*, *The Mayor of Casterbridge* is heavily rhetorical, but this time the rhetoric flows not from a protagonist telling the story from his or her point of view but from an omniscient narrator who is supposed to be objective and reliable. Hardy's omniscient narrator also presents interpretations and judgments that are out of harmony with the mimesis, however. As we saw in the case of *Great Expectations,* novels of education tend to celebrate as growth what they show to be the collapse of one defensive strategy and the adoption of another. Hardy's judgments seem appropriate to the mimesis when Henchard is predominantly aggressive but inappropriate after Henchard's ambitions are crushed and his compliant tendencies emerge. As we saw in the case of *Jane Eyre,* novels of vindication tend to glorify protagonists who have been psychologically damaged in childhood. Hardy never makes clear what was so terrible about Elizabeth-Jane's childhood, but he frequently refers to her early suffering and glorifies her defensive strategies. When analyzed from a Horneyan perspective, the mimetic portrait of Elizabeth subverts Hardy's rhetoric, since it shows what a fearful, rigid, self-imprisoned person she actually is.

The tragic education pattern of Henchard's story is made explicit when he returns to Weydon-Priors, where he had sold his wife over twenty-one years before:

> He experienced not only the bitterness of a man who finds, in looking back upon an ambitious course that what he has sacrificed in sentiment was worth as much as what he has gained in substance; but the super-added bitterness of seeing his very recantation nullified. He had been sorry for all this long ago; but his attempts to replace ambition by love had been as fully foiled as his ambition itself. (Ch. 44)

Henchard's original "crime" is committed in the name of ambition, but he finds his subsequent success empty without human companionship. When his ambition ultimately fails, he tries to replace it with love, but his effort to do so is foiled when he loses Elizabeth-Jane. The narrator tells us that Henchard's "new lights" have allowed him to achieve "higher things than his soul in its half-formed state had been able to accomplish" but that he cannot make use of his "wisdom" because he has lost his zest for living. He has learned the hollowness of ambition and the value of love, but his education is rendered futile by "the ingenious machinery contrived by the Gods for reducing human possibilities of amelioration to a minimum."

From a Horneyan perspective, Henchard is a predominantly aggressive man who has conflicting compliant tendencies that haunt him in the midst of success and become dominant when his fortunes collapse. With the failure of his effort to live for love, he feels everything to be folly and becomes predominantly detached. He changes in much the way the rhetoric suggests—from ambition to love to indifference—but his attachment to Elizabeth-Jane is compulsive and his loss of desire is not the fault of the machinery of the Gods. Hardy's rhetorical treatment of Henchard tends to be crude and may be partly responsible for critics seeing him as having a simple nature driven by elemental forces. The mimetic portrait shows a complicated man who is tormented by inner conflicts at every stage of his life.

Henchard is torn from the beginning by a conflict between ambition and a need for affection. Because of his craving for love, he marries at the age of eighteen but then finds his aspirations thwarted by the responsibilities he has assumed. He soon comes to despise his emotionally needy wife, as he despises the love-hungry side of himself. Terribly oppressed, he tries to defend himself by withdrawing into a "dogged and cynical indifference" (ch. 1). In the opening scene of the novel both partners display a disillusioned resignation as they trudge toward Weydon-Priors.

In the furmity tent, Henchard's frustration, rage, and self-hate rise to the surface under the influence of rum. When the conversation turns to the thwarting "of many a promising youth's high aims and hopes and the extinction of his energies by an early imprudent marriage," he attacks himself as a "fool" for having married and boasts that if he were free he could beat any man in England in the fodder trade and would "be worth a thousand pounds" before he was done (ch. 1). He is angry with himself, his wife, and fate for thwarting his search for glory and tries to gain control of his destiny by selling his wife and child.

Here, as on later occasions, Henchard impulsively acts in a way for which he suffers when the moment has passed and his conflicting feelings emerge. His sale of his wife is felt by the company to be "an indefensible proceeding" (ch. 1), and he too regards it as immoral when his sobriety returns. Some critics depict Henchard as a rebel against social law and the ironies of fortune, but he is a very conventional man who transgresses because he is desperate and then is haunted for the rest of his life by what he feels to be his crime. He punishes himself by swearing not to drink for the next twenty-one years and spends several months and all his money trying to find his wife and child. He fails because he is so ashamed of what he has done that he does not publicize the search effectively.

Henchard is still full of conflict when we see him again, after the passage of nineteen years. A "masterful, coercive" man (ch. 13) with "no pity for weakness" (ch. 5), he has "worked his way up from nothing" to be a wealthy corn factor and Mayor of Casterbridge. Although he has more than fulfilled his boast to be worth a thousand pounds, he confesses to Farfrae that he is not "so thriving in his mind as it seems he might be from the state of his pocket" (ch. 12). Because of the loneliness of his domestic life, he is subject to "gloomy fits" when "the world seems to have the blackness of hell, and like Job, I could curse the day that gave me birth." Having sacrificed his family in order to pursue his ambition, Henchard now suffers from emotional isolation. Although he longs for companionship, he maintains a "haughty indifference" (ch. 13) to the society of women because he fears that he is unlovable and that they will be a hindrance. On becoming involved with Lucetta when she nurses him through an illness, he feels unworthy of her affection and regards her as "foolish" for liking him.

With the reappearance of Susan, Henchard is thrown into a quandary. He is eager to make amends for his earlier treatment of her, but he had intended to marry Lucetta so as to salvage her reputation. Torn between what he owes to each woman, he concludes that his first obligation is to Susan, but he blames himself for having injured Lucetta. He regards his remarriage primarily as a means of restitution and penance. He curses the "pride and mortification at being poor" that led to his earlier unkindness and seeks "to castigate himself with the thorns" that his "restitutory acts" will bring in their train by uniting him with "so comparatively humble a woman" (ch. 13). Henchard often tries to alleviate his guilt and self-hate by punishing himself.

Henchard's relationships with Farfrae and Elizabeth-Jane are profoundly influenced by his inner conflicts. He is so attracted to Farfrae because he promises to gratify the needs for power and human warmth that have hitherto seemed incompatible. Farfrae will be a great help in his business, but it is Henchard's need for "some human object" on whom to pour "out his heart" (ch. 19) that makes him ready to offer Donald almost anything to remain in Casterbridge. Farfrae reminds him of his dead brother, and when he agrees to become his manager, Henchard exults in the feeling that he has at last found a friend. The relationship develops rapidly, on Henchard's side, at least. Explaining that he is "a lonely man" (ch. 12), he impulsively confides in Farfrae and seeks his advice about how he should behave toward Susan and Lucetta. After she moves into Henchard's house, Elizabeth-Jane observes that he always wants Donald near him and has a habit of laying "his arm familiarly on his manager's shoulder, as if Farfrae were a younger brother" (ch. 14). This is an idyllic time for Henchard. He has eased his guilt in relation to Susan, he is growing fond of Elizabeth-Jane, and he has Farfrae as helper and friend.

The Abel Whittle affair puts an end to this happy interlude by activating Henchard's conflicts. When Farfrae revokes his order that the tardy Whittle go to work without his breeches, Henchard is "bitterly hurt" at having been rebuked in front of his men and feels that Farfrae is taking advantage of him because he has told him his secrets (ch. 15). Angry with himself as well as with Farfrae, he calls himself a "fool" for having opened his heart. Although they quickly make up, Henchard continues to berate himself for what he now perceives to be a weakness and feels a "dim dread" at having put himself in Farfrae's power. He becomes insensibly more reserved and gives up his precious intimacy with his friend.

Instead of contributing to Henchard's sense of success, Farfrae now threatens it, since another consequence of the Whittle affair is that Henchard learns that his workers regard Farfrae as the better man and would prefer him as their master. Feeling that he has lost his place as "the most admired man in his circle" (ch. 15), Henchard hopes to outshine Farfrae by offering a lavish entertainment at his own expense after Donald plans one for which admission will be charged. When bad weather spoils his plans while favoring Donald's and he overhears a man asking where his business would be if it were not for his young manager, Henchard is driven to restore his pride by dismissing Farfrae.

Hardy tends to attribute this kind of behavior to broad traits of character such as temper, lack of moderation, and strong-headedness, but Henchard displays such traits only when he feels severely threatened or frustrated. His dismissal of Farfrae is impulsive, to be sure, but it is an act to which he is driven by deep psychological needs. Success for Henchard is less a matter of money than a sense of superiority and triumph. If people think his business depends on Farfrae, "he'll be honeycombed clean out of all the character and standing that he's built up in these eighteen year!" (ch. 16). He has sacrificed everything to achieve his position and cannot bear to be deprived of it. He imagines that once his rival is removed, he will prove he can manage without him and will regain his preeminence.

Henchard's longing for Farfrae's friendship quickly reasserts itself, however, and his "heart [sinks] within him" when he realizes what he has done (ch. 17). He is "hurt" when Farfrae takes his dismissal seriously, showing, as Susan had done earlier, that he does "not mean to put up with his temper any longer." When Susan and Donald thwart his expansive needs, Henchard compulsively rids himself of them but then is shocked and sorry and externalizes his self-hate by blaming them for not knowing that he did not really mean what he had done.

The dismissal of Farfrae is fatal to Henchard's fortunes, but it need not have been so, since the young man is grateful for past friendship and tries to avoid clashing with him. Hardy makes much of the difference in their styles—"Northern insight matched against Southern doggedness" (ch. 17)—and critics have dwelt on the conflict between generations and old and new methods, but as Hardy's famous citation of Novalis suggests, it is Henchard's character that determines his fate. When Donald sets up as a corn and hay merchant on his own account, Henchard feels that he won't be "wo'th a varden" if he "can't overbid such a stripling." Because of his own psychology, he feels himself to be in an all-or-nothing situation. He is an insecure man who is afraid that he will feel worthless if he cannot defeat his rival and win back his glory. His irrational resentment of Farfrae and need for vindictive triumph are primarily responsible for his downfall.

Henchard's rivalry with Farfrae is intensified by the frustration of his need for love. Indeed, without this additional factor, he may never have behaved so rashly as to ruin himself. Soon after his break with Farfrae, Susan dies, and he discovers that Elizabeth-Jane is not his child. This leaves "an emotional void" that he hopes Lucetta will fill (ch. 26). Farfrae's becoming a rival for her affection adds "an inflaming soul" to Henchard's need for competitive triumph, and he hires Jopp, giving him instructions to "grind" Farfrae "into the ground" by a "desperate bid against him for the farmer's custom." Henchard's fortunes now rapidly decline as he gambles on the weather in his desperate effort to crush Farfrae, while Farfrae steadily acquires all that Henchard has lost— Lucetta, his house and business, his civic positions.

Henchard's reactions to his failure reflect his conflicting defenses. Although he often rebels against his fate and seeks to control it, he also has strong tendencies toward detachment. After his bankruptcy, he literally moves away from his fellows, lodging in Jopp's cottage, where he gives orders that he will see no one, not even Elizabeth-Jane. Henchard's impulse toward withdrawal leads him to contemplate emigration, but he relinquishes the idea in response to the kindness of Farfrae, who offers him rooms in his old house, and of Elizabeth-Jane, who insists on nursing him when he becomes ill. Bored with nothing to do, he "stoically" asks to be taken on as a hay-trusser in the business he had formerly owned, saying that honest work is "not a thing to be ashamed of" (ch. 32).

Under the influence of kind treatment and his own resignation, Henchard's injured pride seems for a time to be quiescent. Hardy is careful to point out, however, that he is "a far different journeyman from the one he had been in his earlier days" (ch. 32). Then he had dressed in a clean and colorful outfit appropriate to his station, whereas now he wears "the remains of an old blue cloth suit of his gentlemanly times, a rusty silk hat, and a once black satin stock, soiled and shabby." His apparel expresses his misery, self-pity, and sense of degradation and shows that he cannot let go of his gentlemanly status or of his resentment at having lost it. It is a way of refusing to accept his fate and dramatizing what has been done to him.

Henchard's suppressed anger erupts when he hears that Farfrae will soon be proposed for Mayor, and from this point until their fight in the loft his aggressive tendencies are predominant. Again perceiving Farfrae as a "triumphant rival" who has ridden "rough-shod over him" (ch. 32), he becomes obsessed by the reversal of their positions, which acts "like an irritant poison" upon him (ch. 33).

Henchard seeks to restore his pride by triumphing over Farfrae, but he is inhibited by his inner conflicts. Intending to reveal that the letters in his safe were written by Lucetta, he finds that "such a wrecking of hearts appall[s] even him" (ch. 34). His compunctious side manifests itself again when Lucetta meets him at the Ring and begs him not to destroy her. Remembering his earlier encounter there with Susan, "another ill-used woman," he is "unmanned" and "his heart [smites] him for having attempted reprisals on one of a sex so weak" (ch. 35). The aggressive Henchard can take no satisfaction in hunting such "very small deer," while the compliant Henchard is moved by Lucetta's suffering and would feel guilty if he injured such a fragile creature. He had begun to want Lucetta strongly himself only when she became feisty and was enveloped by the glamour of having inherited money and being courted by another man. Now that he sees her as weak, "his old feeling of supercilious pity for womankind in general" returns. With his contempt for self-effacing females, he feels that Farfrae has "married money, but nothing more," and his envy disappears.

Henchard next tries to restore his pride by greeting the royal visitor, even though the Town Council has refused his request. While everyone else at the festivity "shone in new vesture according to means," Henchard "doggedly retained the fretted and weather-beaten garments of bygone years" (ch. 37). To dress in an appropriate manner would be accepting his position as a common journeyman, whereas through his shabby gentile apparel he seems to be asserting a claim to special status on the basis of past grandeur and the pathos of his present lot. At the same time, he is ensuring that his claim will not be honored and that he will have an additional basis for resentment. He seems to want to feed his sense of outrage. When Farfrae roughly prevents him from greeting the Illustrious Personage, Henchard feels this to be "the crowning degradation" for which the young Mayor must pay (ch. 38).

Henchard means to kill Farfrae when he fights him in the granary, but when Farfrae challenges him to carry out his intent, Henchard's love for him rises to the surface and he cannot do so. Overwhelmed with "shame," "remorse," and "self-reproach," he invites Farfrae to have him arrested and flings himself down in a state of "abandonment" (ch. 38). When Hardy writes that the "womanliness" of his "crouching attitude" sat "tragically on the figure of so stern a piece of virility," he is pointing in his way to the dissonance between the conflicting sides of Henchard's personality.

Henchard had set out to restore his pride by taking revenge on Farfrae and proving himself the better man, but this leads him to the verge of murder, and, tortured by his "self-accusing soul" (ch. 39), he becomes abjectly self-effacing. He seeks pardon for his "mad attack" and agonizes over the thought that Farfrae will hate and despise him forever. When his effort to redeem himself by doing Farfrae a service fails, he is saved from despair by the presence of Elizabeth-Jane, who seems "a pinpoint of light" in "the midst of his gloom" (ch. 40). With all else lost, he begins to "dream of a future lit by her filial presence, as though that way alone could happiness lie" (ch. 41).

Elizabeth-Jane is both a source of affection and a means of restoring his pride. After he discovered that she was not really his daughter, he became irritated with her humble, unrefined ways and wanted her out of his house, but just before she left he caught a glimpse of her accomplishments and wished she would stay. His esteem continued to grow, enabling him to transfer his pride to her after his downfall. He glories in Elizabeth-Jane's self-effacing qualities, her purity and goodness, and satisfies his need for preeminence vicariously through her.

Since there would be "nobody for him to be proud of, nobody to fortify him" (ch. 41) without Elizabeth-Jane, Henchard becomes desperate at the prospect of losing her. His telling Newson she is dead is "the last defiant word of a despair which [takes] no thought of consequences" (ch. 42). In dread of Newson's return, he finds it "unendurable" that he might live for another thirty or forty years to be "scoffed at" or "pitied"(ch. 41) and is on the verge of suicide when he is "resuscitated" by Elizabeth-Jane's proposal that they live together.

Henchard's fear of losing Elizabeth-Jane makes him suppress his aggressive tendencies. He would have declined the offer of a small seed and root business on his own account, but he "fetter[s] his pride sufficiently" to accept it for her sake (ch. 42). Since her "sympathy" is "necessary to his very existence," he becomes a "netted lion" who is "anxious not to pique her." Her "word [is] law" and she has "her own way in everything." He is in anguish at the thought of a renewed acquaintance between Elizabeth-Jane and Farfrae, but he observes her secretly and makes no complaint. Such stealth is not part of his "original make," says Hardy, but "the *solicitus timor* of his love—the dependence on Elizabeth's regard into which he had declined (or, in another sense to which he had advanced)—denaturalized him."

As the preceding sentence shows, it is sometimes difficult to determine Hardy's attitude toward Henchard in this part of the novel. In general, he is critical of the expansive Henchard, whom he compares to Faust— "a vehement gloomy being who had quitted the ways of vulgar men without light to guide him on a better way" (ch. 17); and he is sympathetic toward the self-effacing Henchard, who by his new lights has achieved higher things. Thus he characterizes Henchard's dependence on Elizabeth-Jane's regard as an advance. But he also characterizes it as a decline. It may be the expansive Henchard who is regarding his dependence as a decline, but the sentence does not specifically attribute this sentiment to him. Is Hardy trying to suggest that what Henchard regards as a decline is really an advance? Or is there a conflict in the narrator similar to that in Henchard, so that his expansive side regards the dependence as a decline while his compliant side regards it as an advance? Is Hardy trying to invoke the paradox of the fortunate fall in which Henchard must decline in order to advance? The text provides no clear answer to these questions, and we must wonder if there is an ambivalence in Hardy that is responsible for its imprecise language and slipperiness.

In a later passage Hardy writes that Henchard would have been content if Elizabeth-Jane had lost her heart to any man "than the one he had rivalled, cursed, wrestled with for life in days before his spirit was broken" (ch. 42). From whose perspective has Henchard's spirit been broken? The language does not clearly indicate that the perspective is Henchard's, although we can see from the mimetic portrait that he regards his submissiveness with contempt. If this is the narrator's perspective, then the assertion that Henchard's spirit has been broken is in conflict with the view that he has advanced through his dependence and attained higher things.

A psychological analysis does not show Henchard as having attained higher things but as having changed defensive strategies as a result of the failure of his predominant solution. He still has expansive attitudes that lead him to despise his abjectness, but his need of Elizabeth-Jane is so great that he will go to almost any lengths to remain part of her life. When he sees that she and Farfrae are heading toward marriage, he becomes convinced that they regard him as "an irksome obstacle whom they would be heartily glad to get out of the way," and he has an impulse to "escape those who did not want him, and hide his head forever" (ch. 43). But he clings to the hope that a separation will not be necessary and envisions an alternate scenario in which he will live "like a fangless lion about the back rooms of a house in which his stepdaughter was mistress; an inoffensive old man, tenderly smiled on by Elizabeth, and good-naturedly tolerated by her husband." Although it is "terrible to his pride to think of descending so low," "for the girl's sake he might put up with anything; even from Farfrae; even snubbings and masterful tongue-scourgings." The dependency of this once proud man on Elizabeth-Jane is pathetic.

The reappearance of Newson puts an end to Henchard's oscillation between thoughts of submission and of running away, but he would have had no viable solution even if Newson had not returned. He feels that the "privilege of being in the house" with Elizabeth-Jane "would almost outweigh the personal humiliation" (ch. 43). The crucial word here is *almost*. It is impossible for Henchard to live without Elizabeth-Jane's affection, but it would be agonizing for him to remain with her if she married Farfrae.

After Newson's return, Henchard tries to cope with his pain through self-effacement and resignation. Convinced that Elizabeth-Jane will "hate and despise him" as "an arch-deceiver," he seeks to protect himself from further blows by getting "out of sight" (ch. 43). Accepting his station at last, he dons the apparel of his youth and goes forth as a journeyman haytrusser:

> "If I had only got her with me—if I only had!" he said. "Hard work would be nothing to me then! But that was not to be. I—Cain—go alone as I deserve—an outcast and a vagabond. But my punishment is *not* greater than I can bear!"
>
> He sternly subdued his anguish. . . . (Ch. 43)

Henchard deals with his loss of Elizabeth-Jane in a self-effacing way by telling himself he deserves it. In comparing himself to Cain, he exaggerates his guilt, giving his sins a kind of grandeur. Although he is ashamed of his behavior, he takes pride in his self-condemnation, which is a mark of his high moral standards. He is also proud of his ability to repress his anguish and bear his punishment stoically. Indeed, Henchard is now predominantly detached. We have seen this side of him before in his "cynical indifference" in the opening scene and his resigned response to the discovery of Elizabeth-Jane's parentage: "I am to suffer, I perceive" (ch. 19).

With the collapse first of his ambition and then of his attempt to replace ambition by love, Henchard loses interest in life, which he perceives to be absurd: "It was an odd sequence that out of all this tampering with social law came that flower of Nature, Elizabeth. Part of his wish to wash his hands of life arose from his perception of its contrarious inconsistencies—of Nature's jaunty readiness to support unorthodox social principles" (ch. 44). The guilt-ridden Henchard may well find it puzzling that the wonderful Elizabeth-Jane is the product of the illegitimate union between Susan and Newson that was brought about by his crime, but his desire to wash his hands of life arises from his personal malaise rather than from the "contrarious inconsistencies" of Nature. He is indulging in the same kind of externalization that is so typical of Thomas Hardy: the problem is not in me but in the nature of the universe (see Paris 1976a).

Hardy attributes the departure of Henchard's "zest for doing" to "the ingenious machinery contrived by the Gods for reducing human possibilities of amelioration to a minimum" (ch. 44). Henchard is only forty and, according to Hardy, there is "nothing to hinder his making another start on the upward slope" and achieving higher things than he was capable of before; but he has "no wish to make an arena a second time of a world that had become a mere painted scene to him." His disillusionment has nothing to do with the ingenious machinery of the Gods (or even with the plot contrivances that confirm Hardy's vision of an ironic universe). It is a result of the collapse of his expansive and self-effacing solutions, which are unworkable because they are compulsive, out of touch with reality, and in conflict with each other. Life seems absurd when our defensive strategies fail.

Henchard's sense of the world as "a mere painted scene" is not simply a product of disillusionment but is also a new defense: it reduces his self-hate by attributing his plight to the nature of things and alleviates his pain by suggesting that there are no genuine satisfactions from which he is excluded since all is illusion and vanity. His state of mind at this point is similar to that of Macbeth in his "Tomorrow and tomorrow" speech (see Paris 1991a).

But Henchard cannot achieve the detachment to which he aspires. His "centrifugal tendency" to distance himself from Casterbridge is "counteracted by the centripetal influence of his love for his step-daughter" (ch. 44). Compliance and detachment are so evenly balanced that Henchard's movements toward and away from others cancel each other out. The circle formed by his wanderings around Casterbridge is an objective correlative of his inner conflict. Although he feels that, having seen through its deceptive appearances, he has washed his hands of life, he continues to be obsessed with Elizabeth-Jane, conjecturing what she is doing "every hour—nay, every few minutes."

Henchard calls himself a "fool" and "sneer[s] at himself for his weakness," but when he hears of the upcoming marriage he cannot resist making one more attempt to be reconciled with Elizabeth-Jane: "it was worth the risk of repulse, ay, of life itself" (ch. 44). The issue *is* one of life and death to Henchard, since he feels that he cannot go on alone. Despite his pride in his ability to endure suffering, he is not the stuff of which stoics are made. He determines "to plead his cause" and "endeavour strenuously" to hold a place in Elizabeth-Jane's heart, but when she taxes him with deceit and says that she cannot love him as she did, he does not plead his cause. His lips half part to begin an explanation, but he "shut[s] them up like a vice," while the narrator rehearses the arguments he might have advanced to extenuate his behavior.

To understand Henchard's strange behavior in this scene, we must see it in the context of the oscillations between hope and despair to which he becomes subject once he centers his life on Elizabeth-Jane. After being on the verge of suicide, he is resuscitated when she moves in with him, but once she begins seeing Farfrae, he becomes convinced that he will end his life in "friendless solitude" (ch. 42). He has an impulse to run away but then reflects that "the throbbing pair" may not regard him as an "irksome obstacle" after all and begins to envision the possibility of living with them (ch. 43). When Newson returns, Henchard leaves before Elizabeth-Jane has a chance to denounce him but then begins to wonder if "his own absolute separation from her" is really necessary (ch. 44). Hoping that "his unanticipated presence" will fill a "little unsatisfied corner" of her heart, he decides to attend the wedding, but as the reunion approaches his spirits sink. Fearing "circumstances he would formerly have scorned," he "sadly satirize[s] himself" as a "Samson shorn" and begins to wish he had not come. He asks a housekeeper to announce him as "a humble old friend." When Elizabeth-Jane greets him coldly as "Mr. Henchard" and attacks him for having deceived her and her real father, his hopes collapse, leaving him unable to plead his cause.

Having lost all hope of a reconciliation, Henchard tries to defend himself in a variety of ways. Not wishing to be perceived as a pathetic figure, he addresses Elizabeth-Jane "with proud superiority," telling her not to distress herself on his account (ch. 44). Reverting to his detachment, he presents himself as not needing her concern. He asks forgiveness for having disturbed her on her wedding day, thus presenting himself as concerned about her even though she is unforgiving toward him. This may be a response to her accusations of cruelty and wickedness. He tries to restore his moral position by regarding "only her discomposure" and behaving with a certain gallantry. Beneath his words is a great deal of rage and pain that he conveys indirectly by telling Elizabeth-Jane that he will never trouble her again, not to his dying day, and bidding her not only good night but good-bye. He seems to want to leave her in the position of having wounded him mortally, hoping, perhaps, that she will regret what she has done.

Henchard quickly departs, before Elizabeth-Jane can "collect her thoughts," apparently wanting to nurse his grievance and to leave her feeling uncomfortable (ch. 44). He acts as though he has been harshly rejected, but this is not the case. When he pleads with Elizabeth-Jane to "save a little room" for him, she flushes up and "gently [draws] her hand away." She does not tell him that she no longer loves him but that she cannot love as she "once did a man who has served us like this." Henchard could have explained that he had been deceived by her mother and that his lie to Newson came from his desperate need of her, but he refuses to defend himself. His reticence is partly the result of his not sufficiently valuing himself "to lessen his suffering by a strenuous appeal," but there is also bitterness in it and a determination to feed his despair. A self-dramatizing man to the end, Henchard wants to feel himself the most alienated, abandoned, and misunderstood of mortals. It would have given him satisfaction to know that Elizabeth-Jane relents and seeks "to make her peace with him" (ch. 45), and he would have been pleased that she arrives too late.

Michael Henchard's will reflects the same kinds of conflicting feelings, needs, and defenses that are operative in his last meeting with Elizabeth-Jane. It reasserts his pride by expressing his lack of need of others and indifference to their love and respect. It is also full of self-hate and self-condemnation: he does not deserve to be buried in consecrated ground or to be mourned and remembered. He seems to be continuing his self-punishment from beyond the grave by obliterating himself, an extreme form of self-effacement. The will is also an act of control, an attempt to master his fate in a negative way since he cannot do so triumphantly. Henchard appears to be protective of Elizabeth-Jane by directing that she not be told of his death "or made to grieve on account of [him]" (ch. 45), but there is a good deal of posturing here, as there was in their final encounter. Is not Henchard trying to heighten the pathos of his fate, even while forbidding others to feel for him? For whom is the will written, if not for Elizabeth-Jane? She understands the bitterness and reproach it expresses: "O I would not have minded so much if it had not been for my unkindness at that last parting!" Her regrets for having "misunderstood him on his last visit" and "for not having searched him out sooner" are "deep and sharp for a good while," which is exactly what Henchard would have wanted. He is hardly a caveman or a bull in a china shop, but a very complicated, vulnerable man who is destroyed by his inner conflicts.

While Henchard is the hero of a tragic education plot, Elizabeth-Jane is the protagonist in a comic vindication action. When we first meet her, she is a young woman with excellent qualities whose social and economic deprivations have prevented her from developing her physical and mental potentialities. Her situation quickly changes when her mother's remarriage to Henchard gives her wealth and social position. With nourishing food and new clothes, the plain girl turns into a beauty, and she now has the opportunity to educate herself. Her good qualities are recognized by Donald Farfrae, who would like to marry her. This early transformation of her condition is suddenly reversed when Henchard turns against her on discovering that she is not his daughter and Farfrae falls in love with Lucetta. Elizabeth-Jane suffers greatly from these rejections, despite her efforts at stoicism, and there seems to be little likelihood that she will ever be treated in accordance with her deserts. Her fortunes rise toward the end, however, as those of Henchard and Lucetta decline. The "educated" Henchard worships her, and, after his experience with Lucetta, Farfrae appreciates her all the more. At the conclusion of the novel, the previously slighted Elizabeth-Jane marries the town's most eligible man. When she is reunited with Newson, his "pride in what she had grown up to be was more than he could express" (ch. 43), and her importance to Henchard is such that he cannot live without her.

As is typical in a vindication pattern, Elizabeth-Jane is increasingly surrounded by praise as the novel progresses. She receives tributes from Lucetta, Henchard, and Farfrae, as well as from Newson. As is also typical in this pattern, there are rhetorical devices that convey the implied author's assessment of the protagonist's worth even when she is being devalued by other characters. While Henchard harshly criticizes Elizabeth-Jane for being considerate of the servants, using dialect words, and having served at the Three Mariners, the narrator describes her thoughtfulness and the efforts at self-education of which Henchard is unaware: "Thus she lived on, a dumb, deep-feeling, great-eyed creature, construed by not a single contiguous being" (ch. 20). She is construed by the narrator, however, who enters into her feelings and celebrates her virtues.

Hardy tends to praise Elizabeth-Jane for characteristics that are much like his own, such as her deep feeling, thirst for knowledge, and seriousness of mind. In one passage he has her engaging in metaphysical reflections:

> All this while the subtle-souled girl [was] asking herself why she was born, why sitting in a room, and blinking at the candle; why things around her had taken the shape they wore in preference to every other possible shape. Why they stared at her so helplessly, as if waiting for the touch of some wand that should release them from terrestrial constraint; what that chaos called consciousness, which spun in her at this moment like a top, tended to, and began in. (Ch. 19)

Although these thoughts are not incommensurate with her psychology, as we shall see, they are much more typical of Hardy than they are of Elizabeth-Jane, who does not engage in such reflections again.

If we examine the novel's rhetoric from a Horneyan perspective, we find that for the most part it celebrates Elizabeth-Jane's self-effacing and resigned tendencies, which it contrasts favorably with the expansiveness of Henchard and Lucetta. The mimesis subverts the rhetoric, as it does with the "educated" Henchard, by showing that the behavior being glorified is rigid and defensive.

A timid, unassuming person with low self-esteem, Elizabeth-Jane is compulsively self-minimizing. Feeling safest in a humble position, she becomes anxious when she finds herself raised above others and seeks to diminish herself in some way. She is uncomfortable when she becomes the "town beauty" and tells herself that perhaps she is being admired "by those whose admiration is not worth having" (ch. 15). People would despise her if they only knew "what an unfinished girl" she is, that she cannot "talk Italian, or use globes, or show any of the accomplishments they learn at boarding schools." Although Hardy assures us that she is more beautiful and intelligent than Lucetta, Elizabeth-Jane regards Lucetta as vastly superior, subordinates herself to her, and thinks it natural that Farfrae should find her more attractive. The narrator attributes the behavior toward servants that so irritates Henchard to Elizabeth-Jane's "considerate disposition" (ch. 20), but it is another instance of her compulsive need to avoid a position of superiority. She goes to the kitchen instead of ringing, gets down on her knees to gather spilled coals, and "persistently thank[s] the parlour-maid for everything."

Elizabeth-Jane has numerous other self-effacing traits. She feels it degrading to serve at the Three Mariners, but, like the mother on whom she models herself, she always has "a willingness to sacrifice her personal comfort and dignity to the common weal" (ch. 4). Susan returns to Henchard mainly "to advance Elizabeth." When Henchard scolds her for using dialect words, Elizabeth-Jane humbly apologizes, and when he treats her so cruelly that she wishes she were dead, she blames herself instead of him: "All is owing to my defects, I daresay" (ch. 20). After Henchard is disgraced, she "believe[s] in him still," although no one else does, and wants "to be allowed to forgive him for his roughness to her, and to help him in his trouble" (ch. 31). Although Henchard has treated her unfairly, she cannot allow herself to feel resentment and is ready to turn the other cheek. She has no basis for her belief in him except the needs of her own defense system. She wants to help him in his trouble in part because she has no life of her own and gains a sense of meaning and purpose by living for others. When Henchard wants her out of the house in his days of prosperity, she becomes deeply "depressed by a sense of her own superfluity" (ch. 20).

Elizabeth-Jane is by no means entirely self-effacing. Like Henchard, she has inner conflicts. She responds to her sense of lowliness and inadequacy not only by being modest, submissive, and self-sacrificial, but also by developing a compensatory desire for elevation and triumph. She simultaneously needs to be humble and to feed her pride. Although she is uncomfortable when she assumes her position as mayor's daughter, she feels an initial "elation" at "discovering herself akin to a coach" (ch. 5). She is immediately drawn to Farfrae because he is "respectable and educated—far above the rest of 'em in the inn" (ch. 8), just as she wishes to be herself. Despite her humility, she is hurt when he leaves without saying good-bye, indicating that she has lofty claims. Elizabeth-Jane's ambition is most evident in her intense desire for "wider knowledge" and "higher repute" (ch. 4). She feels inferior because she lacks the accomplishments that girls learn at boarding schools, and her mind runs "on acquirements to an almost morbid degree" (ch. 22). She is driven to engage in the laborious study that the self-taught Hardy so admires by her profound sense of inadequacy and her desire to rise.

Another of Elizabeth-Jane's morbid preoccupations is her concern with respectability. This, too, is apparently compensatory, but Hardy's account is so confusing that it is hard to tell what she is compensating for. When she takes the uncompromising position that in view of their past relationship Lucetta must marry Henchard or no one at all, the narrator explains that any suspicion of impropriety was to Elizabeth-Jane like a red rag to a bull. Her craving for correctness of procedure was, indeed, almost vicious. Owing to her early troubles with regard to her mother a semblance of irregularity had terrors for her which those whose names are safeguarded from suspicion know nothing of. (Ch. 30)

Earlier, Elizabeth-Jane had told Lucetta that Henchard was cold toward her "because he does not think I am respectable. I have tried to be so more than you can imagine, but in vain! My mother's separation from my father was unfortunate for me. You don't know what it is to have shadows like that upon your life" (ch. 24).

This is confusing because near the beginning of the novel we are informed that Susan had not told Elizabeth-Jane about Henchard and had no misgivings about her union with Newson. It was not until her daughter was close to eighteen years of age that a friend ridiculed Susan's acceptance of her position and destroyed her peace of mind. Perceiving this, Newson had news sent that he had been lost at sea, and Susan felt free to seek out Henchard, whom she described to Elizabeth-Jane simply as a relative. If, as the narrator tells us, Elizabeth-Jane "had grown up in the belief that the relations between the genial sailor and her mother were the ordinary ones that they had always appeared to be" (ch. 4), what were the early troubles and the shadow upon her life that produced her intense craving for respectability?

Whatever the source, Elizabeth-Jane has an anxiety about being respectable that makes her punctilious in her own behavior and moralistic in her dealings with others. This is in keeping with her overall sense of deficiency, for which she needs to compensate by gaining higher repute. Driven by tyrannical shoulds, she compulsively complies with established manners and morals and has a great fear of the increased self-contempt she would feel if she failed to do so. She is so ready to blame herself and to accept criticism from others because she is ashamed of her origins and of what she feels to be her personal inadequacies.

Elizabeth-Jane is driven in opposite directions: toward meekness, humility, and unobtrusiveness on the one hand and toward social elevation, personal accomplishment, and moral superiority on the other. Her predominant defense, however, is detachment. She is deeply resigned. She feels that life is "a tragical rather than a comical thing; that though one could be gay on occasion, moments of gaiety were interludes, and no part of the actual drama" (ch. 8). During the "triumphant" time when she is being indulged by Henchard, she guards herself against her "lighter moods" (ch. 14). Because she had "known rough times, light-heartedness seemed to her too irrational and inconsequent to be indulged in except as a reckless dram now and then; for she had been too early habituated to anxious reasoning to drop the habit suddenly." Thus she tempers her triumph "by circumspection": "she had still that field-mouse fear of the coulter of destiny despite fair promise, which is common among the thoughtful who have suffered early from poverty and oppression" (ch. 14).

Here and elsewhere Hardy attributes Elizabeth-Jane's guardedness to her harsh childhood, just as he had attributed her craving for correctness to early troubles. Again, however, the few details he provides about her childhood give a different picture from his broad characterizations of it. Susan Henchard goes with Newson to Canada, where her daughter by Henchard dies and she has another child whom she also names Elizabeth-Jane. Although they live there "without any great worldly success," Susan works hard "to keep their cottage cheerful and well-provided" (ch. 4). When Elizabeth-Jane is twelve years old, they return to England, where Newson makes a living as boatman and general handy shoreman. They cannot provide the child with opportunities for development, but they are not impoverished, and it is difficult to see why Elizabeth-Jane is habituated to anxious reasoning and has come to regard life as tragic. Her mother is devoted to her, and she tells Henchard that Newson "was very kind—O so kind!" (ch. 19). From what "oppression" has she suffered?

There is one passage, I think, that can help us to understand the sources of Elizabeth-Jane's resignation. After receiving news of Newson's death, Susan sits one day "survey[ing] her daughter thoughtfully":

> Her face, though somewhat wan and incomplete, possessed the raw materials of beauty in a promising degree. There was an under-handsomeness in it, struggling to reveal itself through the provisional curves of immaturity, and the casual disfigurements that resulted from the straitened circumstances of their lives. She was handsome in the bone, hardly as yet handsome in the flesh. She possibly might never be fully handsome, unless the carking accidents of her daily existence could be evaded before the mobile parts of her countenance had settled to their final mould.
>
> The sight of the girl made her mother sad. . . . They both were still in that strait-waistcoat of poverty from which she had tried so many times to be delivered for the girl's sake. The woman had long perceived how

zealously and constantly the young mind of her companion was struggling for enlargement; and yet now, in her eighteenth year, it still remained but little unfolded. The desire—sober and repressed—of Elizabeth-Jane's heart was indeed to see, to hear, and to understand. How could she become a woman of wider knowledge, higher repute—'better,' as she termed it—this was her constant inquiry of her mother. She sought further into things than other girls in her position ever did, and her mother groaned as she felt she could not aid in the search. (Ch. 4)

Before I comment on the psychological implications of this passage, let me observe that in addition to the narrator Elizabeth-Jane's mother appreciates her from the beginning. She seeks out Henchard in a "desperate effort to advance" her daughter, and as a result Elizabeth-Jane ultimately becomes all that her mother had envisioned. From one point of view, Elizabeth-Jane's is the story of the fulfillment of her mother's dream of glory for her. Newson's pride in what Elizabeth-Jane has grown up to be is what Susan would feel as well if she were alive and suggests that he and Susan had similar hopes for their daughter, although Newson has a far more cheerful and easy-going temperament that may have made him more content than his "wife" and daughter with their lot.

My interpretation of Elizabeth-Jane is that she, like the younger Henchard, has suffered from thwarted ambition. She is a bright, curious girl who has intellectual aspirations that cannot be fulfilled because of the family's social and economic position. Her mother recognizes her potentialities, both of mind and of body, and engages in the kind of anxious reasoning Hardy attributes to Elizabeth-Jane. Perhaps Elizabeth-Jane caught it from her. Her mother's anxiety is not about survival but about how to foster the development of this special child, how to give her the opportunities she longs for and deserves. Aware of her own abilities and her parents' high regard for them, Elizabeth-Jane develops a sense of herself as superior to her condition in life. In the atmosphere of frustrated hopes in which she lives, she sees no possibility of achieving the "wider knowledge" and "higher repute" to which she aspires, however, and responds by becoming resigned.

Henchard developed a "cynical indifference" when his ambitions were frustrated by his early marriage (ch. 1), but his search for glory was irrepressible and drove him to sell his wife. He reverts to detachment later, when having lost both his position and Elizabeth-Jane, he sees the world as a mere painted scene. His is a bitter resignation in which he wants to wash his hands of a life that he sees as capricious. Even then, as I have said, he is not the stuff of which stoics are made, and he remains obsessed with Elizabeth-Jane.

Elizabeth-Jane *is* the stuff of which stoics are made. Her resignation does not have the bitterness of Henchard's but is rather a defense against such bitterness. A major difference is that she develops a dark view of life early on and does not expect her desires to be fulfilled. Thus she is not subject to the rage and frustration that comes with intense desires and high aspirations like Henchard's. She begins by wanting a great deal, but once she is convinced she cannot have it, her desires become "sober and repressed." She detaches herself from her feelings, becomes an onlooker at life, and protects herself against disappointment by always anticipating the capriciousness of fate. She no doubt derives her resignation to some extent from her mother, as she does her ambition and self-effacement. When we see Susan trudging toward Weydon-Priors with Henchard at the beginning of the novel, she has "the hard, half-apathetic expression of one who deems anything possible at the hands of Time and Chance except, perhaps, fair play" (ch. 1). Many years later, when Elizabeth-Jane is eighteen, Susan still sees the world as one in which "everything" has been "inopportune" (ch. 4).

Elizabeth-Jane's resignation is so important to her and so deeply fixed in her psyche that she clings to it when her mother marries Henchard and her prospects greatly improve. She remains sober and repressed not only because she distrusts fate but also because she thinks too poorly of herself to feel that she deserves her good fortune. Hardy presents Elizabeth-Jane as a wonderful person whom the characters in the novel come to appreciate, but she measures herself against an idealized image of herself as she would have been had she received the upbringing and education she desired, and as a result she always feels herself to be wanting. When Farfrae remains in Casterbridge partly at her urging but does not resume his courtship, Elizabeth-Jane concludes that "her appearance on the evening of the dance [was] such as to inspire a fleeting love at first sight" and that by this time he has "discovered how plain and homely was the informing spirit of that pretty outside" (ch. 17). When she feels "her heart going out to him," she says to herself, "No, no, Elizabeth-Jane—such dreams are not for you!" Hardy hints that Farfrae might have been more aggressive with encouragement (Lucetta has not yet appeared), but Elizabeth-Jane tries to prevent herself from seeing and thinking of him.

Although Hardy is capable of seeing the morbidity of Elizabeth-Jane's cravings for acquirements and correctness, he is blind to the compulsiveness of her resignation and its negative effects. Perhaps this is because it corresponds to his own predominant defense and is founded on a basic distrust of life that he shares (see Paris 1976a). I am speaking here of Hardy the implied author, but I suspect that on this matter there is no great distance between the implied author of *The Mayor of Casterbridge* and Hardy the person. The rhetoric of the novel consistently celebrates Elizabeth-Jane's resignation, which it describes as the product of "wisdom" (ch. 14) and a "straightforward mind" (ch. 25). Because she does not allow herself to be "too gay," Elizabeth-Jane experiences "none of those ups and downs of spirit which beset so many people without cause" (ch. 14)—Henchard and Lucetta, for example. "The reasonableness of almost everything" she does is well illustrated by her refusal to "make a fool of herself" by dressing up when she has the money to do so. The resigned defense is designed above all to prevent us from making fools of ourselves. The "unsophisticated girl" keeps "in the rear of opportunity in matters of indulgence" by "an innate perceptiveness that [is] almost genius."

Elizabeth-Jane is proved to have been wise in not allowing herself to be deceived by good fortune when Henchard turns against her and she loses Farfrae to Lucetta. Her defenses fail momentarily when she feels that Henchard scorns her: "quite broken in spirit," she exclaims, "O, I wish I was dead, with dear mother!" (ch. 20). She is rescued from her "unbearable position" when Lucetta invites her to be her companion and is soon able to resume her usual subdued but not depressed state of mind. She does much better with regard to Farfrae, quenching her interest in him "with patient fortitude." She "stoically" contemplates "her fate" when he begins courting Lucetta (ch. 25) and "cork[s] up the turmoil of her feelings with grand control" when she learns of their marriage (ch. 30).

Elizabeth-Jane defends herself against troubling emotions by distancing herself from difficult situations and finding them curious or amusing. She is initially "terrified" when Henchard tries to greet the royal personage, but "her interest in the spectacle as a strange phenomenon [gets] the better of her fear" (ch. 37). The pain she experiences "from the almost absolute obliviousness to her existence" shown by Henchard and Farfrae while both are courting Lucetta is "at times half dissipated by her sense of its humourousness. When Lucetta had pricked her finger they were as deeply concerned as if she were dying; when she herself had been seriously sick or in danger they uttered a conventional word of sympathy at the news, and forgot all about it immediately" (ch. 25). Whereas Henchard is maddened by the fickleness of fate, Elizabeth-Jane regards life as a curious spectacle. She anticipates "the wreck of each day's wishes" but has observed that life is less "a series of pure disappointments" than "a series of substitutions": "Continually it had happened that what she had desired had not been granted her, and that what had been granted her she had not desired." When she loses Farfrae, she wonders with a certain amusement "what unwished-for thing Heaven might send her in place of him." Thanks to her detached perspective, she is able to think of the days when he was her undeclared lover with "an approach to equanimity."

Her detachment may account for Elizabeth-Jane's speculations about why she was born, why things have the shape they do, and where consciousness came from, since these questions arise when we are not involved in life but are contemplating it from a distance. To a significant extent, Elizabeth-Jane is alienated from her own feelings and from the world around her. Her defensiveness makes it impossible for her to experience anything in a spontaneous, wholehearted way.

When things turn out well for her at the end, Elizabeth-Jane clings grimly to her defenses, as she had done during her earlier period of prosperity. She has regrets about her behavior toward Henchard, but they fade, as do "the lively and sparkling emotions of her early married life," and she finds "herself in a latitude of calm weather" in which she is blessed with "an equable serenity" (ch. 45). Her mission becomes not to fulfill herself or to relax and enjoy life but to teach her defenses to others:

> the finer movements of her nature found scope in discovering to the narrow-lived ones around her the secret (as she had once learnt it) of making limited opportunities endurable; which she deemed to consist in the cunning enlargement, by a species of microscopic treatment, of those minute forms of satisfaction that offer themselves to everybody not in positive pain; which, thus handled, have much of the same inspiriting effect upon life as wider interests cursorily embraced. (Ch. 45)

There is wisdom in this philosophy, of course, especially when our opportunities have been narrowed by forces over which we have no control and it behooves us to relish the small pleasures available to us. But there are wider interests within Elizabeth-Jane's reach that she seems afraid to embrace lest the gods become jealous. While magnifying minute satisfactions, she tends to devalue larger ones, which need not be cursorily embraced. In the midst of plenty she continues to defend herself against poverty and gives meaning to her life by teaching the secret of endurance to the less fortunate.

Although Elizabeth-Jane has desired social elevation, she has ambivalent feelings about it because of her inner conflicts. She needs both to have her worth vindicated and to be humble and unassuming. Now that she is the wife of the most prominent man in town, she finds there is "no great personal difference between being respected in the nether parts of Casterbridge and glorified at the uppermost end of the social world" (ch. 45). She at once defends herself against taking pride in her position by depreciating its worth and protects herself against a possible reversal of fortune by feeling that its loss would not matter very much. If she enjoys her triumph at all, it is in a guarded, indirect way.

Elizabeth-Jane remains sober and repressed. Her position seems to afford "much to be thankful for," but she is presented as being too wise to be "demonstratively thankful":

> Her experience had been of a kind to teach her, rightly or wrongly, that the doubtful honour of a brief transit through a sorry world hardly called for effusiveness, even when the path was suddenly irradiated at some half-way point by daybeams rich as hers. But her strong sense that neither she nor any human being deserved less than was given, did not blind her to the fact that there were others receiving less who had deserved much more. And in being forced to class herself among the fortunate she did not cease to wonder at the persistence of the unforeseen, when the one to whom such unbroken tranquillity had been accorded in the adult stage was she whose youth had seemed to teach that happiness was but the occasional episode in a general drama of pain. (Ch. 45)

This remarkable passage shows the lengths to which Elizabeth-Jane goes in her effort to maintain her resignation at a time when most people would rejoice.

Elizabeth-Jane feels threatened by her prosperity and must keep reminding herself of its meaningless and impermanence. Thus she continues to see the world as an absurd place in which there is no relation between people's fates and their deserts and in which frustration is far more frequent than happiness. Whereas a predominantly self-effacing person would see happiness as a reward for virtue and feel a strong obligation to be "demonstratively thankful," for Elizabeth-Jane being thankful would imply that she was the beneficiary of a just order and that goodness was a means of controlling fate. If this were the case, she might reasonably expect to continue being happy, but such an expectation frightens her and she must remind herself that there are "others receiving less who had deserved much more." She turns her "unbroken tranquillity," which is one of the highest values of the resigned person, into another reason for distrusting life. It is further evidence of the unpredictability of fate, since her youth had held out no such hope, and of its unfairness, since rewards are not distributed according to deserts. By affirming that no one deserves less than is given, Elizabeth-Jane asserts the claims on which her sense of injustice is based, while by feeling that many deserve more than she, she maintains her humility.

Uncomfortable at being "forced to class herself among the fortunate," Elizabeth-Jane soothes herself by remembering that happiness is "but the occasional episode in a general drama of pain." This enables her to remain steeled against misfortune, instead of being deluded by her happiness, and it is also a method of warding off misfortune. In her belief system fate is not only capricious, it is also sometimes malicious, and seeing oneself as fortunate invites being struck down. By refusing to feel very happy, she shows a proper fear of the coulter of destiny and preserves a state of obscurity that will not arouse the enmity of the powers that be.

This is one of the strangest happy endings in literature. Elizabeth-Jane's is the story of a woman who ultimately gets what she wants but who cannot allow herself to want it very much or to enjoy the fulfillment of her desires. Presented as a victim of fate at the beginning, she is clearly a victim of her defenses at the end. Hardy does not see this because these are his defenses as well. He is as uncomfortable with happy endings as his heroine and has created a resolution that is compatible with his dark view of life. We are to understand that fate has more disappointments in store for Elizabeth-Jane and that her present happiness is but a passing episode. We are also to understand that Elizabeth-Jane will not be crushed by misfortune, like Henchard, because she will never allow herself to be tricked into expecting much from life.

11

Madame Bovary

At first glance *Madame Bovary* and *The Mayor of Cast-erbridge* may not seem to have much in common, but from a Horneyan perspective they are interesting to compare. Emma and Henchard are both restless, aspiring people who demand a great deal from life and whose search for glory leads them to behave in self-destructive ways. Their sufferings are treated with sympathy, but they are criticized for the character flaws that bring misery to themselves and others. The dominant solution in each novel is detachment, with Hardy's being expressed primarily through his celebration of Elizabeth-Jane and Flaubert's through the narrator's voice and a variety of ironic devices. Both authors seem to be disillusioned romantics who need to defend themselves against the dissonance between desire and reality. Since the pursuit of happiness exposes us to such pain, it is better to see through the vanity of human wishes and expect little from life.

Like Hardy, Flaubert has not received due credit for his genius in mimetic characterization. During the composition of *Madame Bovary* he wrote to Louise Colet, "The reader will not notice, I hope, all the psychological work hidden under the form, but he will sense its effect" (De Man 1965, 317). This wish has been granted. Although Emma Bovary is one of the most celebrated characters in literature, Flaubert's "psychological work" has gone largely unnoticed. A Horneyan approach will help us to recover Flaubert's psychological intuitions and to appreciate the brilliance of his portrait of Emma.

Because we have detailed accounts of their childhoods, we can readily understand the compensatory needs that lead characters like Pip and Jane Eyre to idealize themselves and embark upon searches for glory. We know almost nothing about Emma Bovary's childhood, however, and her need for glory, like Henchard's, is an aspect of her character that is simply there when we meet her. In the fullest psychological study of the novel to date, Giles Mitchell tries to explain Emma's romanticism as the product of "pathological narcissism," "a personality disorder characterized by intense, excessive, and sometimes fatal devotion to the ego-ideal" (1987, 107). Her narcissism is "a flight from humanness, from mortality and bodily vulnerability, from being-in-the-world" (115). Although Flaubert seems to suggest "that Emma's falsely romantic ideals derive from her reading," Mitchell contends that they "were formed in response to something far more existential" (116). The problem with Mitchell's view of Emma as "a universal figure" (125) is that we are all confronted with our human limitations, but we do not all respond like Madame Bovary.

Nonetheless, I think Mitchell is correct in saying that Emma's destructive "ideals" are not just caused by her reading. Flaubert's detailed description of the influences to which she is exposed during her stay in the convent leaves us with the impression that her romanticism is the product of these influences and that her frustration results from the contrast between the bourgeois existence to which she is destined and the unrealistic expectations that have been fostered by the "tantalizing phantasmagoria of sentimental realities" (I, vi) to which she has been exposed.[1] But influence is always a matter of *interaction* between external stimuli and individual psychology, and there must be something in Emma's character that makes her so responsive to romantic elements in her culture.

I believe that Emma has a narcissistic personality, but in Karen Horney's sense of that term rather than in Freud's or in that of the self and existential psychologists cited by Mitchell. For Horney, narcissism is a reactive rather than a primary phenomenon, and an inability to come to terms with the human condition is a *product* of grandiosity rather than a cause of it. Self-idealization occurs in all the solutions Horney describes, but whereas most people develop an idealized image to compensate for feelings of weakness, inadequacy, and low self-esteem, as do Pip and Jane Eyre, narcissists derive an exalted conception of themselves from the admiration and indulgence of others. Horney observes that the narcissist "often is gifted beyond average, early and easily won distinctions, and sometimes was the favored and admired child" (1950, 194). Emma Bovary was an only child, and what little information we have suggests that she was indulged by her father, who thought her "too clever for farming" (I, iii). She develops a sense of superiority to her surroundings, to which she makes little effort to accommodate herself.

By the time Emma goes to school at the convent, she has a vague idea of herself as an exceptional being who is destined for glorious things. "The comparisons of betrothed, husband, celestial lover, and eternal marriage" that she hears repeated in sermons stir "within her soul depths of unexpected sweetness" (I, vi) because, like the images she finds in novels, ballads, and keepsakes, and on the painted plates depicting the story of one of Louis XIV's mistresses, they give shape to her aspirations for an exalted existence.

These aspirations take a variety of forms. Emma is drawn to religion by "the mystic languor exhaled in the perfumes of the altar" and "the sonorous lamentations of romantic melancholy re-echoing through the world and eternity!" (I, vi). Christ, whom she would wed if she became a nun, is the first of her phantom lovers. Novels, romantic ballads, history, and paintings stock her mind with images of persecuted ladies, brave gentlemen, famous women of the past, impossibly exotic places, and exquisite scenes of love. These "pictures of the world," as Flaubert ironically describes them, provide material from which she forms idealized images of herself and also of her life, of the kind of lover, home, furnishings, clothes, travel, friends, and experiences she ought to have.

As is characteristic of the narcissistic person, Emma has lofty claims but relatively weak shoulds. Because Horneyan narcissists *are* their idealized selves, they are not driven by punitive inner dictates into trying to become what they feel they ought to be. Their object is not to actualize their idealized image but rather to hold onto it, to confirm the sense of specialness they already have. One of their primary means of doing this is to insist on their claims, which they feel the world must eventually honor. Even if their claims are being frustrated at the moment, they feel assured of future glory if they continue to assert them. Because they have "an unquestioned belief" in their "greatness and uniqueness" and in the power of their claims, narcissists have a "buoyancy and perennial youthfulness," a "resiliency" in the face of disappointment, that is lacking in the other groups (Horney 1950, 194). Although her dreams are repeatedly crushed, Emma retains her "ever young illusions" (II, xii).

But beneath their surface optimism, narcissists experience "undercurrents of despondency and pessimism" (Horney 1950, 196). While Emma keeps rebounding from her disappointments, in the intervals she has intense feelings of rage and despair. One reason for the narcissist's pessimism is that "measuring by the yardstick of infinitude, of the attainment of fantastic happiness, he cannot help sensing a painful disparity in his life." Since he is not given to conscious self-doubts, he feels that "the discrepancy is not in him but in life as such. Thus he may see a tragic quality to life, not the one that does exist but the one which he brings to it." This seems to me a more accurate description of Emma than Mitchell's version of her as a universal figure suffering from existential problems.

From a Horneyan perspective, then, *Madame Bovary* is the story of a woman whose romantic dreams are the product of an interaction between the phantasmagoria of sentimental realities she encounters in her culture and a narcissistic personality that makes her highly responsive to such influences. Although she is repeatedly disillusioned, she is extraordinarily resilient and soon finds a new dream. Her search for glory takes a variety of forms, as she swings from one solution to another. She becomes more and more self-destructive as her desperation grows and increasingly divorced from reality in her pursuit of escapes and consolations.

Madame Bovary may seem to be very different from *The Mayor of Casterbridge* in that Hardy's attitudes toward his characters are evident whereas Flaubert is famous for his rhetorical restraint. "Nowhere in my book," he wrote to Louise Colet, "must the author express his emotions or his opinions" (De Man 1965, 311). Earlier he had written, "No lyricism, no comments, the author's personality absent" (310). I think that Flaubert is deluding himself about his personality being absent, but a surprising number of critics have agreed with him. According to Sainte-Beuve, "The novelist refrains from taking sides; he is present only in order to watch, to reveal and to say everything, but not even his profile appears in a single corner of the novel" (De Man 1965, 327). Erich Auerbach contrasts Flaubert with Stendhal and Balzac, in whose works "we frequently . . . hear what the writer thinks of his characters and events" (1957, 428). In *Madame Bovary,* the writer "expresses no opinion and makes no comment" (429). I believe that the implied author's attitudes and judgments are very much present in this novel, which is highly rhetorical. Flaubert not only portrays but satirizes Emma's search for glory.

An author is present in a novel not only in comments (which Flaubert, in fact, makes with some frequency) but also in his arrangement of the materials. One of Flaubert's favorite rhetorical devices is to mock Emma's dreams by showing the contrast between her illusions and the truth. He often lets us know in advance that Emma is out of touch with reality and is bound to be disappointed. Although Emma is the subject of the novel, the first two chapters are largely devoted to Charles, and one of their functions is to make us aware of Emma's mistake in idealizing him before she is aware of it herself. Charles is introduced as an awkward boy wearing an absurd cap who is made to conjugate *ridiculus sum* twenty times on his first day at school. A mediocre student, he must work very hard to stay in the middle of the class. Dominated by his mother and then by his first wife, he is a pathetic figure who could never satisfy Emma's craving for a gallant lover, or at least a distinguished husband.

Another function of the introductory chapters is to establish the basic pattern of the novel, which is that of foolish hopes followed by disappointment. This is a novel neither of education nor of vindication; it is, like *Vanity Fair,* a novel of disenchantment (see Paris 1974). Charles's father, a retired assistant-surgeon-major, takes advantage of his fine figure to "get hold of a dowry of sixty thousand francs in the person of a hosier's daughter who had fallen in love with his good looks" (I, i). He spends money recklessly, becomes indignant when his father-in-law dies leaving little, and fails in the textile business and farming. He then withdraws from the world, "soured, eaten up with regrets, cursing his luck, jealous of everyone." He cares nothing for his wife and is annoyed by her servile adoration. As a result, the once "lively," "expansive," and "affectionate" woman becomes "ill-tempered, grumbling, irritable." She transfers all her "broken little vanities" to her son and dreams "of high station" for him. Although we are only a few pages into the novel, we have already seen enough of Charles to know that his mother will be disappointed.

Charles's story, too, is part of the pattern of disenchantment. After he finally passes his examination and is ready to enter practice, his mother arranges a marriage with a forty-five-year-old widow who has an income of twelve hundred francs. Despite the fact that Madame Dubuc is "ugly, as dry as a bone, her face with as many pimples as the spring has buds," Charles welcomes the marriage as "the advent of an easier life" in which "he would be more free to do as he liked with himself and his money" (I, i). His wife is master, however, and the marriage is miserable. When he returns home in the evening, she "stretche[s] forth two long thin arms from beneath the sheets, put[s] them round his neck," and complains that he is neglecting her. She turns out not to be rich, and Charles's father accuses his wife "of having caused the misfortune of their son by harnessing him to such a harridan" (I, iii). It is no wonder that Charles is attracted to Emma during his visits to the Bertaux. He is caught up in a romantic dream that is the most tenacious, perhaps, in the novel, since he remains blind to Emma's betrayals and pants "like an adolescent under the vague desires of love" even after his wife has died and he has learned the truth about her (III, xi). Flaubert keeps us aware throughout of the folly of Charles's love, of disparity between his adoration of Emma and her scorn of him.

Emma's story begins with a series of disenchantments. In the convent, she is swept up by the romance of religion and seems destined to become a nun, but she rebels against the mysteries of the faith, and its discipline, "as something alien" to her sensuous, self-indulgent nature (I, vi). She thinks she has achieved glory when her mother dies and she engages in romantic excesses of grief. Her father is afraid she is ill, but Emma is "secretly pleased that she had reached at a first attempt the rare ideal of delicate lives, never attained by mediocre hearts." Emma soon grows tired of her grief, however, and is "surprised to feel herself consoled." When she returns home, she relishes the pleasure of ruling over the servants, but this, too, soon passes. Growing "disgusted with the country," she becomes nostalgic for the convent. She thinks herself "quite disillusioned, with nothing more to learn, and nothing more to feel," when she is roused from her apathy by Charles, whose presence "sufficed to make her believe that she at last felt that wondrous passion which, till then, like a great bird with rose-coloured wings, hung in the splendour of poetic skies." Marriage leads to her greatest disappointment so far. She had thought herself in love, but "since the happiness that should have followed failed to come," she concludes that she must have been mistaken and tries to find out what one means exactly "by the words *bliss, passion, ecstasy*, that had seemed to her so beautiful in books" (I, v).

It is impossible to separate the psychological portrait of Emma from Flaubert's attitude toward her, since in this novel rhetoric and mimesis are often indistinguishable. A surprising number of critics feel that Flaubert presents Emma as a superior being who is the victim of a bourgeois society that is discordant with the fineness of her nature. Flaubert satirizes the mediocrity, materialism, and dreariness of bourgeois life, to be sure, but he also ridicules Emma's romanticism, which he presents as equally conventional and full of clichés. To "taste the full sweetness" of her honeymoon,

> it would no doubt have been necessary to fly to those lands with sonorous names where the days after marriage are full of the most suave laziness! In post-chaises behind blue silken curtains, one rides slowly up steep roads, listening to the song of the postilion re-echoed by the mountains, along with the bells of goats and the muffled sound of a waterfall. At sunset on the shores of gulfs one breathes in the perfume of lemon-trees; then in the evening on the villa-terraces above, one looks hand in hand at the stars, making plans for the future. It seemed to her that certain places on earth must bring happiness, as a plant peculiar to the soil, and that cannot thrive elsewhere. Why could not she lean over balconies in Swiss chalets, or enshrine her melancholy in a Scotch cottage, with a husband dressed in a black velvet coat with long tails, and thin shoes, a pointed hat and frills? (I, vii)

There are many such passages that portray and mock Emma simultaneously.

It is above all her husband that Emma finds wanting, since he does not correspond to her romantic conception of a man. A man should "know everything, excel in manifold activities, initiate you into the energies of passion, the refinements of life"; but Charles can "neither swim, nor fence, nor shoot, and one day he could not explain some term of horsemanship to her that she had come across in a novel" (I, vii). She wants to "experience love with him" in "accord with the theories she believed right," and, in a comic scene, she recites to him by moonlight in the garden "all the passionate rhymes" she knows by heart and sings "many melancholy adagios." But she finds herself "as calm after this as before, and Charles seem[s] neither more amorous, nor more moved." She decides that his "passion [is] no longer very ardent."

Flaubert explains, however, that Emma is incapable "of understanding what she did not experience or of believing anything that did not take on a conventional form" (I, vii); and he shows that despite his limitations, Charles loves Emma with a passion that might have gratified her had she been able to recognize it:

> In bed, in the morning, by her side, on the pillow, he watched the sunlight sinking into the down on her fair cheek, half hidden by the ribbons of her nightcap. Seen thus closely, her eyes looked to him enlarged, especially when, on waking up, she opened and shut her eyelids rapidly many times.

Black in the shade, dark blue in broad daylight, they had, as it were, depths of successive colors that, more opaque in the center, grew more transparent towards the surface of the eye. His own eyes lost themselves in these depths and he could see himself mirrored in miniature, down to his shoulders, with his scarf round his head and the top of his shirt open. (I, v)

This is the romantic love of an unromantic lover, one who wears a scarf round his head. As Charles rides off after breakfast, he reproaches himself for not loving Emma enough, turns back, and runs "up the stairs with a beating heart." He cannot "keep from constantly touching her comb, her rings, her scarf." Sometimes he gives her "great sounding kisses" on her cheeks, "or else little kisses in a row all along her bare arm from the tip of her fingers up to her shoulder." Because Charles's love does not take the form her reading has led her to expect, it fails to register on Emma, who suffers from ennui and begins to fantasize what life would have been like with the man of her dreams.

Emma's visit to Vaubyessard gives her for the first time a taste of the life she feels she deserves. She is spellbound by the social elegance and material refinements of this world, but Flaubert subverts her view of it by calling attention to its sordid features. Emma is fascinated by the Marquis' father-in-law because "he had lived at court and slept in the beds of queens" (I, viii). Flaubert depicts him as a revolting old man who has "lived a life of loud dissipation" and now sits eating like a child, "letting drops of gravy drop" from his "hanging lips." To Emma, the people at the ball are like figures out of her dreams; she wants "to know their lives," "to blend with them." Flaubert describes the "indifferent eyes" of the men as having "the appeased expression of daily-satiated passions" and observes that through "all their gentleness of manner pierced that peculiar brutality that stems from a steady command over half-tame things, for the exercise of one's strength and the amusement of one's vanity—the handling of thoroughbred horses and the society of loose women."

When Emma returns to Tostes, she dwells on the memory of the ball, and although the details fade, a "wistful feeling remain[s]" (I, viii). She imagines that the green silk cigar-case Charles had found belonged to the Viscount with whom she had danced and weaves a romance around it that sets her dreaming of Paris. Her fantasies are again quite conventional, and Flaubert's depiction of them is satirical. In the world of high society, as Emma imagines it, the duchesses are all pale, and they all get up at four in the afternoon. The men all have "talents hidden under a frivolous appearance" and ride "horses to death at pleasure parties" (I, ix). In the bohemian quarter, writers and actresses are "prodigal as kings, full of ambitious ideals and fantastic frenzies. They [live] far above all others, among the storms that rage between heaven and earth, partaking of the sublime."

In an effort to maintain a sense of connection with Vaubyessard and the Paris of her dreams, Emma begins the pursuit of elegance and material refinements that ultimately becomes a major cause of her downfall. She turns her servant into a lady's-maid and buys fashionable clothes, trinkets, and furnishings. She devises new ways of "arranging paper sconces for the candles" and extraordinary names for simple dishes (I, ix). Flaubert comments that "in her wistfulness, she confused the sensuous pleasures of luxury with the delights of the heart, elegance of manners with delicacy of sentiment."

Emma feels that, despite his coarseness, marriage to Charles would be tolerable if he were at least "one of those silently determined men who work at their books all night, and at last . . . wear a string of medals on their ill-fitting black coat" (I, ix). Thwarted in her dreams of romantic love and a glamorous social life, Emma craves "this name of Bovary, which was hers, to be illustrious, to see it displayed at the booksellers', repeated in the newspapers, known to all France." Emma's search for glory could take the form of identifying with Charles if he were the kind of man who could feed her pride, but he is unambitious and even tells her how he has been humiliated in a consultation with another doctor. Full of rage and shame, she feels "a wild desire to strike him." It injures her pride to bear his name, and she displaces onto him her anger with herself for having married him. His mediocrity is so threatening to Emma because it represents her despised image, what she could not bear to become. His presence is a constant reminder of the disparity between what is and what ought to be.

We can see some of Flaubert's fine psychological work in his portrayal of Emma's reactions when she feels she has nowhere to turn in her effort to escape her unbearable existence. At first she waits for an "act of fortune" (I, ix) that will transform her life, but nothing happens, and when her hopes for another ball at Vaubyessard are dashed, she despairs: "The future was a dark corridor, with its door at the end shut tight." Life seems meaningless to Emma unless she has the prospect of some form of glory that will confirm her idealized image of herself. She gives up music: "Since she could never, in a velvet gown with short sleeves, striking with her light fingers the ivory keys of an Erard concert piano, feel the murmur of ecstasy envelop her like a breeze, it was not worth while boring herself with practicing." She gives up drawing, embroidery, and reading as well and finds herself lonely and bored. Feeling hopeless, she lets everything go: "She who was formerly so careful, so dainty, now spent whole days without dressing, wore grey cotton stockings, and used tallow candles to light the house." She grows "difficult, capricious," and "no longer conceal[s] her contempt" for the people around her. She experiences mood swings and suffers from psychosomatic symptoms that Charles cannot cure.

Emma's behavior is not entirely the result of despair. Her suffering is an expression of rage at having her claims denied. She feels that she is "the equal of all the women who were living happily. She had seen duchesses at Vaubyessard with clumsier waists and commoner ways, and she hated the divine injustice of God" (I, ix). Emma's bargain with fate is evident here. Because of her beauty and refinement, she deserves a luxurious life, and her misery is a protest against the unfairness of her lot. She is showing the world what it has done to her. Accepting her lot would mean giving up her claims, whereas suffering is a way of holding onto them, of compelling fate by demonstrating that life is intolerable as it is. Emma's suffering is, finally, a manipulative technique, one that succeeds in bringing about a change. She is suffering at God, at the world, and especially at Charles, who is driven to give up his flourishing practice in an effort to alleviate her misery. As soon as he mentions the idea of leaving Tostes, Emma drinks "vinegar to lose weight, contract[s] a little cough, and [loses] all appetite." Her palpitations are real, but this passage suggests that some of her other behavior may also be contrived.

One of Emma's most persistent illusions is that her misery is entirely the result of external conditions and that happiness comes from without, is granted by fortune or found. While she has no recognition of the internal sources of her frustration, for Flaubert, as for Hardy in *The Mayor of Casterbridge*, character is fate. He emphasizes Emma's inner emptiness, her superficiality, and her unrealistic expectations. The life she dreams of does not exist in the world and would not be worth having if it did. Emma thinks that things are bound to be better in a new place, but through his description of Yonville-l'Abbaye before her arrival, Flaubert once again lets us know that she is deluding herself. The land is poor, the cheese is bad, the decaying church has neither organ nor stained glass, and there is only one street, which is "a gunshot long and flanked by a few shops" (II, i). The town is as dreary as Tostes. Things do change for Emma, however, in that she meets new people, first Léon and then Rodolphe, on whom to focus her dreams.

In the midst of her misery at Tostes, Emma longs for a life of adventure, "for masked balls, for shameless pleasures that were bound, she thought, to initiate her to ecstasies she had not yet experienced" (I, ix). But, although she longs for shameless pleasures, she is not yet ready to engage in them. Indeed, she hopes that her child will be a male so that she can fulfill her desires through him: "a man, at least, is free; he can explore all passions and all countries, overcome obstacles, taste of the most distant pleasures" (II, iii). A woman is "always drawn by some desire, restrained by some rule of conduct." Emma dreams of revenging "all her impotence" by having a son, but this hope is shattered when she gives birth to a girl.

Although Emma feels that she would be able to follow her dreams if only she were a man, Flaubert's linking her with Léon suggests that he sees her temperament rather than her gender as the primarily source of her plight. Many critics regard Emma as vastly superior to Léon, but Flaubert presents them as kindred spirits, with Léon showing, perhaps, what Emma might have been like had she been a male. The two experience an immediate rapport when they discover that they both love sublime landscapes, dreamy music, and "stories that rush breathlessly along" (II, ii). Emma expresses scorn for "commonplace heroes and moderate feelings, as one finds them in nature," and Léon assents: "since these works fail to touch the heart, they miss, it seems to me, the true end of art. It is so sweet, amid all the disenchantments of life, to be able to dwell in thought upon noble characters, pure affections, and pictures of happiness." Both are bored, disillusioned romantics who feel wasted in the provinces and console themselves by escaping into imaginary worlds. They share the same stock of superficial tastes and sentimental clichés. Léon is enchanted by Emma's elegance, and she notices "his nails, which were longer than one wore them in Yonville. It was one of the clerk's chief concerns to trim them, and for this purpose he kept a special knife in his writing-desk." (II, iii). Each sees in the other a means of escaping a mundane existence, and both are caught between desire and fear.

Her love for Léon, and his for her, throws Emma into conflict. Deliriously happy, she wants to consummate their relationship, but, restrained by rules of conduct, she represses her desire and finds another path to glory by resisting temptation and becoming a model wife and mother. She goes to church regularly, brings Berthe home from the nurse, and warms Charles's slippers by the fire. The object of everyone's admiration, she seems "to be passing through life scarcely touching it, bearing on her brow the slight mark of a sublime destiny" (II, v). She fears that she has lost Léon by repulsing him too much, but the "pride, the joy of being able to say to herself, 'I am virtuous,' and to look at herself in the mirror striking resigned poses" consoles her in some degree "for the sacrifice she [thinks] she [is] making."

Emma's virtue is unreal, another romantic pose, but so, Flaubert makes clear, is her love. She *thinks* she is making a sacrifice. She seeks solitude in order to delight in Léon's image, but "his physical presence trouble[s] the voluptuousness of this meditation" (II, v). She thrills "at the sound of his step," but, to her astonishment and sorrow, the emotion subsides when he appears. Emma is sacrificing an unreal love in order to glory in a pretended virtue. She feels victimized by fate because she did not meet Léon before she married Charles, but Flaubert suggests that if she had, he would not have satisfied her either. No real man can compete with her imaginary lovers.

Beneath her pose of serene virtue, Emma is "eaten up with desires, with rage, with hate" (II, v). She bewails "the clothes she did not have, the happiness she had missed, her overexalted dreams, her too cramped home." It is Flaubert, presumably, who sees her dreams as "overexalted." As at Tostes, she cultivates her suffering, but this time Charles is oblivious of her torment, and she hates him for his conviction that he is making her happy. She consoles herself with "wild extravagance" and has "shocking thoughts" of adultery and revenge, but she is still restrained by rules of conduct, and a "dark, shapeless chasm" opens within her at the thought of fleeing with Léon. Her realization that there is no relief from her misery leaves her "shattered, exhausted, frozen, sobbing silently, with flowing tears." Her attempt to find consolation in religion does not succeed, and after Léon's departure for Paris, "the evil days of Tostes [begin] again" (II, vii). Filled with "a numb despair," Emma regrets "her sterile virtue." She spends money lavishly, becomes increasingly unstable, and develops psychosomatic ailments. Her despair is so great that she reacts with indifference when she begins to spit blood: "what does it matter?"

Emma's spirits are revived by the attentions of Rodolphe, who seems to be exactly the kind of man for whom she has been looking. Once again, Flaubert creates ironic effects by showing us in advance that Emma is bound to be disappointed. Rodolphe is a calculating seducer who worries about "how to get rid of her afterwards" before he begins the relationship (II, vii). Emma and Léon were truly kindred spirits, but Rodolphe plays the role of the melancholy romantic because he knows it appeals to her. Bemoaning "provincial mediocrity, . . . the lives it stifles, the lost illusions," he tells Emma that he is "sinking in gloom" and longs to join those who are lying in moonlit graveyards (II, viii). He may have had an aim in life if only he had met a woman he could love, and he clings to the belief that one day happiness will come. When one is near despair, a voice suddenly cries, " 'It is here!' You feel the need of confiding the whole of your life, of giving everything, sacrificing everything to this person." There is "no need for explanations" because the other has been met "before in dreams." Sensing Emma's desperation, Rodolphe easily manipulates her by employing the romantic clichés for which she is looking and presenting himself as the man of her dreams.

Rodolphe differs from Léon not only in cynically exploiting a romanticism he does not really share, but also in enabling Emma to resolve the conflict between rules of conduct and her desires. One's real duty, he says, is not to "accept all the conventions of society with the hypocrisy it forces upon us" but to "cherish the beautiful," "to feel what is great" (II, viii). The passions are "the one beautiful thing on earth, the source of heroism, of enthusiasm, of poetry, music, the arts." When Emma objects that one must accept the world's morality to some extent, Rodolphe distinguishes between two moralities: "the petty one, the morality of small men," and the eternal morality that governs people like them. In the petty morality, the "noblest feelings, the purest feelings are persecuted," but the eternal morality sanctions a beautiful passion like theirs that had its origin "in some previous state of existence" (II, viii). Her moral qualms allayed, Emma plunges into the affair, which becomes a source of pride rather than of shame.

For the first time since her mother's death, Emma feels that she has succeeded in rising above the mediocrity that surrounds her. Before the affair is consummated, Rodolphe flatters her skillfully, telling her that although he has tried to stay away he cannot "struggle against Heaven; it is impossible to resist the smile of angels; one is carried away by the beautiful, the lovely, the adorable" (II, ix). Emma's pride unfolds "languidly in the warmth of this language, like someone stretching in a hot bath." After the affair is consummated, Emma feels neither anxiety nor remorse but rather that she has fulfilled at last "the love-dream of her youth" (II, ix). She sees herself as having joined the "lyric legion" of adulterous women about whom she has read and feels that she no longer need envy them. She is to know the "joys of love" at last, "that fever of happiness of which she had so despaired!" For the first time in her life, her dream of glory seems attainable. She feels herself surrounded by a blue space, with "ordinary existence" appearing "only intermittently between these heights, dark and far away beneath her." It has been Emma's object to separate herself from ordinary existence, and now she looks down on it from the heights of her illusory grandeur.

Emma has experienced what Karen Horney calls a vindictive triumph. She felt, says Flaubert, "a satisfaction of revenge. How she had suffered! But she had won out at last" (II, ix). She has revenged herself on an uncomprehending world by defying its moral code and gaining the happiness it wished to deny her. And she has had her revenge on Charles as well, whose mediocrity has been so humiliating. Another feature of a vindictive triumph is proving one's true grandiosity. Emma has been in despair when it has seemed that her claims would never be fulfilled, but they have been honored at last, validating her bargain and confirming her exalted conception of herself. She so conflates reality with her dreams that she conducts her affair in a reckless manner, feeling no concern for discovery, and exercises caution only at Rodolphe's insistence.

When Rodolphe becomes bored and takes her for granted, Emma is disenchanted once more and knows "what it [is] to repent" (II, x). Reviewing her life, she mourns all her lost illusions, but she is soon caught up in a new dream of glory when Homais proposes the operation on Hippolyte. She urges Charles on in the hope that "his reputation and fortune will be increased" and that she will have something "more solid" to lean on "than love" (II, xi). But the operation fails, and Emma is humiliated by the fact that "she, who was so intelligent—could have allowed herself to be deceived again." The remnants of her virtue crumble "away beneath the furious blows of her pride," and she resumes her affair with Rodolphe.

Her relationship with Rodolphe is characterized now by a morbid dependency in which she abases herself and glorifies him: "I am your servant, your concubine! You are my king, my idol! You are good, you are beautiful, you are clever, you are strong!" (II, xii). Emma transfers her pride to Rodolphe and seeks to exalt herself by merging with him. One of her objects in proposing that they elope is to bind him to her in a mutual dependency: "You are everything I have, and I'll be everything to you. I'll be your family, your country; I'll look after you." "The longer we live together," she proclaims, "the more it will be like an embrace, every day closer, more complete." This prospect is unbearably oppressive to a detached person like Rodolphe, who values his freedom and "holds back his emotions in any engagement." The more fiercely Emma clings to him, the more inevitable it becomes that he will abandon her.

As we have seen, Emma's search for glory takes many forms: she tries to confirm her idealized conception of herself through religious fervor, romantic love, devotion to duty, and her husband's achievements. As each solution fails, she turns to another, or she escapes into memories, reading, and dreams. When nothing works and the future looks hopeless, her rage and despair lead to inconsistent behavior, cynicism, and psychosomatic illnesses. Through almost all of these changes, Emma has a persistent desire for material refinements, which are a symbol of the exalted existence she craves.

After Rodolphe abandons her, Emma has a momentary impulse toward suicide and then retreats from a life she cannot bear into a long and serious illness. When she receives the sacrament at the height of her illness, her search for glory revives. She feels herself "mounting toward God" and faints "with celestial joy as she advance[s] her lips to accept the body of the Saviour presented to her" (II, xiv). She hears "the music of seraphic harps" and perceives God "on a golden throne" ordering "angels with wings of fire to carry her away in their arms." As she recovers, she tries to hold onto this "splendid vision" and aspires "to become a saint": "Her soul, tortured by pride, at length found rest in Christian humility, and tasting the joy of weakness, she saw within herself the destruction of her will opening wide the gates for heavenly grace to conquer her."

Flaubert satirizes this religious phase as another form of romanticism in which submission to God replaces Emma's wish to merge with Rodolphe. As she kneels on her Gothic prie-Dieu, she addresses "to the Lord the same suave words that she had murmured formerly to her lover in the outpourings of adultery" (II, xiv). Through Christian humility she hopes to gain "a bliss that can replace happiness," a love that will "grow forever!" Emma feels she has found a celestial lover who will raise her to the heights and whom she can control through humility and self-abnegation. She is not really humble, of course, but takes "pride [in] her devoutness," comparing herself "to those grand ladies of long ago whose glory she had dreamed of" and "who, trailing with so much majesty the lace-trimmed trains of their long gowns, retired into solitude to shed at the feet of Christ the tears of hearts that life had wounded." She "fancie[s] herself seized with the finest Catholic melancholy ever conceived by an ethereal soul."

In the absence of earthly delights, Emma wearies of religion and arises from her prayers "with aching limbs and the vague feeling that she [is] being cheated" (II, xiv). With the failure of this solution, she is once again torn by inner conflicts between resignation, aggression, and a wish to be good. Wrapping "all things in the same mood of indifference," she combines "gentleness of speech with such haughty looks" that one can "no longer distinguish selfishness from charity, or corruption from virtue."

When Charles takes her to see *Lucia di Lammermoor,* Emma's dream of love is reawakened. She feels herself "carried back to the reading of her youth, into the midst of Sir Walter Scott" (II, xv). As Lucie longs for wings, Emma, too, wants "to flee away from life, locked in a passionate embrace." In Lucie's "melodious lamentations," she recognizes "all the intoxication and the anguish that had brought her close to death," but she feels that, unlike Lucie, she has never been loved by the right man. Once she married Charles there was bound to be conflict between desire and rules of conduct; but if "before the degradation of marriage and the disillusions of adultery, she could have anchored her life upon some great, strong heart," she believes that all her needs could have been met: "virtue, affection, sensuous pleasure, and duty would have combined to give her eternal bliss."

Once again, Flaubert mocks Emma's illusion, and, indeed, for a moment she sees through it herself. She realizes that the bliss of which she dreams is "a lie, a mockery to taunt desire" (II, xv). Knowing "how small the passions [are] that art magnifie[s]," she strives for "detachment" and smiles "inwardly in scornful pity" when the hero reappears. But her "critical detachment" is quickly "swept away by the poetic power of the acting; and, drawn to the man by the illusion of the part," she begins to imagine the "extraordinary, magnificent" life of the tenor, Edgar Lagardy, "the life that could have been hers" if only fate had brought them together. She would have traveled with him through all the kingdoms of Europe, sharing his triumphs and being the sole object of his desire. She becomes possessed by the "mad idea" that he is looking at her now, and she longs to run into his arms, crying out "Take me away! . . . All my passion and all my dreams are yours!" In his characteristic way, Flaubert makes us aware of Emma's self-deception by having previously described Edgar Lagardy as a "charlatan type, in which there was something of the hairdresser."

Meeting Léon at the opera, Emma soon transfers her romantic dreams to him. Flaubert's account of their dialogue is deliciously comic. Emma expatiates "on the frailty of earthly affections, and the eternal isolation that stifles the human heart"; and Léon, "to show off, or in a naive imitation of this melancholy," declares that he has been "dreadfully despondent" (III, i). Both speak of what they have dreamed and what they have suffered, and Emma says that there would be some consolation if her pain could at least be of use to others. At this, Léon starts "off in praise of virtue, duty, and silent immolation, having himself an incredible longing for self-sacrifice." Emma would like to work in a hospital as a nursing Sister, and Léon praises the "holy vocation" of doctor. Emma wishes she had died in her illness, and Léon is "quick to express his own longing for 'the quiet of the tomb.' " Listening to Léon, Emma feels her existence expand: "it was like some sentimental immensity to which she had returned."

Emma's relationship with Léon follows a predictable course. No man has "ever seemed to her so beautiful" (III, i), and, although she fears things might change, she feels once again that her dream is coming true. To Léon, she is "the mistress of all novels, the heroine of all the dramas, the vague 'she' of all the volumes of verse" (III, v). After an idyllic interval, full of romantic clichés, disenchantment sets in. When Léon allows himself to be delayed by Homais, he seems to Emma "incapable of heroism, weak, banal, more spiritless than a woman, avaricious and timorous as well" (III, vi). On his side, Léon resents Emma's domination and the "increased absorption of his personality into hers." It was as though he were her mistress, observes Flaubert, rather than she his. Since he is soon to become head clerk, he feels it is time to settle down, to give up "his exalted sentiments, his poetic imagination." "In the flush of his youth," says Flaubert, "every bourgeois" has "believed himself capable of immense passions, of lofty enterprises. . . . every notary bears within him the débris of a poet." Emma differs from Léon in the persistence of her youthful illusions, but Flaubert does not present her "exalted sentiments" as any less ludicrous than his.

Becoming "as sick of [Léon] as he [is] weary of her," Emma wonders "how to get rid of him" (III, vi), much as Rodolphe had wondered how to get rid of her. She becomes reckless in her behavior and lascivious in her love-making in a desperate effort to keep her passion alive, but she destroys "every pleasure by always wishing for it to be too great." Disappointed again by life, she reads lurid novels in order to gain vicarious excitement and sees another man in her mind's eye while writing to Léon. He is "a phantom fashioned out of her most ardent memories, of her favorite books, her strongest desires." Her phantom lover becomes "so real, so tangible" that she feels he will "ravish her entire being in a kiss."

Emma's affair involves her in an elaborate tissue of lies and contributes to her undoing by plunging her more deeply into debt. She borrows to pay for her trysts with Léon and rejects his suggestion that they meet at a less expensive hotel. It is her luxurious habits, more than anything else, that ultimately lead to her downfall. She needs to surround herself with material refinements in order to confirm her sense of grandeur and avoid the feeling that she is sinking into the mire of ordinary life. Her various forms of romanticism are linked in her mind with elegant accoutrements. Love seems inseparable "from boudoirs with silken curtains and thick carpets, well-filled flower stands, . . . the flashing of precious stones and the golden braid of liveries" (I, ix). When she aspires to become a saint, she buys rosaries, wears holy medals, and wishes to have by her bed "a reliquary set in emeralds" (II, xiv). The romance of motherhood is spoiled before Berthe is born because she cannot spend as much as she would like "on a suspended cradle with rose silk curtains, and embroidered caps" (II, iii). Emma compulsively buys things as a way of keeping up her morale and "soften[ing] the bitterness of her life" (III, vii). Flaubert meticulously details her purchases after every disappointment. The more her other resources fail her, the more she consoles herself with material luxuries, which are a symbol to her of romantic glamour and social superiority.

Emma's compensatory needs, combined with her sense of entitlement, lead her to fall prey to Lheureux. Absorbed in her passions and feeling that she deserves the best, she worries "no more about money matters than an archduchess" (III, vi). Lheureux tempts her with goods and easy credit, and as a result of buying, borrowing, and renewing notes, she runs up of debt of eight thousand francs while having only a dim awareness of what she is doing. When her money troubles close in, she deals with them at first by denial, wishful thinking, and longings for escape. She wants "not to be alive," "to be always asleep," or "to take wing like a bird, and fly off far away to become young again in the realms of immaculate purity" (III, vi). Finally forced to cope with her debt, Emma employs a series of desperate measures. She appeals to Léon, whom she urges to steal the money, and then to the notary, Monsieur Guillaumin, who insults her by seeking sexual favors. Despite her indignation with him, she makes advances to the timid Binet and finally goes to Rodolphe, "unaware that she was hastening to offer what had so angered her a while ago, not in the least conscious of her prostitution" (III, vii). With Rodolphe's refusal, her world crumbles, and she feels that she is going mad.

With all her solutions failing, Emma turns, like Hedda Gabler, to suicide. Like Hedda's, her self-destruction is partly an escape from an intolerable situation and partly a vindictive triumph. Her feeling that she is going mad is a product of both her disappointment in love and her impending financial disaster. Léon has let her down, and Rodolphe, after telling her that he loves her, says that he does not have the money for which she is asking. She had been confident that "one single glance would reawaken" his ardor (III, vi), and at first she seems to have succeeded. Her request for money chills him, however, and the rage and despair Emma felt when he deserted her are revived, along with her profound sense of injustice: she would have "sold all," would "have begged on the high-roads," for a smile or a look from him. At first she "suffer[s] only in her love," but when she returns to Yonville, "her plight, like an abyss, loom[s] before her" (III, viii).

Although her suicide is an escape, and perhaps also a revenge on those who did not take her plight seriously, Emma's mood is not one of despair. She takes arsenic in "an ecstasy of heroism" that makes her "almost joyous," and when no symptoms immediately appear, she believes that death is "but a little thing": "I shall fall asleep and all will be over" (III, viii). Emma is almost joyous because she thinks she has found a way to escape all her suffering in a way that seems glorious to her. She will have fulfilled her duty not to others but to her romantic conception of herself; instead of being a pathetic victim, she will at last have mastered her fate.

Literature is full of protagonists who are granted romantic deaths, who feel that they have actualized their idealized images and then die before they are subject to continued failure, despair, and self-hate. Shakespeare's Antony and Cleopatra (Paris 1991b), Stendhal's Julien Sorel (Paris 1974), and Conrad's Lord Jim (Paris 1974) come to mind; and there are many others, including Antigone, Hedda Gabler, and, as we shall soon see, Edna Pontellier. It is precisely such a death that Flaubert denies Emma Bovary. He describes her physical agony in horrible detail, and the appearance of the hideous blind man shatters the dream of "celestial glory" (III, viii) that had been induced in Emma by the last sacraments. The blind man, who sings of how a young girl loses her virtue by dreaming her heart away, had filled Emma with dread while she was in the midst of her affair with Léon, and when he reappears as she is dying, she is seized by a fear of damnation. At the sound of his "raucous voice," she begins

> to laugh, an atrocious, frantic, desperate laugh, thinking she saw the hideous face of the poor wretch loom out of the eternal darkness like a menace.
>
> The wind blew very hard that day
> It blew her petticoat away.
>
> A final spasm threw her back on the mattress. She had ceased to exist. (III, viii)

At the end, Emma is wedded not to her dream of glory but to her nightmare.

As we have seen, the author's personality is by no means absent from this novel, as both Flaubert and many critics have claimed it to be. There are numerous authorial comments and a satirical treatment of almost every character and set of values. The primary object of Flaubert's satire is Emma's romanticism, which is shown to be foolish, derivative, and destructive. Many critics feel that Flaubert sympathizes with Emma's frustrations, which are blamed on the meanness of bourgeois society. I think that they are not entirely wrong in sensing that it is not only Emma but also Flaubert who is a thwarted romantic. The implied author has inner conflicts that are evident in his ambivalent attitudes.

While the expansive side of Flaubert empathizes with Emma's craving for glory, his moralistic side condemns her, in rather conventional ways, for her pride and adultery. He describes her as corrupt, degenerate, her soul "all shriveled up, like the duke of Clarence in his butt of malmsey" (II, xii). His account of the priest's administration of extreme unction when Emma is dying reflects orthodox attitudes:

> First, upon the eyes, that had so coveted all worldly goods; then upon the nostrils, that had been so greedy of the warm breeze and the scents of love; then upon the mouth, that had spoken lies, moaned in pride and cried out in lust; then upon the hands that had taken delight in the texture of sensuality; and finally upon the soles of the feet, so swift when she had hastened to satisfy her desires. . . . (III, viii)

Flaubert sometimes expresses sympathy with Emma's "poor oppressed heart," but his moral judgment of her is unremitting and severe. When Charles affects bohemian manners after her death, Flaubert describes Emma as corrupting him from beyond the grave.

The dominant side of Flaubert's personality is, of course, his detachment. This results not in the disappearance of the author but in the presence of a pervasive irony which is his defense against the frustration, humiliation, and despair that are the lot of those who allow themselves to expect very much from life. Those who have extremely limited goals, like Binet, or who aggressively pursue crass ones, like Lheureux and Homais, may succeed; but those who hope for more are bound to be mocked by fate. As author, Flaubert plays the role of fate himself, making fools of his dreamers and rewarding only those whose success is not worth the having. What Emma lacks most of all is the "critical detachment" that she momentarily attains during the intermission at the opera and that leads her to smile "inwardly in scornful pity" when the hero reappears (II, xv). Scornful pity is what Flaubert feels toward Emma through most of the novel.

Seemingly afraid both of himself and of life, Flaubert seeks to become invulnerable by repressing his desires. Emma represents a side of himself that he despises, pities, and fears. He needs to expose her folly again and again in order to reinforce his own resignation. What he is telling himself through Emma's story is that there, but for his bitter wisdom, goes he. It is this wisdom in which Flaubert's pride is invested. He pursues his own search for glory by means of critical detachment. He sees men as the victims of their illusions, the sordidness of society, and the mockery of fate. Like Hardy, he seeks to rise above the common lot by being permanently disillusioned, by despising worldly success, and by escaping the mockery of fate through his own superior irony.

There is one character in the novel whom Flaubert admires. This is Dr. Larivière, who is as glamorous a figure as any Emma creates in her fantasies:

> Disdainful of honors, of titles, and of academies, hospitable, generous, fatherly to the poor, and practicing virtue without believing in it, he would almost have passed for a saint if the keenness of his intellect had not caused him to be feared as a demon. His glance, more penetrating than his scalpels, looked straight into your soul, and would detect any lie, regardless of how well hidden. He went through life with the benign dignity that goes with the assurance of talent and wealth, with forty years of hardworking, blameless life. (III, viii)

Dr. Larivière is supposed to have been modeled on Flaubert's father, but he is also an expression, I believe, of Flaubert's idealized image of himself. He harmonizes Flaubert's conflicting needs for goodness, greatness, and critical detachment. He has the insight, talent, and wealth that Flaubert possesses but which are denied to Emma. He is Flaubert's vision of himself as the venerated, disdainful, demonic, benign, dedicated, dignified, and, above all, omniscient artist.

12

The Awakening

The Awakening has frequently been compared to *Madame Bovary*. Like Emma Bovary, Edna Pontellier craves a kind of passion she does not find in marriage, has an extra-marital affair, and commits suicide. Some critics feel that a major difference between the novels is that "the ironic distance of *Madame Bovary* is replaced by a high degree of narrative sympathy" (Walker 1993, 144). As Chopin tells it, Edna's is not a story of romantic folly but of a woman's awakening. Others agree with Willa Cather that Edna Pontellier and Emma Bovary both "belong to a class, not large, but forever clamoring in our ears, that demands more romance out of life than God put into it" (1899, 6).

These contrasting responses reflect one of the major features of the criticism of *The Awakening*: lack of agreement as to the nature of the story. For some the novel is a feminine *Bildungsroman* that depicts a woman's liberation, while for others it is the tale of a woman who does not grow up or who regresses to an early stage of development. There are many other versions of the story as well. The ending has been the subject of the greatest controversy. Is Edna's death a victory or a defeat, a triumph over the forces that would thwart her authenticity or the consequence of psychological problems that compel her to destroy herself?

The critical disagreements are the product not only of differing perspectives but also of contradictions within the novel itself. The indictment of the social system and claims for self-realization that Edna seems intended to illustrate are contradicted by the mimetic depiction of her character, which shows, as Elizabeth Fox-Genovese has observed, that "we are dealing with personal pathology . . . not with social or sexual injustice at all" (Culley 1994, 262). The situation is further complicated by the fact that there are tensions not only between rhetoric and mimesis but within the rhetoric itself. Although the narrator usually presents her heroine as a woman struggling toward freedom and self-realization, she engages at times in a Flaubert-like mockery of Edna's romanticism and describes her as foolish or immature. There are moments when the narrator sees Edna quite clearly. In order to understand the relation between rhetoric and mimesis in this novel, we must first separate the strands of the rhetoric and see how they conflict with each other.

Although the rhetoric is full of contradictions, the mimetic portrait of Edna is consistent. She is not as fully drawn as Emma Bovary, but she is still a well-conceived and fascinating character. Her puzzling behavior has often been misunderstood, but it is intelligible, I believe, if approached from a Horneyan perspective. A psychological analysis of Edna will show that she is far from finding herself and that she is driven to suicide not by external conditions, as many critics contend, but by her inner conflicts.

There is little question that Chopin wants us to see Edna as undergoing a process of liberation and psychological growth. Edna awakens out of a "life-long stupid dream" (ch. 36) of habitual submission to her husband and her society's expectations of her as a woman. She will not be one of the mother-women who idolize their children, worship their husbands, and esteem it "a holy privilege to efface themselves as individuals and grow wings as ministering angels" (ch. 4). During the summer at Grand Isle, she begins to resist her husband's domination, and on her return to New Orleans she frees herself from one after another of her social obligations. She gets in touch with feelings she has suppressed, including her sexuality, and has a sense of becoming more and more herself.

Chopin surrounds these developments with a celebratory rhetoric. When, back in New Orleans, Edna goes out on her at-home day and begins to do as she likes, her husband cannot see that she is "becoming herself and daily casting aside that fictitious self which we assume like a garment with which to appear before the world" (ch. 19). This favorable rhetoric is supported by Dr. Mandelet's observation that Edna has been transformed "from the listless woman he had known" into a being who seems "palpitant with the forces of life. . . . There was no repression in her glance or gesture. She reminded him of some beautiful, sleek animal waking up in the sun" (ch. 24). Later Chopin tells us that every step Edna takes "toward relieving herself from obligations add[s] to her strength and expansion as an individual" (ch. 32). She now apprehends "the deeper undercurrents of life" and no longer feeds on opinion. The narrator does not specify what Edna apprehends, but the reference may be to her sexual awakening. After she is aroused by Arobin's kiss, Edna feels that a "mist [has] been lifted from her eyes," enabling her to comprehend "the significance of life" (ch. 29). She liberates herself not only from the sexual constraints of her culture but also from its treatment of women as property, proclaiming to Robert that she is no longer "one of Mr. Pontellier's possessions" (ch. 36). This is all very stirring and has understandably sparked feminist interest in the novel.

Edna can be seen as a more courageous Hedda Gabler or as a Nora Helmer who must face the consequences of her rebellion. Since *A Doll's House* ends with Nora storming out into the night, Ibsen does not have to imagine what will happen to his heroine. Chopin seems aware from the outset that Edna will not be able to translate her emancipation into a viable way of life. After telling us that Edna has begun to recognize her relation to internal and external realities, Chopin foreshadows the end of the story:

> This may seem like a ponderous weight of wisdom to descend upon the soul of a young woman of twenty-eight—perhaps more wisdom than the Holy Ghost is usually pleased to vouchsafe to any woman.
>
> But the beginning of things, of a world especially, is necessarily vague, tangled, chaotic, and exceedingly disturbing. How few of us ever emerge from such beginning! How many would perish in the tumult! (Ch. 7)

Edna is presented as a pioneer in the struggle for women's liberation who perishes because she knows too much and because the beginning of things is tangled, chaotic, and disturbing. This vague explanation is not developed in the novel, and by the time we reach the end it does not seem to apply to what has happened to Edna.

When Edna learns to swim, Chopin introduces a variation on the theme that she perishes because she is too far in advance of her time. Exulting in her new-found power, Edna grows "daring and reckless," overestimates her strength, and wants "to swim far out, where no woman had swum before" (ch. 10). As she swims out alone, she seems "to be reaching out for the unlimited in which to lose herself." When she realizes how far she has gone, she has "a quick vision of death" and struggles "to regain the land." She tells her husband, "I thought I should have perished out there alone," but he assures her that she had not gone very far and that he was watching her. The message here seems to be that those who try to go where no others have gone before are in danger of perishing. The rhetoric is no longer exculpatory, since it seems to suggest that Edna is too reckless, that she overestimates her strength, and that she is a kind of Icarus figure who aspires to transcend the human condition.

Another important strand of the rhetoric presents Edna as failing to achieve her goals because she lacks sufficient courage. She has a good deal of courage, of course, and acts out her desires rather than trying to gratify them safely through a male, like Hedda Gabler. When she leaves no excuse for being absent on her at-home day, Léonce says "people don't do such things" (ch. 17), and this is certainly something that Hedda never would have done. Hedda's first and last act of rebellion is committing suicide. However, Chopin suggests through Mademoiselle Reisz that, bold though she is, Edna does not have "the courageous soul," "the brave soul," "the soul that dares and defies" (ch. 21). Mademoiselle Reisz tells Edna that "the bird that would soar above the level plain of tradition and prejudice must have strong wings" and that it is "a sad spectacle to see the weaklings bruised, exhausted, fluttering back to earth" (ch. 29).

The bird imagery is important in the novel. When Mademoiselle Reisz plays the piece at Grand Isle that Edna entitles "Solitude," Edna envisions "the figure of a man standing beside a desolate rock on the seashore. He was naked. His attitude was one of hopeless resignation as he looked toward a distant bird winging its flight away from him" (ch. 10). This seems to express Edna's hopelessness at this point about her ability to soar above the level plain. The nakedness of the figure and the fact that it is a man may express her desire for freedom from inhibition and her flight from womanhood. At the end, of course, Edna stands naked on the seashore, hopeless about her ability to soar. A "bird with a broken wing" is "beating the air above, reeling, fluttering, circling disabled down, down to the water" (ch. 39). This is the sad spectacle of which Mademoiselle Reisz had spoken. In her final thoughts, Edna imagines Mademoiselle Reisz laughing, perhaps even sneering, at her: "And you call yourself an artist! What pretensions, Madame! The artist must possess the courageous soul that dares and defies" (ch. 39).

What, according to Chopin, does Edna lack the courage to do? Her list of accomplishments is impressive. She has sloughed off all of her duties and does as she likes. She has freed herself from her husband's domination, had an affair, and declared her love to Robert: "I suppose this is what you would call unwomanly," she says, "but I have got into the habit of expressing myself" (ch. 36). The one thing she cannot do is to be totally indifferent to the welfare of her children. When Chopin introduces Mademoiselle Reisz, she describes her as a "self-assertive" woman with "a disposition to trample upon the rights of others" (ch. 26). Must Edna be ready to trample on the rights of others if she is to soar above the level plain of tradition and prejudice in order to fulfill herself? Is Chopin saying that Edna is destroyed because she is only at the beginning of a movement that will eventually allow women to pursue their desires without being concerned about their children? This seems to be one implication of the rhetoric.

While the rhetoric usually presents Edna's getting in touch with her desires and acting them out as a good thing, one of its strands presents this in a negative way. Emma's experience during her summer at Grand Isle is portrayed both as an awakening and as a regression to the state she was in when she ran through the green meadow as a child. When she explains to Adèle that she was "running away from prayers," her friend asks if she has been running away from prayers ever since: " 'No! oh, no!' Edna hastened to say. 'I was a little unthinking child in those days, just following a misleading impulse without question' " (ch. 7). "Sometimes I feel this summer," she goes on, "as if I were walking through the green meadow again; idly, aimlessly, unthinking, and unguided."

Is Edna getting in touch with herself and striving to develop her human potentialities or unthinkingly following misleading childish impulses? Chopin seems to be supporting both positions. On the day Edna goes to *Chênière* with Robert, she is described as "blindly following whatever impulse moved her, as if she had placed herself in alien hands for direction, and freed her soul of responsibility" (ch. 12). This does not sound like a movement toward self-realization and authenticity. Later, in the same chapter in which Edna is described as "becoming herself" when she gives up her Tuesdays at home, we are informed that she uses her new freedom to lend herself "to any passing caprice" (ch. 19). Robert tells Edna that she lacks "forethought" (ch. 12), and near the end, Madame Ratignolle says that she seems "like a child": "You seem to act without a certain amount of reflection which is necessary in this life" (ch. 33). Are we supposed to see Edna as freeing herself from the social institutions and conventions that infantilize women or as throwing off adult responsibilities so that she can behave in an idle, aimless, unguided way?

Finally, Chopin presents Edna with Flaubertian mockery as a woman who is given to romantic fantasies about unattainable men. Before she reaches puberty Edna becomes "passionately enamored of a dignified and sad-eyed cavalry officer who visit[s] her father" (ch. 7). She cannot "remove her eyes from his face, which [is] something like Napoleon's, with a lock of black hair falling across the forehead." The cavalry officer melts "imperceptibly out of her existence," but in her early teens "her affections [are] deeply engaged" by the fiancé of a lady on a neighboring plantation. The realization that she herself is "nothing, nothing, nothing to the engaged young man [is] a bitter affliction" to Edna, but he, too, goes "the way of dreams." Evidently her passions were not as deep as she had imagined them to be. As a grown young woman, she is "overtaken by what she suppose[s] to be the climax of her fate," as "the face and figure of a great tragedian [begin] to haunt her imagination and stir her senses. The persistence of the infatuation lent it an aspect of genuineness. The hopelessness of it colored it with the lofty tones of a great passion." The tone here is similar to that of *Madame Bovary*.

Courted by Léonce while she is "in the midst of her secret great passion," Edna decides to accept him when she realizes that "the acme of bliss, which would have been a marriage with the tragedian, was not for her in this world" (ch. 7). It is not long before the tragedian goes the way of "the cavalry officer and the engaged young man and a few others." When she marries, Edna feels that she has closed "the portals forever behind her upon the realm of romance and dreams" and has entered the world of reality. She takes satisfaction in the fact that "no trace of passion or excessive and fictitious warmth" colors her affection for her husband, "thereby threatening its dissolution."

Chopin presents Edna's attraction to Robert Lebrun not only as a sexual awakening but also as a return to the realm of romance and dreams, which was not forever closed to her after all. When Robert leaves for Mexico, Edna recognizes in her despondency "the symptoms of infatuation" she had experienced a number of times before, but, like Emma Bovary, she cannot view herself with critical detachment:

> The recognition did not lessen the reality, the poignancy of the revelation [of her love for Robert] by any suggestion or promise of instability. The past was nothing to her; offered no lesson which she was willing to heed. The future was a mystery which she never attempted to penetrate. The present alone was significant; was hers, to torture her as it was doing then with the biting conviction that she had lost that which she had held, that

she had been denied that which her impassioned, newly awakened being demanded. (Ch. 15)

The narrator, who possesses the detachment that Edna lacks, seems almost to make fun of her heroine's impassioned being in this passage. If Edna could heed the lesson of the past, she would realize that what she feels for Robert is just an infatuation that will go the way of her other dreams. But, like a child, she lives entirely in the present and is unable either to imagine the future or learn from the past. Chopin seems sympathetic toward Edna's pain, which is real, but scornful of her immaturity. When Edna returns to New Orleans, she is described as being "still under the spell of her infatuation" (ch. 18).

In part at least, *The Awakening* is, like *Madame Bovary,* a novel of disenchantment. Like Emma, Edna is presented as an unstable person who is happy when she is living in her romantic dreams and despondent when it seems "as if life were passing her by, leaving its promise broken and unfulfilled" (ch. 25). Her depressions do not persist because she is repeatedly "led on and deceived by fresh promises which her youth [holds] out to her." Like Emma Bovary, she is an irrepressible romantic who is doomed to ultimate disenchantment because she demands more of life than it can give.

Edna's final awakening is presented as a recognition of life's realities. After attending Madame Ratignolle's accouchement, during which Adèle urges her to remember the children, Edna tells Dr. Mandelet that she does not want to be forced into doing things, that no one has the right to make demands of her, except perhaps the children.

> "The trouble is," sighed the Doctor, grasping her meaning intuitively, "that youth is given up to illusions. It seems to be a provision of Nature; a decoy to secure mothers for the race. And Nature takes no account of moral consequences, of arbitrary conditions which we create, and which we feel obliged to maintain at any cost."
>
> "Yes," she said. "The years that are gone seem like dreams—if one might go on sleeping and dreaming—but to wake up and find—oh! well! perhaps it is better to wake up after all, even to suffer, rather than to remain a dupe to illusions all one's life." (Ch. 28)

Dr. Mandelet sounds a bit like Thomas Hardy here. The lure of parenthood is one of Dame Nature's vulpine tricks that perpetuates the race but brings misery to individuals. Once people procreate, they are trapped by conditions they feel obliged to maintain. This may not be a problem for nurturing women like Adèle Ratignolle, but Edna, like Hedda Gabler, feels oppressed by "a responsibility for which Fate had not fitted her" (ch. 8). Through much of the novel Edna manages to unburden herself of her children, but at the end she realizes that she cannot escape her maternal responsibilities.

Edna tells Robert that her encounter with him on Grand Isle awakened her out of a life-long stupid dream of habitual submission, but she seems to fall immediately into another dream. On the night she refuses to go to bed despite her husband's insistence, she is eventually forced to yield by fatigue: "Edna began to feel like one who awakens gradually out of a dream, a delicious, grotesque, impossible dream, to feel again the realities pressing into her soul" (ch. 9). Edna is awakening here not from the old dream that had led her to conform but from the new dream of asserting her will and having the freedom to follow her whims. She lives in this second dream after her return to New Orleans but finds it to be grotesque and impossible of fulfillment when the reality of motherhood presses into her soul.

In terms of plot and rhetoric, then, *The Awakening* is a confusing novel. It seems to be telling a number of different stories that are often incompatible with each other. Is it a story of awakening, liberation, and psychological growth, or one of a woman who throws off her adult responsibilities and behaves in an aimless, unthinking, misguided way? Or is it the story of a foolish and irrepressible romantic who is ultimately disenchanted and chooses death to escape reality? Or is it the story of a victim of nature's entrapments who finds herself in a maternal role for which she is not fitted but that she cannot disregard? Is Edna a pioneer in the struggle for women's liberation who perishes because the beginning of things is tangled and chaotic? Or does she perish because she is too daring and reckless, overestimates her strength, and aspires to go where no woman has gone before? Or does she lack the courageous soul that dares and defies, making her unable to rise above the level plain of tradition and prejudice? We can make sense of the novel in terms of each of its strands if we ignore the others, but it seems impossible to integrate them into a unified whole and to say what the novel is really about.

So far I have focused on plot and rhetoric, but another way of approaching the novel is to look at the mimetic depiction of Edna and to ask what story it tells. Although Chopin did not know what to make of

her heroine, she understood her intuitively and had a gift for characterization. A Horneyan approach to the novel will help us to recover
Chopin's psychological intuitions and appreciate her mimetic achievement. When we understand Edna in motivational terms, we shall see
that some of the author's interpretations are more appropriate than
others but that none is adequate to the richness and complexity of the
psychological portrait.

I believe that Elizabeth Fox-Genovese is correct in saying that a
recognition of Edna's personal pathology turns "the indictment of society" into "an individual case history" (Culley 1994, 262). *The Awakening* resembles *Great Expectations* in this respect. Chopin does not begin
by dwelling on Edna's early life, as Dickens dwells on Pip's, but she
provides enough information to enable us to see that the protagonist's
difficulties derive more from compulsive needs and inner conflicts generated in childhood than they do from social conditions. Indeed, it is
impossible to envision any social changes that would have enabled Edna
to feel that she could have a satisfactory life. It is striking that the more
she frees herself from her conventional roles, the more despondent she
becomes. Her problems are related to the patriarchal nature of her
society insofar as it influenced the behavior of her father, the fate of her
mother, and her experiences in the family, but they have little to do with
the conditions against which she rebels as an adult. She reacts to these
conditions so intensely and self-destructively because of a hypersensitivity to constraint that has its origins in her family history.

It is through her father that the young Edna experiences the oppression of the patriarchal order. The only distinct picture we have of her
response to him in childhood is her memory of "running away from
prayers, from the Presbyterian service, read in a spirit of gloom by my
father that chills me yet to think of" (ch. 7). Léonce tells Dr. Mandelet
that Edna's father "used to atone for his week-day sins with his Sunday
devotions" (ch. 23). The Colonel's week-day sins seem to have included
gambling away his blue-grass farm in Kentucky. Our most important
information about Edna's father comes when he reproaches Léonce for
being "too lenient, too lenient by far" with his wife: "Authority, coercion are what is needed. Put your foot down good and hard; the only
way to manage a wife. Take my word for it" (ch. 25). Chopin observes
that "the Colonel was perhaps unaware that he had coerced his wife
into her grave."

Edna grows up, then, with a gloomy, tyrannical father who believes that women must be managed with authority and whose coercion has driven her mother into the grave. She has an impulse to run away from his stern, hypocritical religiosity, but she has nowhere to turn. Her older sister "has all the Presbyterianism undiluted" (ch. 22), and her younger sister is hostile. Edna deals with this situation by retreating into herself: "At a very early period she had apprehended instinctively the dual life—that outward existence which conforms, the inward life which questions" (ch. 7). In order to preserve a sense of inner freedom, she keeps others at a distance and envelops herself in a "mantle of reserve." In describing the adult Edna, Chopin observes that "she had all her life long been accustomed to harbor thoughts and emotions which never voiced themselves. They had never taken the form of struggles. They belonged to her and were her own, and she entertained the conviction that they concerned no one but herself" (ch. 16).

In Horneyan terms, Edna defends herself by becoming detached. She avoids conflict with her environment by being outwardly compliant and keeping her thoughts and emotions to herself. Her compliance is not that of the self-effacing person: she conforms not from a desire to win love, protection, and approval but in order to avoid friction that would disturb her peace and intrude on her inner life. Her secret thoughts and feelings do not generate struggles because she does not consider acting on them. Her environment is too threatening for that. She resigns herself to outward conformity and tries to preserve a sense of freedom by guarding her inner life.

Edna's detachment is a response not only to a coercive environment but also to the absence of love. She loses her mother at an early age and is "not very warmly or deeply attached to her father" (ch. 23). Her older sister Margaret, to whom she must look for nurturing, is described as "practical" rather than "effusive." She is "matronly and dignified, probably from having assumed matronly and house-wifely responsibilities too early in life." Her younger sister, Janet, is a "vixen" with whom Edna quarrels a lot. With no warmth available to her in her family, Edna tries to do without it, especially since intimacy seems dangerous in view of her secret thoughts. Her occasional girl friends all seem to have been "of one type—the self-contained. She never realized that the reserve of her own character had much, perhaps everything, to do with this" (ch. 7). Edna is somewhat startled by the warmth and candor of Adèle Ratignolle, since she is not "given to confidences" herself and is unaccustomed "to an outward and spoken expression of affection."

Edna wants to be self-sufficient, but she cannot help hungering for intimacy and love. Her hunger expresses itself in infatuations that inwardly disturb her "without causing any outward show or manifestation" (ch. 7). Edna "wonder[s] at" this "propensity" because it is so out of keeping with her need for self-control and reserve. Existing secretly in her imagination, her infatuations reflect both her craving for love and her fear of intimacy and emotion. They comprise the love life of a very detached person. Edna is attracted to unavailable men and has no real relationships before her marriage to Léonce. Her passion for the great tragedian perfectly suits her psychological needs. By keeping his picture on her desk, she can engage in her fantasy under everyone's nose "without exciting suspicion or comment." Indeed, she takes a wicked delight in expressing "admiration for his exalted gifts" while passing his photo around. When alone, she sometimes picks up the photograph and "kisse[s] the cold glass passionately." She can kiss it passionately because it is cold glass and not a flesh-and-blood human being. Her mental image of the tragedian "stir[s] her senses" far more than does the actual presence of Léonce Pontellier.

Edna is attracted to Léonce in part because there is "no trace of passion" in her feeling for him (ch. 7). She marries him as a way of getting out from under the paternal roof without having her privacy invaded or subjecting herself to another authoritarian male. Léonce is really a very easy-going husband for the time. He offers her "absolute devotion" and a dignified place in the world. The fact that her father and Margaret are violently opposed to her marriage to a Catholic is an additional attraction, since it gives Edna an opportunity to act out some of her rebellious impulses. She submits to the conventions of marriage, represses her desires for intensity, passion, and merger, and relinquishes her romantic dreams. These never amounted to anything anyway, since they were so out of keeping with her need for emotional distance.

Edna carries the need for distance into her marriage, in which she behaves in a very detached way. Léonce's primary complaint is that while she is "the sole object of his existence," she evinces "little interest in things which concerned him" (ch. 3). She is also inattentive to her children and feels a great sense of relief whenever they are taken off her hands. As a married woman, Edna follows her practice of conforming outwardly in order to be left alone. There is less struggle than ever because her conformity seems to have deadened her inward questioning. She habitually yields to Léonce's desires, "not with any sense of submission or obedience to his compelling wishes, but unthinkingly, as we walk, move, sit, stand, go through the daily treadmill of the life which has been portioned out to us" (ch. 12). She awakens from this almost somnambulistic state during the summer on Grand Isle.

One of the major changes that occurs in Edna during that summer is that she moves from a passive, resigned form of detachment to an active rebellion against the constraints imposed by marriage, motherhood, religion, and society's expectations of her as a woman. When Léonce reproaches her for "her habitual neglect of the children," "an indescribable oppression" fills "her whole being with a vague anguish," and she has a crying spell (ch. 4). Edna "could not have told why she was crying," but she appears to be oppressed by both her husband's reproaches and her duties as a mother, against which she has passively rebelled by being inattentive. Edna's detachment involves a resistance to obligations that is intensified, ironically, by her intimacy with Adèle. While this relationship makes her less detached in that it breaks down her reserve, it also leads her to get in touch with some of the rebellious feelings she has repressed.

The memory that surfaces as she talks with Adèle is of the day when she ran away from prayers read in a spirit of gloom by her father. She had been religious "by habit" since the age of twelve, but now she begins to question her unthinking conformity (ch. 7). Edna feels that she is returning this summer to the aimless, impulsive, unguided state that she was in when she walked through the green meadow that day. This had been a passing episode in her youth, but it is memorable to her because she was acting out her detached desires to follow her impulses and to be free of authority. She reenacts it, in a way, when she blindly follows her impulses by going to Chênière with Robert and then flees from "the stifling atmosphere of the church" she attends there (ch. 13).

Once they rise to the surface, Edna's desires to be free of authority and to follow her impulses become stronger and stronger, first on Grand Isle and then in New Orleans. When Léonce tries to assert his authority by telling her that he "can't permit" her to stay outside and that she "must come in the house instantly," Edna's "will" blazes up, "stubborn and resistant," and she cannot understand why she had "submitted to his command" before (ch. 12). "Don't speak to me like that again," she tells him; "I shall not answer you." It seems likely that Edna had long harbored desires to rebel against the coerciveness of her father but had never dared to act upon them, except, perhaps, in the matter of her marriage. Léonce, however, is a much less formidable figure. He is a doting, indulgent husband, emotionally bound to her, who cannot cope with her defiance. The feebleness of his response intensifies her rebelliousness and allows her to experience her need for freedom with increasing urgency.

Edna's growing impulsiveness should be understood, I think, not as a regression to an infantile state but as an expression of her detached personality, with its need for freedom and independence. No doubt because of her father's coerciveness, she has a hypersensitivity to all forms of constraint that she has repressed and concealed because of its dangerousness. She deals with it by resignation, automatic conformity, and the cultivation of a secret inner life that is nobody's business but her own. When her repression and conformity break down during the summer on Grand Isle, her hypersensitivity rises to the surface, and she begins to behave impulsively as a way gaining the sense of freedom and independence she craves.

The more randomly Edna behaves, the more she feels that she is her own master. By "blindly following whatever impulse move[s] her" (ch. 12), she "free[s] her soul" of the "responsibility" that is so oppressive to detached people like Edna, Jake Horner, and Hedda Gabler. Once she learns to swim, that activity becomes associated in her mind with the power to do what she wants, to go her own way. She plunges and swims "about with an abandon that thrill[s] and invigorate[s] her" (ch. 16). As she sails to the *Chênière Caminada* with Robert, she delights in the feeling that she is "being borne away from some anchorage which had held her fast, whose chains had been loosening . . . leaving her free to drift whithersoever she chose to set her sails" (ch. 12). Edna has felt like a prisoner in chains. As is characteristic of the detached person, she craves *freedom from* constraint rather than *freedom to* fulfill herself. The main thing she wants to do with her freedom is to drift.

Edna's rebellion against authority escalates when she returns to New Orleans. She goes out on her at-home day and allows herself to feel her anger when Léonce, dissatisfied with dinner, storms out to dine at the club. Such scenes had "often made her very unhappy," but now they fill her with rage. She takes off her wedding ring, flings it on the carpet, and tries to crush it with her heel. When she cannot even make a mark upon it, she shatters a glass vase against the hearth: "She wanted to destroy something. The crash and clatter were what she wanted to hear" (ch. 18). Chopin tells us that Edna is "seeking and finding herself," and in a sense this is true. She is getting in touch with the resentment and fury she has been suppressing, first in her father's house and then in her marriage. This is not the same thing as finding her real self, however, since what she is uncovering are her responses to oppressive conditions rather than the spontaneous feelings she would have had in a nurturing environment. In a therapeutic setting, experiencing such rage can be a stage in psychological growth, but getting in touch with her anger does not help Edna to find herself.

Edna does not repeat her outburst but instead throws off her outward compliance and begins "to do as she like[s], and to feel as she like[s]" (ch. 19). She abandons her Tuesdays at home, does not return the visits of callers, and gives up the effort "to conduct her household *en bonne ménagère.*" She takes up painting, but in a dilettantish way, since she has no ambition and only wants to work "when in the humor" (ch. 25). For the most part, she seeks to gain a sense of freedom by coming and going "as it suit[s] her fancy" and lending herself to any passing caprice (ch. 19). Chopin describes such behavior as "becoming herself," and perhaps that is the way Edna experiences it, but I think that Léonce is right "to wonder if his wife were not growing a little unbalanced mentally." Instead of becoming more herself, she is becoming more compulsively impulsive and detached.

When Léonce is shocked and angered by "her absolute disregard for her duties as a wife," Edna responds by telling him, "Let me alone; you bother me" (ch. 19). Edna wants to be left alone, not to be bothered, and Chopin so arranges things that she is granted her wish. Léonce leaves for a long stay in New York, and the children visit their grandmother. These departures give Edna a pang, but "a radiant peace settle[s] upon her when she at last [finds] her self alone" and her time is "completely her own to do with as she like[s]" (ch. 25). A "sense of restfulness invade[s] her, such as she ha[s] not known before."

After Léonce's departure, Edna takes additional steps to free herself. She moves out of their house to a small one, dubbed "the pigeon-house." One of her reasons for doing this is that she is "tired of looking after" the large house with all its servants; she wants fewer burdens and responsibilities (ch. 26). Her primary motive is to achieve a greater "feeling of freedom and independence" by no longer relying on Léonce. She will support herself out of her inheritance from her mother, her winnings at the racetrack, and the sale of her sketches; and when she moves, she takes only the things that are hers. She resolves "never again to belong to another than herself" and feels that her financial autonomy frees her of her "allegiance" to her husband. She exercises this freedom by having an affair with Alcée Arobin.

Perhaps a less conscious motive for her move to the pigeon-house is that it is too small for a family. "Where on earth," asks Adèle, "was she going to put Mr. Pontellier in that little house, and the boys?" (ch. 33). There is no place in Edna's new life for either her husband or her children. When she tells the boys about the house during a visit to Iberville, they ask where they and papa will sleep. Edna's reply is that "the fairies would fix it all right" (ch. 32). She is living in a dream from which she awakens at the end.

At Edna's dinner party, given on her twenty-ninth birthday (Hedda Gabler's age) before she moves out of Léonce's house, she seems to be in control of her life: "There was something in her attitude . . . which suggested the regal woman, the one who rules, who looks on, who stands alone" (ch. 30). But Chopin goes on to say that, as Edna sat among her guests,

> she felt the old ennui overtaking her; the hopelessness which so often assailed her, which came upon her like an obsession, like something extraneous, independent of volition. It was something which announced itself; a chill breath that seemed to issue from some vast cavern wherein discords wailed. There came over her the acute longing which always summoned into her spiritual vision the presence of the beloved one, overpowering her at once with a sense of the unattainable. (Ch. 30)

Edna seems to have attained the power to make her own choices and the freedom from interference to which she has aspired, but she feels an ennui and hopelessness over which she has no control and is full of inner discords. Since her hopelessness seems to derive from her longing for an unattainable beloved, she is *not* the regal woman who is content to look on and stand alone. To comprehend why Edna is so unhappy despite the progress she seems to have made, we must return to the summer at Grand Isle.

In addition to her wish to be free of authority and to follow her impulses, other desires are aroused in Edna that summer. As we have seen, the young Edna had cravings for intimacy and love that expressed themselves in the form of romantic fantasies about inaccessible men. Under the influence of Adèle Ratignolle and Robert Lebrun, this side of Edna's nature reemerges, more highly eroticized than before. There are passages suggesting not only the stirrings of desire in relation to Robert but also autoerotic feelings and a homoerotic attraction to Adèle. Much has been made of Edna's sexual awakening, and I do not wish to minimize its importance, but the revival of her romanticism is the more significant development, since it is the source of much of her later hopelessness and inner discord.

Edna's latent romanticism is stirred by her "night in a dream" (ch. 11). That afternoon, "the unaccustomed taste of candor" in her conversation with Adèle had "muddled her like wine, or like a first breath of freedom" (ch. 7). Edna had never before opened herself to another person. In the evening, Mademoiselle Reisz's playing further liberates her feelings, and she experiences a pang of self-pity as she recognizes her hopelessness about ever fulfilling her dreams. This is followed by Robert's suggestion that they all go into the water "at that mystic hour and under that mystic moon" (ch. 10), and, after having tried unsuccessfully all summer, Edna finally learns to swim. Intoxicated by "her newly conquered power," she wants to "swim far out, where no woman has swum before." Roused from her hopeless resignation, Edna immediately begins to dream of great things.

The climax of the evening is Edna's conversation with Robert, in which she wonders if "any night on earth will ever again be like this one" (ch. 10). Robert exalts her as a demi-goddess who has been selected by the spirit who haunts the gulf and fears that perhaps she "will never again suffer a poor, unworthy earthling to walk in the shadow of her divine presence." Feeling herself to be the object of a grand passion, Edna experiences "the first-felt throbbings of desire" and refuses to go in at Léonce's command. The delicious impossible dream from which she awakens when fatigue forces her to go to bed is not only of freedom but also of romantic fulfillment.

Edna reenters her dream of freedom and romance on the following day, when, under the aegis of the "mystic spirit," she is borne away from the anchorage in which she had been held fast in chains and sails to *Chênière* with Robert. They fantasize about further excursions, in one of which the Gulf spirit will direct Edna to the island where treasures are hidden. Later in New Orleans, when stories are being exchanged at a dinner party, Edna tells "of a woman who paddled away with her lover one night in a pirogue and never came back. They were lost amid the Baratarian Islands, and no one ever heard of them or found trace of them from that day to this" (ch. 24). The narrator tells us that the story is "a pure invention"; "perhaps it was a dream she had had."

The fantasy Edna has woven around Robert helps us to understand why she is so distraught when he goes to Mexico: he has reawakened her longing for a grand romance and then left her frustrated. She has become so emotionally dependent on him that his departure takes "the brightness, the color, the meaning out of everything," leaving "a void and wilderness behind" (ch. 16). Her "whole existence [is] dulled, like a faded garment which seems to be no longer worth wearing."

Edna's experience in her family generated needs for freedom and for love. In youth, she deals with the conflict between these needs by developing romantic fantasies about inaccessible men. When she marries, she gives up her fantasies but remains detached and becomes passive and resigned. During the summer on Grand Isle, her needs for freedom and romance are both reawakened, and they become more intense as the novel proceeds. Neither need can be satisfied, since Edna wants absolute freedom and a grand passion that occurs only in dreams. To make matters worse, the needs are in conflict with each other. The more obsessed Edna becomes with freedom, the less possible it is for her to be emotionally bound to another person.

As an adult, Edna tries once again to reconcile her contradictory needs through fantasy, but she does not always succeed. On her happy days she likes "to wander alone into strange and unfamiliar places. She discovered many a sunny, sleepy corner, fashioned to dream in. And she found it good to dream and to be alone and unmolested" (ch. 20). She has here both the solitude and freedom from interference that she craves and dreams of love through which she can escape her sense of isolation. There are unhappy days, however, "when it did not seem worthwhile to be glad or sorry, to be alive or dead; when life appeared to her like a grotesque pandemonium and humanity like worms struggling blindly toward inevitable annihilation. She could not work on such a day, nor weave fancies to stir her pulses and warm her blood." On such days, she seems to be suffering from what Jake Horner calls cosmopsis, the cosmic view, which paralyzes her as it does him.

Edna oscillates between losing herself in dreams and feeling that life is absurd. In a way, she is a combination of Emma Bovary and Flaubert. Like Emma, she often feels that life is leaving its promise unfulfilled but is repeatedly led on by youthful dreams. Like Flaubert, she is a detached observer who sees through the illusions and follies of mankind. There are times when she looks at life from a very great distance indeed. She remembers awakening after having given birth "to find a new little life to which she had given being, added to the great unnumbered multitude of souls that come and go" (ch. 38). This is an extraordinary reaction for a new mother. Her detachment here is perhaps closer to Hardy's than to Flaubert's.

Edna oscillates also between seeking freedom and independence— aspiring to be the regal woman who looks on and stands alone—and feeling despair because of her "acute longing" for Robert, which overpowers her "with a sense of the unattainable" (ch. 30). She becomes increasingly despondent despite her growing liberation because of her hopelessness about fulfilling her romantic dreams. Edna has no inner core, no self-realizing aspirations that her freedom enables her to pursue. Like the shallow-living detached people whom Horney describes, she needs external stimulation, perhaps even danger, to dispel her ennui, fill her inner emptiness, and make her feel alive.

Although Edna's romantic dreams are an expression of her need for love, she is not looking for the kind of domestic bliss that her friend Adèle has found. To her the "fusion" of the Ratignolles is repugnant, and she feels that "domestic harmony" such as theirs would bring "an appalling and hopeless ennui" (ch. 18). She pities their "colorless existence," the "blind contentment" that would never give them a "taste of life's delirium." Like Emma Bovary, Edna is often "restless and excited" and wants "something to happen—something, anything" (ch. 25). She pursues excitement by gambling at the racetrack and associating with a man like Alcée Arobin. It is only a grand passion, however, such as she envisions with Robert, that can give her a taste of life's delirium. Thus, despite the celebration of her impending freedom at her birthday dinner, she feels overtaken by ennui.

The aspect of Edna's behavior that I have the most difficulty understanding is her becoming involved with Alcée Arobin just after she learns from Mademoiselle Reisz that Robert left because he loved her and that he is about to return. She responds to Arobin's kiss that evening, and she begins an affair with him the night that she moves out of her husband's house. Nonetheless, she expects Robert to seek her out "at the very first hour" of his return and to express or betray "in some way his love for her" (ch. 33). I do not quite know what to make of this. In terms of rhetoric, Chopin may be emphasizing the speciousness of Edna's romanticism by having her become involved in a purely physical relationship with Arobin despite the imminence of Robert's return. But what is Edna's motivation? Is it simply an ungovernable craving for immediate sexual gratification? She has been sexually awakened, to be sure, but her needs thus far do not seem to have been overpowering. How does she reconcile her affair with Arobin with what she feels to be her exalted passion for Robert and her expectation that he will declare his love? Thematically, her relationship with Arobin seems to parallel Robert's liaison with the Vera Cruz girl. Is Chopin saying that if men can have casual sex while romantically devoted to another, women can do the same? Is she attacking the double standard? Perhaps, but such a thematic reading does not explain Edna's motivations. Does the prospect of Robert's return arouse her fears of emotional closeness and dependency, and does she need to confirm her sense of freedom and independence by having an affair? While longing for union with Robert, does she need to prove that she does not belong to any man? This may be the best explanation.

In any event, when Robert returns it seems at first "as if [Edna's] dreams [are] coming true after all" (ch. 33). She becomes "a prey to despondency" when he does not call on her after their initial reunion (ch. 35). Then she meets him by chance, boldly declares her love, and tries to take possession of him: "Now you are here we shall love each other, my Robert. We shall be everything to each other. Nothing else in the world is of any consequence" (ch. 36). But she is called away to be with Adèle during her delivery, and when she returns Robert has left because he loves her too much to destroy her standing in society. Edna does not commit suicide because of Robert's departure, however, but because of problems she would have had even if he had remained.

What happens at the end is that Edna awakens from her dream of freedom and love and feels trapped by reality and her inner conflicts. Her suicide, like Hedda Gabler's, has many motives, serves many needs, and is both a triumph and a defeat.

Edna's dream of freedom is shattered when Adèle, after having had a difficult delivery, urges her to "Think of the children. . . . Oh think of the children! Remember them!" (ch. 27). Edna, of course, has been trying to forget the children. We are told early on that she is not one of the mother-women, like Adèle, but she is drawn to Adèle, admires her, and cannot free herself entirely from her sense of maternal responsibility. This clashes with her need for freedom, which has become so intense that she has a phobic reaction to anything that impinges on her. When Dr. Mandelet asks if she will be going abroad with Léonce when he returns, she says, "I'm not going to be forced into doing things. . . . I want to be let alone. Nobody has any right—except children, perhaps—and even then, it seems to me—or it did seem—" (ch. 38). Edna's bargain has been that if she asked nothing of anyone else, no one would have a right to ask anything of her—hence her need not to be beholden to her husband. But once Adèle asserts the rights of the children, Edna can no longer maintain her claim to be let alone. "I don't want anything," she explains to Dr. Mandelet, "but my own way. That is wanting a good deal, of course, when you have to trample upon the lives, the hearts, the prejudices of others—but no matter—still, I shouldn't want to trample upon the little lives."

Edna's inner conflict has been indicated by the fact that she is drawn to both Madame Ratignolle and Mademoiselle Reisz, women who embody opposite solutions. Madame Ratignolle is a self-effacing woman, whereas Mademoiselle Reisz has a self-assertive temper and a disposition to trample on the rights of others. At first, Mademoiselle Reisz's influence appears to be stronger; but she cannot ignore Madame Ratignolle's pleas to think of the children, to remember them. When Dr. Mandelet says that she should not have been at the delivery, Edna answers "indifferently," "I don't know that it matters after all. One has to think of the children some time or other" (ch. 38). She recognizes that she would eventually have had to confront her maternal responsibilities and resigns herself to the fact that she could not have brought herself to disregard them. It is her inability to free herself from her sense of obligation to her children that prevents her from soaring above the level plain of tradition and prejudice.

Even before she returns home to find Robert gone, Edna feels doomed by her determination to think of the children, which "had driven into her soul like a death wound" (ch. 38). Her dilemma is that she can neither free herself of her responsibilities nor bear the feeling of being coerced by them: "The children appeared before her like antagonists who had overcome her; who had overpowered and sought to drag her into the soul's slavery for the rest of her days" (ch. 39). Edna's feeling of enslavement is, in part at least, the result of her hypersensitivity to any form of constraint, which has become intolerable to her. She has entirely lost her capacity for outward conformity. The children would interfere with her life not only by disrupting her plans for an independent existence in the pigeon-house but also by depriving her of sexual freedom: "She had said over and over to herself: 'To-day it is Arobin; tomorrow it will be some one else. It makes no difference to me, it doesn't matter about Léonce Pontellier—but Raoul and Etienne!' " She feels that she would be indifferent to the consequences of her behavior and that Léonce's suffering does not matter, but the children would be socially stigmatized. She decides "to elude them" by committing suicide.

As Edna conceives it, her suicide is a way not only of eluding her children but also of fulfilling her responsibility to them. During one of her conversations with Adèle on Grand Isle, she had said that "she would never sacrifice herself for her children, or for any one": "I would give my life for my children; but I wouldn't give myself" (ch. 16). Not understanding Edna's distinction, Adèle replies that "a woman who would give her life for her children could do no more than that." Since she identifies her "self" with the freedom to follow her impulses, Edna feels that if she remained alive she would have to sacrifice her self for her children. By sacrificing her life, she will avoid the unbearable feeling of being enslaved and will protect her children from the shame she would have brought upon them if she insisted on having her own way. Neither they nor Adèle will be able to reproach her. As she swims out to her death, she thinks of Léonce and the children: "They were a part of her life. But they need not have thought that they could possess her body and soul" (ch. 39).

One reason why Edna commits suicide, then, is that, in her society, if she behaves as she likes she will harm her children, and she cannot resolve her inner conflict between the need to be absolutely free and the need to fulfill her responsibilities as a mother. It is important to recognize, however, that if Edna had possessed the courageous soul that dared to defy the duties of motherhood, or if she had lived in a society in which her sexual behavior would not have harmed her children, she would still have been trapped by her conflicting needs for freedom and love. Her romantic fantasies would still have collapsed, leaving her to face the prospect of continued loneliness and despondency in a series of meaningless liaisons. There are no social changes that could resolve Edna's psychological problems.

It is not only her dream of freedom from which Edna awakens at the end but also her dream of romantic love. Robert's departure is a blow, of course, but she knows that he still loves her. The decisive factor is her realization "that the day would come when he, too, and the thought of him would melt out of her existence, leaving her alone" (ch. 39). This is the realization she fails to have when Robert leaves for Mexico—that her infatuations are not the grand passions she thinks them to be and that they will all go the way of dreams. She tells Robert that they will be everything to each other, that nothing else is of any consequence, but her vision of their relationship could never have been actualized. Before she knows that Robert has left, she tells Dr. Mandelet that she wants to be let alone and that she does not want anything but her own way. Her detachment is the most powerful force in her personality and is hardly compatible with her romantic dream of merger with her lover. Her freedom is more important to her than anything else.

After Edna returns to find Robert gone, she becomes despondent and plans her suicide. She is so disenchanted and paralyzed that there is "no one thing in the world that she desire[s]" (ch. 39). Every desire seems either futile or in conflict with another. Suicide provides an escape from her inner conflicts and external pressures, while giving her a sense both of freedom and righteousness. Although she is driven to it by her dilemma, she has the illusion of choice.

Edna seems to experience committing suicide, in part at least, as a triumph, as a fulfillment of her desires for freedom and love. There are a number of images of freedom. Disliking the confinement of clothing, like many detached people, she throws off her "unpleasant, pricking garments," stands "naked under the sky," and feels like a "new-born creature" (ch. 39). As she swims out, she thinks "of the blue-grass meadow that she had traversed when a little child, believing that it had no beginning and no end." The meadow is associated with her flight from her father's coercion. Instead of being narrow and restrictive, like her everyday world, the meadow seems to present a limitless expanse. In this respect, it resembles the sea in which she is immersing herself. As exhaustion begins to overcome her, she hears the voices of repression (her father and her sister Margaret) and "the barking of an old dog that was chained to the sycamore tree." She may be reminding herself through these images of confinement of the enslavement she is escaping.

Edna's merger with the sea is presented as a kind of erotic fulfillment: "The touch of the sea is sensuous, enfolding the body in its soft, close embrace" (ch. 39). The sea is a lover with whom she can be alone and unencumbered. It offers her the combination of solitude, freedom, and union that she requires because of her inner conflicts. She has found this combination before only in her fantasies, one of which recurs as she hears "the spurs of the cavalry officer" just before she drowns. This seems to suggest that she dies with an illusory sense not only of freedom but also of romantic fulfillment.

Edna also experiences committing suicide as a defeat. She imagines that Mademoiselle Reisz would laugh, perhaps even sneer, at her "if she knew"—if she knew, presumably, that Edna was killing herself because she lacked "the courageous soul that dares and defies" (ch. 39). Edna despises herself because she cannot actualize her idealized image of herself as the woman who goes where no other has gone, who can soar above the level plain of tradition and prejudice. She is caught, as we have seen, in a crossfire of conflicting shoulds: if she lives up to the inner dictates of her detached solution she will hate herself for trampling upon the little lives, but if she does her duty as a mother she will hate herself for allowing herself to be enslaved. She tries to escape her self-hate by committing suicide, and she partially succeeds, but she cannot help imagining the truly unencumbered woman, Mademoiselle Reisz, sneering at her.

In a relatively brief novel, Kate Chopin has created a remarkably rich mimetic portrait of her heroine. She has grasped Edna's conflicting needs and portrayed her behavior with considerable subtlety. At the same time, she has presented a bewildering picture of Edna in terms of plot and rhetoric. She seems confused about the nature and meaning of her heroine's story. Her confusion may be partly the result of Edna's complexity, which escapes her conscious understanding, but it is also the result of her psychological conflicts. I am speaking here of the implied author, the Chopin we infer from the text.

Like her heroine, Chopin oscillates between detached, self-effacing, and aggressive tendencies. The detached side of Chopin sympathizes with Edna's desire for freedom and independence, celebrates her rebellion against the constraints imposed by marriage, family, and her feminine role, and mocks Edna's dreams of romantic love and her deception by the fresh promises held out to her by her youth. Her aggressive side is aligned with her detachment. She seems to criticize Edna for not having the courage to trample on the rights of others, including her children, when that is what she must do in order to gain her freedom. Her self-effacing side is expressed in her admiration for Madame Ratignolle, through whom she insists on Edna's maternal responsibilities, in her repeated suggestions that Edna's capriciousness is misguided and immature, and in her sympathy with Edna's longings for love and merger.

Chopin cannot resolve the conflict between these tendencies, any more than can Edna, and she is ambivalent toward all of them. She is attracted to both Madame Ratignolle and Mademoiselle Reisz, but she is also critical of each from the point of view of the opposing solutions they represent. She is also ambivalent toward Edna's demands for freedom and her desire to follow her passing caprices. Sometimes she presents Edna's impulsiveness as a sign that she is being true to herself, while at other times she seems aware of how compulsive and self-destructive is Edna's need for absolute freedom and how little happiness she derives from her increasing independence. While presenting her heroine's story as one of a woman's liberation, she seems to know that Edna is in deep psychological trouble and that she cannot find her way out of it.

Because of her inner conflicts, Chopin creates a thematic morass out of which she cannot find *her* way. From an aggressive perspective Edna's rebellion does not go far enough, but from a self-effacing one it goes too far. The dream of freedom from which Edna awakens when fatigue forces her to go to bed is described as "grotesque" as well as "delicious" (ch. 12). When Léonce remonstrates with Edna for spending so much of her time in her atelier, Edna replies: "I feel like painting. . . . Perhaps I shan't always feel like it." "Then in God's name paint!" says Léonce, "but don't let the family go to the devil" (ch. 19). This is not, on the face of it, unreasonable. Léonce wonders if his wife is "not growing a little unbalanced mentally." Although Chopin dismisses this by saying that he "could not see that she was becoming herself," Chopin has allowed Léonce to give expression to some of her own misgivings.

Chopin's ambivalences are what make the novel, and especially the ending, open to so many conflicting interpretations. She mocks Edna's fantasies, but, like Flaubert, she empathizes with the protagonist's romantic aspirations even as she satirizes them, and she sympathizes with Edna's frustrations even though they are the fruit of her folly. Unlike Flaubert, she takes pity on her heroine and grants her a death in which her cravings for love and freedom are fulfilled, if only fleetingly, in her erotic union with the sea. But she cannot resist introducing Edna's fears that Mademoiselle Reisz is sneering at her and also the bird with the broken wing that is "reeling, fluttering, circling disabled down, down to the water" (ch. 39).

13

Wuthering Heights

In the opening chapter of this book, I observed that a Horneyan approach has led me to see that in realistic literature there are almost bound to be disparities between representation and interpretation, mimesis and rhetoric, and that I have also come to realize that these disparities can be either exacerbated or reduced by the choice of narrative technique. They are exacerbated by omniscient narrators, who by convention are supposed to be authoritative, and diminished by first person narration, in which interpretations and judgments express the point of view of a character. First person narration may not eliminate the tensions between rhetoric and mimesis, however, since the perspectives of self-serving narrators, such as Pip and Jane Eyre, often seem to be endorsed by the implied authors. As we have just seen in the case of *The Awakening*, in addition to disparities between rhetoric and mimesis, there may also be inconsistencies within the rhetoric. Chopin presents Edna from a variety of perspectives that cannot be reconciled with each other.

A comparison of *Wuthering Heights* with the other novels we have studied will show just how much difference narrative technique can make. Because Emily Brontë employs multiple narrators, none of whom is endowed with authority, I do not find a disparity between rhetoric and mimesis in this novel. Indeed, it is very difficult to locate the implied author's rhetorical stance. She seems to have disappeared from this novel, much as Flaubert *thought* he had done from *Madame Bovary*. As in *The Awakening*, characters are presented from a variety of perspectives, leaving us with a sense of bewilderment, but *Wuthering Heights* avoids thematic confusion through its impressionistic technique. Each of its narrators gives us an *ex parte* account of events, but since no perspective is privileged, its limitations belong to the character rather than to the implied author, and we do not have to reconcile it with the others. Emily Brontë had at least as many inner conflicts as Kate Chopin, but she found a way of giving expression to the different sides of her personality that enriches rather than damages her art.

Before we examine the novel's narrative technique, we must first consider the characters whose story is being told. Unlike most critics, I believe that Heathcliff and Cathy are imagined human beings whose behavior can be understood in motivational terms. One of the major questions in both the novel and the criticism is what kind of a being is Heathcliff. In the novel, the question is posed most directly by Isabella: "Is Mr. Heathcliff a man? If so, is he mad? And if not, is he a devil?" (ch. 13). When she flees from the Heights, Isabella calls him an "incarnate goblin" and a "monster" and wishes that "he could be blotted out of creation" (ch. 17). Nelly replies, "Hush, hush! He's a human being" and urges Isabella to "be more charitable." Nelly is the chief proponent of Heathcliff's human status. Watching his agony at the death of Catherine, she thinks, "Poor wretch!. . . you have a heart and nerves the same as your brother men!" (ch. 16). Near the end, however, even Nelly wonders if Heathcliff is "a ghoul, or a vampire" (ch. 34).

The issue for critics has not been whether Heathcliff is a ghoul or a human being, but whether he is a realistically drawn figure or some other kind of character about whom it is inappropriate to ask motivational questions. A common view has been that as a character in a Gothic romance, he is an archetype, symbol, or projection of the unconscious who is not supposed to be understood as though he were a person. I believe that Emily Brontë meant Heathcliff to be perceived as a human being, since despite the aura of mystery with which she surrounds the question of his nature, she is at pains to make his behavior seem naturalistically motivated. As Frances Russell Hart observes, the Gothic represents not "a flight from novel to romance," but "a naturalizing of myth and romance into novel" (1968, 103). The central experience it offers is a "dreadful, sublime shock to one's complacently enlightened idea of human character and the reality to which it belongs" (88). In order for the Gothic to achieve this shock, its characters must be imagined human beings whose behavior, however strange, is psychologically credible.

Heathcliff retains his human status, however fiendlike he becomes, because Emily Brontë keeps telling us that he has been victimized and that his viciousness arises from his misery. Perhaps the strongest evidence that she meant us to see his cruelty as a natural phenomenon is the fact that several characters articulate the principle that bad treatment leads to vindictiveness and several others illustrate its operation. Even the pampered, innocuous Linton girls turn savage after a brief exposure to Heathcliff. After her escape, Isabella lusts for revenge. Sounding much like Heathcliff, she wants to "take an eye for an eye, a tooth for a tooth; for every wrench of agony [to] return a wrench, [to] reduce him to my level" (ch. 17). And Nelly observes of the young Catherine that "the more hurt she gets, the more venomous she grows" (ch. 30). Abuse quickly generates powerful vindictive impulses in these girls, and their sufferings are trivial compared to what Heathcliff endured in childhood.

I believe that the failure to understand Heathcliff as a person has two main sources. The first is that many critics have entertained a view of the novel as predominantly metaphysical, lyric, or Gothic that has prevented them from even attempting to make sense of Heathcliff's behavior. The second is that Heathcliff's love for Cathy and his vindictiveness toward the Earnshaws and the Lintons have seemed so extreme as to be beyond the pale of human nature. Critics have deemed Heathcliff unrealistic, in effect, because his behavior has escaped their comprehension. There is always the possibility that the author's intuitive grasp of psychological phenomena is deeper than our conceptual understanding. We can recover Emily Brontë's intuitions, I believe, with the aid of Karen Horney, assisted by R. D. Laing and Abraham Maslow. Heathcliff's vindictiveness and devotion to Cathy are both intelligible as defensive reactions to the deprivation and abuse to which he was subjected in childhood.

According to Abraham Maslow (1970), all humans have a set of basic needs that must be reasonably well met if they are to develop in a healthy way. In the order of their potency, these are physiological survival needs, needs for safety, for love and belonging, for esteem, and for self-actualization. Frustration of the basic needs arrests development and leads individuals to develop defensive strategies for making up their deficiencies. If we consider Heathcliff's childhood with the basic needs in mind, it is evident that he was severely deprived. Mr. Earnshaw finds him at about the age of six "starving and houseless, and as good as dumb in the streets of Liverpool" (ch. 4). He appears to have been abandoned by his family and to have lost, or never fully acquired, the art of language. When Mr. Earnshaw picks him up, his very survival is in jeopardy. He has been living, for we know not how long, in a state that is radically devoid of safety, love and belonging, and esteem.

When Mr. Earnshaw brings him home, Heathcliff has a protector at last; but he meets with contempt and rejection from the other members of the household. Everyone refers to him as "it"; and Nelly, the children, and Mrs. Earnshaw would all like him to disappear. He gradually gains a place in the family, but it is never a secure one, and he is always an object of hostility. When Mr. Earnshaw dies, Heathcliff is entirely dependent on Hindley, who hates him. He has only one relationship that makes him feel secure, and that is with Cathy. It is no wonder that he clings to her with such intensity.

Heathcliff is a severely deprived, frequently abused child who develops all three of Horney's interpersonal strategies of defense. The very reserved Lockwood describes him as "a man who seemed more exaggeratedly reserved than myself" (ch. 1). In addition to his exaggerated withdrawal, Heathcliff displays extreme forms of aggression and compliance. All the suggestions of demonism, vampirism, and ghoulishness derive from his unrelenting vindictiveness and his sadistic delight in the suffering of his victims. His frantic dependency on Cathy is one of the most intense emotions in all of literature. It is so extreme that many critics feel it can be explained only in metaphysical terms. Unlike most of the people Horney describes, Heathcliff avoids inner conflict not by subordinating any of his trends, but by a process of compartmentalization. He moves toward Cathy, against Hindley and the Lintons, and away from everyone else.

Heathcliff's initial defense is detachment. When Mr. Earnshaw brings him to the Heights, he protects himself against the hostility he meets there by trying to be invulnerable: "He seemed a sullen, patient child," says Nelly, "hardened, perhaps, to ill-treatment: he would stand Hindley's blows without winking or shedding a tear, and my pinches moved him only to draw in a breath, and open his eyes as if he had hurt himself by accident, and nobody was to blame" (ch. 4). Heathcliff is showing them, in effect, that they cannot hurt him. His only way of gaining a sense of control in a hostile world is by not reacting to what is done to him. He follows the same pattern during his illness: whereas Cathy and Hindley harass Nelly terribly, Heathcliff is "as uncomplaining as a lamb, though hardness, not gentleness, made him give little trouble." He gives little trouble because he does not expect anyone to be concerned about him, and it is important for him to feel that he is not dependent on them.

Heathcliff practices a resignation to suffering that removes him from the power of other people and makes him impervious to the slings and arrows of outrageous fortune. He denies that anything is impinging on him and distances himself from his own feelings. Since he has no reason to trust other people or to expect anything but pain from his dealings with them, he is sullen, withdrawn, and unsociable. When his situation worsens after the death of Hindley's wife, "his naturally reserved disposition was exaggerated," says Nelly, "into an almost idiotic excess of unsociable moroseness" (ch. 8).

Heathcliff complains so little of his injuries that Nelly thinks he is not vindictive, but there is a burning rage beneath his stoical exterior. He does not show his rage because to express hostility would expose him to retaliations against which he is powerless to defend himself. The favoritism of Mr. Earnshaw allows Heathcliff's aggression to surface; it gives "rich nourishment to the child's pride and black tempers" (ch. 5). Heathcliff is a rejected and abused child on the one hand and a spoiled one on the other. The rejection and abuse generate a great deal of anger, and the protection of Mr. Earnshaw allows him to begin to express it.

Heathcliff's aggression is directed primarily against Hindley, who is his chief tormentor. He controls Hindley by absorbing his abuse and then threatening to have him punished by his father. He forces Hindley to exchange horses, for example, by threatening to tell Mr. Earnshaw "of the three thrashings you've given me this week, and show him my arm, which is black to the shoulder" (ch. 4). When Hindley menaces him with an iron weight, Heathcliff invites him to throw it, "and then I'll tell how you boasted that you would turn me out of doors as soon as he died, and see whether he will not turn you out directly." Hindley's rage toward the "beggarly interloper" whom he sees as "a usurper of his parent's affection and his privileges" is kept in check as long as Mr. Earnshaw is alive; but after his father's death, Hindley has his revenge. This, in turn, fuels Heathcliff's anger, which he expresses through his rebelliousness while he is a child and by revenging himself upon Hindley as soon as he has the power. *Wuthering Heights* resembles an Elizabethan revenge tragedy in which there is a seemingly endless cycle of injury and retaliation.

Heathcliff's chief defense is his attachment to Cathy. *Wuthering Heights* is above all the story of the formation of that attachment and of the sufferings of the partners when their bond with each other is threatened. Heathcliff's needs for love, warmth, and companionship have been repressed because it has seemed impossible that they would ever be satisfied. They emerge in the presence of Cathy, however, and he becomes completely dependent upon her. She is his first and only friend, his sole companion, the only person to whom he risks exposing himself emotionally. Since Mr. Earnshaw rejects Cathy because of her naughtiness, she and Heathcliff are outcasts together. They are in league against the others, and Cathy is the leader. They share a code that exalts mastery, toughness, and revenge. When their situation becomes much worse after the death of Mr. Earnshaw, they take refuge in each other, feed each other's pride, and reinforce each other's vindictiveness. They react to Hindley's abuse by running off to the moors, forgetting "everything the minute they were together again, at least the minute they had contrived some naughty plan of revenge" (ch. 6). They compensate for being outcasts by belonging to each other, and they assuage the pain of their mistreatment by plotting retaliation. Whereas each would feel helpless alone, together they have a feeling of solidarity and power that enables them to laugh at their oppressors.

Although Heathcliff is far from being the typical subordinate partner in a morbid dependency relationship, we must recognize that in relation to Cathy he is quite self-effacing. He submits himself to her, obeys her commands, and glories in her greatness. He is able to gratify both his need for love and his need for aggressive triumph through her. After he has been scorned by the Lintons when Cathy is injured by their dog, he restores his pride by dwelling on their admiration of her: "she is so immeasurably superior to them—to everybody on earth, is she not, Nelly?" (ch. 6). He gains an intoxicating sense of worth through his identification with this marvelous being to whom *he* is an object of love. Since Heathcliff pursues glory through his idealized image of Cathy, he must maintain his sense of her superiority. When he beats her in the race from the Heights to the park, he excuses her defeat by pointing out that she was barefoot. He reports that when the Linton's bulldog bit into Cathy's ankle, "She did not yell out—no! She would have scorned to do it, if she had been spitted on the horns of a mad cow." She was sick, he insists, "not from fear . . . but from pain." Heathcliff is spellbound by Cathy's aggressive qualities and needs to deny that she could ever show weakness. Heathcliff is not envious of Cathy because he shares in her triumphs. Her love and superiority are so important that he represses his vindictive impulses toward her when she hurts him and displaces them onto others. If she extends her protection to others, he will not attack them directly. Her wishes account for his initial restraint toward both Edgar and Hindley.

Cathy saves Heathcliff from deep feelings of unlovableness and self-contempt. She is the one person who finds him admirable and who promises to fulfill his overwhelming need for affection. This gives his feeling for her the neurotic intensity that makes it so romantic and that Horney associates with morbid dependency. For the dependent partner in such a relationship, love appears "as the ticket to paradise": "no more feeling lost, guilty, and unworthy. . . . love seems to promise protection, support, affection, encouragement, sympathy, understanding. It will give him a feeling of worth. It will give meaning to his life. It will be salvation and redemption. . . . To love, for him, means . . . to merge with another being, to become one heart and one flesh" (1950, 239–40). This passage helps us to understand Heathcliff's feeling that he has been cast into hell when Cathy rejects him (she has been his salvation) and his anguished cry upon her death—"I *cannot* live without my life! I *cannot* live without my soul!" (ch. 16).

It is essential to recognize that the relationship is as important to Cathy as it is to Heathcliff and that it serves her psychological needs as well as his. According to Nelly, within a few years of Heathcliff's arrival, Cathy was "much too fond" of him: "The greatest punishment we could invent for her was to keep her separate from him" (ch. 5). It is because Cathy needs him almost as much as he needs her that Heathcliff can open himself to her. While Heathcliff gains a sense of power and glory through his identification with Cathy's superiority, she has these needs met through his deference and adulation, which mean all the more to her because he is an aggressive person whom she respects. Although her childhood is certainly better than Heathcliff's, Cathy, too, experiences deprivations that intensify her needs for love and belonging. She loses her mother when she is eight and is severely rejected by her father, who tells her that he cannot love her and that he and her mother "must rue that ever we reared thee!" (ch. 5). Cathy and Heathcliff are both alienated, emotionally deprived children who feel a profound affinity and who cling to each other with passionate intensity. Cathy identifies with Heathcliff as completely as he does with her and feels truly at home in the world only through his existence.

Heathcliff and Cathy seem to be engaged, in effect, in a mutual morbid dependency which is so intense that they do not have a sense of themselves as autonomous beings with separate identities. As a result, each feels that existence is unbearable without the other. The degree of their need for each other is the product not only of their alienation from the world around them but also of their alienation from themselves. The pathological conditions of their childhoods are such that they are suffering from what R. D. Laing calls "ontological insecurity," that is, an insecurity about the distinctness and substantiality of their own identities. According to Laing, the ontologically secure person experiences "his own being as real, alive, whole; as differentiated from the rest of the world . . . so clearly that his identity and autonomy are never in question; . . . as having an inner consistency, substantiality, genuineness, and worth; as spatially coextensive with the body; and, usually, as having begun in or around birth and liable to extinction with death" (1965, 42). The ontologically insecure person has the opposite feelings. Heathcliff and Cathy do not feel real, alive, and whole in and of themselves but only when they are joined with each other. They do not feel intrinsically genuine and worthwhile; they do not have a sense of personal autonomy; they do not believe that the self is coextensive with the body; and they do not feel that their beings will end with their individual deaths.

Laing's description of the way in which ontologically insecure people relate to each other explains in a psychological way Cathy and Heathcliff's most extreme utterances about their indivisibility and what many critics have taken to be the metaphysical dimension of their relationship:

> A lack of sense of autonomy implies that one feels one's being to be bound up in the other, or that the other is bound up in oneself, in a sense that transgresses the actual possibilities within the structure of human relatedness. It means that a feeling that one is in a position of ontological dependency on the other (i.e., dependent on the other for one's very being), is substituted for a sense of relatedness and attachment to him based on genuine mutuality. Utter detachment and isolation are regarded as the only alternative to a clam- or vampire-like attachment in which the other person's life-blood is necessary for one's own survival. . . . Therefore, the polarity is between complete isolation or complete merging of identity rather than between separateness and relatedness. (1965, 53)

Heathcliff and Cathy's relationship is not based on genuine mutuality, especially after Cathy becomes more refined and Heathcliff begins to degenerate, but on a sense of necessity. Cathy explains to Nelly that her love for Linton "is like the foliage in the woods. Time will change it. . . . My love for Heathcliff resembles the eternal rocks beneath—a source of little visible delight, but necessary. Nelly, I am Heathcliff—he's always, always in my mind—not as a pleasure, any more than I am always a pleasure to myself—but as my own being" (ch. 9). Although he is less articulate about it, it is clear that Heathcliff's sense of being is equally bound up with Cathy. He does not wish to survive her: "oh God! would you like to live with your soul in the grave?" (ch. 15). When they are merged with each other, they feel at home in the world, but when they are separated, they feel completely isolated in a universe that has turned into "a mighty stranger" (ch. 9).

Wuthering Heights is above all a novel about merger and separation. Cathy and Heathcliff are embattled children who become ontologically dependent on one another and who find in their alliance a mutual support that saves them from feeling alone in the world and gives meaning to their lives. They become embedded in this relationship and are unable to grow beyond it or to feel themselves whole beings with separate identities. The novel explores what happens when people who are so bound to each other are torn apart. After their union is shattered, they spend the rest of their lives looking back upon it as a paradisal state from which they have fallen and looking forward to a reattainment of their bliss, if not here, then hereafter. The most radical separation occurs when Catherine dies. There is an eventual movement back toward merger, which occurs at the end when Heathcliff joins her in the grave.

The first turning point in the relationship occurs when Hindley deprives Heathcliff of the instruction of the curate, drives him into the company of the servants, and makes him a common laborer. Heathcliff bears his "degradation pretty well at first, because Cathy [teaches] him what she learn[s], and work[s] or play[s] with him in the fields" (ch. 6); but the social difference Hindley has created becomes important after Cathy's stay at the Linton's and her sister-in-law's efforts to make her into a lady. Before both had been "rude as savages"; now Cathy looks at Heathcliff from a distance and gives him the message that something is wrong with him. Cathy had been his sustaining source of affirmation, the withdrawal of which exposes him to painful feelings of inadequacy and self-hate. He becomes envious of Edgar Linton and feels that in order to please Cathy he must become something quite different from what he is. As the social and cultural gap between them grows, Heathcliff becomes increasingly demoralized.

Their estrangement is almost as painful to Cathy as it is to Heathcliff. Her visit to Thrushcross Grange throws her into inner conflict by giving a new form to her search for glory, one that separates her from Heathcliff and forces her to repress some of the strongest components of her own personality. Instead of feeding her pride through a spirited rebellion, she now craves the approval of the Lintons, who represent the conventional world. She wants to triumph by becoming "the greatest woman of the neighborhood" (ch. 9), but in order to do this she must give up her unladylike ways and conform to accepted manners and mores. She must also give up Heathcliff, at least as a mate. It is unthinkable for her to marry this coarse, ragged, impoverished young man. Since her need for social conquest is in conflict with her need to remain bonded to Heathcliff, she is bound to experience frustration and regret whatever she does.

By marrying Edgar, Cathy will fulfill her ambition, but she knows that she can never feel at home at the Grange, where she is expected to be submissive, calm, restrained, and civilized. Heathcliff is the same psychological type, whereas Edgar is her opposite. Heathcliff worships her for the untamed, rebellious, masterful spirit of which the Lintons disapprove. Edgar is a self-effacing person whose compliance she at once exploits and despises. "I have such faith in Linton's love," she later tells Nelly, "that I believe I might kill him, and he wouldn't wish to retaliate" (ch. 10). Cathy can be spontaneous at the Heights, but by marrying Edgar Linton she dooms herself to a permanent sense of constraint.

The effects of Cathy's decision on Heathcliff are even more devastating than they are upon her. By marrying Edgar, Cathy satisfies at least some of her conflicting needs, but she leaves Heathcliff with nothing. Even the unromantic Nelly understands this: "he'll be the most unfortunate creature that ever was born! As soon as you become Mrs. Linton, he loses friend, and love, and all! Have you considered how you'll bear the separation, and how he'll bear to be quite deserted in the world?" (ch. 9). Perhaps the severest blow of all is to Heathcliff's sense of worth, which is based almost exclusively on Cathy's love and approval. We do not know what Heathcliff did during his mysterious three-year absence, but his objective is clear. Ever since Cathy's return from the Lintons', Heathcliff had wanted to be rich and refined like Edgar; and he runs away when he hears Cathy telling Nelly that it would degrade her to marry him now. His objective is to restore his pride by acquiring wealth and polish, to show Cathy that he is as good as Edgar and that she was wrong to have despised him.

Cathy does not expect to lose Heathcliff. She intends to marry Edgar and become the greatest woman of the neighborhood, using her new wealth to rescue Heathcliff from the clutches of Hindley and help him to rise. Heathcliff will remain as devoted to her as always, and they will retain their intimate bond. Under the pressure of her inner conflicts, Cathy develops a fantasy in which all of her needs will be satisfied. She envisions Edgar and Heathcliff accepting an arrangement that would be extremely repugnant to both but that she must have if she is to fulfill her contradictory needs.

Cathy's reaction to Heathcliff's departure is intense. She falls into a delirium, becomes seriously ill, and emerges from her illness more domineering than ever. Because of her suffering she feels entitled to total submission from everyone else. Although she marries Edgar after a couple of years and seems happy with him at times, she remains in a state of chronic depression. She is moody and demanding and is kept in temper only by the entire compliance of Edgar and Isabella. Her domineering behavior is an indirect expression of her rage and grief.

While he is away, Heathcliff fears that Cathy has forgotten him, and he expects nothing from the future but *"death* and *hell"* (ch. 14). On his return, he intends to display his accomplishments to Cathy, to kill Hindley, and then to kill himself. Cathy's reception assures him of her love and gives him a motive for living. The meaning of his life now lies in maintaining his contact with her and pursuing his revenge. He will attempt to wipe out his earlier humiliations by a series of vindictive triumphs that will subject others to the same kind of suffering they had inflicted on him. He is enraged not only with Hindley and Edgar, but also with Cathy, who he feels has treated him "infernally" (ch. 11). He tells her that he shall not "suffer unrevenged"; but his old taboo against being vindictive toward her is still in operation, and he plans to take out his rage on others.

Cathy now has both Edgar and Heathcliff and is beginning "to be secure and tranquil" (ch. 11). This precarious situation deteriorates rapidly, however, when Heathcliff and Cathy argue over his intentions toward Isabella and the worm, Edgar, turns, forbidding Heathcliff admission to the house and telling Cathy that she must choose between them. This renewed separation, coming so soon after their reunion, is more than Cathy can bear. Enraged by the thwarting of her claims, she retaliates by becoming self-destructive: "I'll try to break their hearts by breaking my own." Her strategy succeeds, for through her death she poisons Edgar's life and reduces Heathcliff to utter desolation. I believe that Emily Brontë means us to see Heathcliff as wronged most of all by Cathy, whose betrayal and death inflict psychological torments that account for much of his demonic behavior.

Cathy seeks death not only as a means of revenge, but also as a way of achieving reunion with Heathcliff. She is eager to die in order to escape into a "glorious world," which is not heaven but a place like the Heights where she will be at one with *her* Heathcliff. This is not the angry man at her side in the final scene, who mingles curses with his kisses, but the Heathcliff she retains "in [her] soul" (ch. 15). She tells Nelly that when she achieves this union, she will be "incomparably beyond and above" them all.

Heathcliff cannot bear the thought of their final separation any more than could Cathy, and after her death he turns to his belief in ghosts as a refuge from his loneliness. Cathy has accused him of killing her. He prays that her spirit will not rest, that she will haunt him as long as he lives: "Be with me always—take any form—drive me mad! only *do* not leave me in this abyss where I cannot find you!" (ch. 16). Cathy's ghost is presented so ambiguously that it is impossible to say whether we are meant to believe in its actual existence, but we do not need to believe in the ghost to account for Heathcliff's sense of being haunted by Cathy. Since life without her is truly unbearable, he must believe in her continued existence in order to assuage his anguish, just as she had to believe that she would be reunited with him after her death.

In childhood Heathcliff develops two ways of compensating for mistreatment, merging with his glorified image of Cathy and plotting retaliation. The first half of the novel is the story of Heathcliff's love; the second is the story of his revenge. At first Heathcliff is the object of our sympathy as victim and lover; it is not until the death of Cathy that he becomes a monster. The stories of his love and his revenge are closely intertwined, since his rage is fueled in part by his anger with Cathy and his despair at losing her, and it subsides only when he senses the prospect of achieving reunion.

The harshness of his early experience leads Heathcliff to develop arrogant-vindictive trends. He is obsessed with a desire to retaliate for his humiliations and to prove his superiority to those who have damaged his pride. He needs to hurt his enemies more than they have hurt him: his schemes are designed to reduce his persecutors and their representatives to a state of misery and degradation greater than his own. His sadistic behavior is fueled also by his grief at Cathy's loss; he tries to assuage his pain by making sure that everyone else bears him company in his misery.

The first object of Heathcliff's vindictiveness is Hindley Earnshaw, whose treatment of him was enough, says Nelly, "to make a fiend of a saint" (ch. 8). His behavior toward Hindley follows the *lex talionis:* he wants to vent his rage and restore his pride by doing to Hindley what Hindley has done to him. He spends much of his childhood waiting for the time when he will be powerful enough to even the score: "at least while I'm thinking of that, I don't feel pain" (ch. 7). Hindley literally ruins Heathcliff's life by demeaning him in such a way that he is separated socially from Cathy. Heathcliff retaliates by contributing to Hindley's degradation and gaining control of his possessions, rendering Hindley as powerless and frustrated as he had been. He repays Hindley for all those childhood floggings by kicking and trampling on him and dashing his head against the flags while he is unconscious. His rage toward Hindley is immense. Hindley's self-inflicted end gives him great satisfaction, but his need to even the score is not yet satisfied, and so his revenge continues into the next generation. He exults at having the opportunity to degrade Hareton now as Hindley had degraded him. He revels in the feeling that he has got Hareton "faster than his scoundrel of a father secured me" and that his victim is "damnably fond" of him (ch. 21). He imagines Hindley seeing what he has done and suffering at having been "outmatched."

Heathcliff has not been abused by the Lintons as he has by Hindley, but he still has ample motives for revenge. On his first encounter with the family, when Cathy is bitten by their dog, they treat him with contempt and hostility. Heathcliff has an overwhelming need to restore his pride through a series of vindictive triumphs over them. It gives him immense satisfaction to be adored by the once scornful Isabella while he despises her. He wants to turn the tables on the Lintons by gaining power over them and putting them in the position he once occupied. His sadistic behavior toward Isabella and Cathy II is fueled in part by his particular animosity toward Edgar, who has taken Catherine away from him. Since he is restrained by Cathy's regard for Edgar, he uses Edgar's sister and daughter as proxies in suffering.

Heathcliff's viciousness toward the Lintons can be attributed in part to the fact that they are the opposite psychological types. Cathy and Heathcliff both have contempt for Edgar's self-effacing qualities. Heathcliff is outraged that Edgar has, in fact, triumphed over him; like Iago (see Paris 1991a), he has a need to demonstrate his superiority to soft people like that. He shows that their strategy does not work by treating them more harshly when they appeal for pity and using their self-effacing qualities against them. He knows that the Lintons cannot resist an appeal to their sympathy or affection; and this, combined with his own contempt for all such appeals, makes them easy victims. His conquests vindicate his own character traits, which were rejected for theirs, and demonstrate their inferiority.

Heathcliff is so cruel to the Lintons also because he is threatened by their self-effacing behavior, to which he reacts with extraordinary intensity. The reaction of the arrogant-vindictive person to self-effacing behavior is so extreme, explains Horney, because "it is prompted by his need to fight all softer feelings in himself" (1945, 69–70). He despises in others "their compliance, their self-degrading, their helpless hankering for love. In short, he despises in them the very self-effacing trends he hates and despises in himself" (1950, 207). Heathcliff's self-effacing behavior is all channeled toward Cathy. He romanticizes its intensity, but he, too, displays the compliance and has the helpless hankering for love that he despises in Isabella. Indeed, his enslavement is far more extreme than hers. Isabella suggests this by her comment on his behavior after Cathy's death: "if I were you, I'd go stretch myself over her grave and die like a faithful dog. The world is surely not worth living in now, is it?" (ch. 17). The Linton women are constantly appealing to the softer side of Heathcliff's nature. If he allowed himself to respond, he would have to despise himself for being like them and to condemn himself for his cruelty. The more they plead, the harsher he becomes in his effort to avoid self-hate.

Heathcliff's vindictiveness serves a number of psychological functions. It restores his pride, expresses his rage, and helps him forget his pain. Cathy II understands very well the relationship between his lovelessness, his misery, and his cruelty: "You have nobody to love you; and, however miserable you make us, we shall still have the revenge of thinking that your cruelty rises from your greater misery! You *are* miserable, are you not? Lonely, like the devil, and envious like him?" (ch. 29). What contributes most to the sadistic person's callousness toward others, observes Horney, is his "bitter envy" of them, which "stems from his feeling excluded from life" (1950, 211). Heathcliff tries to assuage his suffering by persecuting others so that they will be "as defeated and degraded as he" and will share in his misery (1945, 202).

Heathcliff's end is in keeping with what we know of his personality. The turning point is the scene in which the young Cathy defies Heathcliff to strike her and announces that she and Hareton are allies. He seems about to tear her in pieces when he stops, gazes intently in her face, draws his hand over his eyes, and lets her go. Heathcliff is disarmed by the alliance of Cathy and Hareton, which reminds him of his own alliance with the first Cathy, and by Cathy's eyes, which are those of her mother. The resemblance between Hareton and the first Cathy is even stronger, especially after his mental faculties have been awakened, and Heathcliff's taboo on vindictiveness toward Cathy now becomes operative toward Hareton as well. Hareton reminds him of his earlier self, moreover. Hareton's aspect, he tells Nelly, is "the ghost of my immortal love, of my wild endeavours to hold my right, my degradation, my pride, my happiness, and my anguish" (ch. 33). Heathcliff has been doing unto others what he feels has been done unto him; but once he begins to identify Cathy II and Hareton with Cathy and himself, he sees them as victims rather than as enemies and loses his desire to strike.

Heathcliff's loss of vindictiveness is also the result of his growing indifference to everything around him as he becomes more and more absorbed by the idea that his reunion with Cathy is near. This development is triggered by the resemblances we have just examined and by his experience of seeing Cathy's as yet uncorrupted body in her coffin when Edgar is buried. Both of these things give him a stronger sense than he has yet had of the proximity of his beloved. With his loss of interest in revenge and his sense of Cathy's nearness, his energies now concentrate on a single objective. He longs for death, as Cathy had done earlier, as the only means by which he can reestablish their union. After he loosens one side of Cathy's coffin, he bribes the sexton to pull it away when he is laid there and to slide out a side of his coffin too so that "by the time Linton gets to us, he'll not know which is which!" (ch. 29). His dream of merger now takes the form of the mingling of their dust so that they can no longer be identified as separate entities. He dies with a "gaze of exultation" in his eyes that Nelly is unable to remove. He has finally reentered his heaven.

Except for the possible presence of ghosts, whose actual existence is never confirmed, *Wuthering Heights* is as realistic as most other Victorian novels. Heathcliff, Cathy, the Lintons, Lockwood, and Nelly are all mimetic characters whose behavior is intelligible in terms of their psychological traits. In its presentation of the devastating effects of traumatic childhood experiences, *Wuthering Heights* is one of a long line of nineteenth-century novels, and it is more perceptive than most in its recognition of the destructive effects of abuse on the human personality. What often happens in Victorian fiction is that abused characters develop self-effacing trends which are then glorified because of their seeming unselfishness. Suffering is presented as ennobling, a source of moral growth. Emily Brontë understands better than most of her contemporaries that bad treatment is harmful to people, and she vividly portrays its destructive consequences. Heathcliff is such a memorable character not because he is a demon, symbol, or principle, but because he acts out in an extreme way responses we have all had to loneliness and rejection. We find him a frightening yet sympathetic figure because he shows us some very real potentialities of our nature.

Although Clifford Collins says that there is perhaps "no other novel in English which it is possible to interpret strictly in terms of thematic development" (Sale 1963, 314), I find *Wuthering Heights* to be extremely difficult, if not impossible, to interpret thematically. It is one of those novels about which Wayne Booth (1961) complains in which the author has disappeared. The story is told largely by Nelly, through Lockwood, and there is little agreement about Emily Brontë's relation to her narrators. Mark Schorer feels that Emily Brontë set out to celebrate "the moral magnificence of unmoral passion" but that, partly as a result of her narrative technique, the triumph at the end "is on the side of the cloddish world, which survives" (1950, xii). The "voice that drones on is the perdurable voice of the country, Nelly Dean's" (xv). John K. Mathison represents a large body of critics, however, when he says that "as Nelly contentedly provides her superficial interpretations of motive . . . we are constantly directed toward feeling the inadequacy of the wholesome, and toward sympathy with genuine passions, no matter how destructive or violent" (Sale 1963, 338).

There is clearly a system of contrasts in the novel involving Heathcliff, Cathy, and the Heights on the one hand and the Lintons, Nelly, and the Grange on the other; but what exactly is being contrasted? According to Schorer, Brontë is presenting through Heathcliff and Cathy "a devastating spectacle of human waste" (1950, xi), but many other critics feel that theirs is the story of a splendid passion, the grandeur of which is emphasized by the contrast with ordinary experience. What is Emily Brontë's attitude toward Heathcliff and Cathy, Nelly and the Lintons, the Heights and the Grange? Why does she tell her story of extreme love and hate through the medium of Nelly and Lockwood, never speaking in her own voice?

From a Horneyan perspective, the Heights represents extreme forms of both aggressive and self-effacing behavior (there is extreme detachment, too), whereas the Grange represents a moderate form of self-effacing behavior combined with a moderate detachment. Both Hindley and Heathcliff are inconsolable on the death of the woman they love and are destructive to themselves and others, whereas Edgar, though grief-stricken, is eventually comforted. Heathcliff, Cathy, and Hindley are all highly vindictive people, while the Lintons represent a more charitable attitude. They turn vindictive when they are persecuted, but this is a passing phase for them rather than a fixed trait of character. In the second generation, the characteristics associated with both Heights and Grange are combined and softened.

The novel's system of contrasts is developed not only through the juxtaposition of Heights and Grange, but also through its narrative technique. The story of extreme love and hate is told by the moderate and predominantly self-effacing Nelly to the detached Lockwood, who tells it to us. All three of the Horneyan trends are present in the novel in varying degrees of intensity and in various combinations.

Where does Emily Brontë stand in this system of contrasts? If, as Mark Schorer says, it is Nelly's voice that endures at the end, Brontë would seem to be favoring the moderate self-effacing position. A good case can be made for this. Nelly represents the standard compliant values of her culture. She is the voice of the community and perhaps also of the implied author. She stands for forgiveness as opposed to revenge. "It is for God to punish wicked people," she admonishes Heathcliff when he swears to even the score with Hindley; "we should learn to forgive" (ch. 7). She later urges Isabella to "be more charitable" toward Heathcliff and scolds her for her vindictiveness: "One might suppose you had never opened a Bible in your life" (ch. 17). She disapproves of Cathy's vanity and arrogance and hopes they will be chastened. Of Heathcliff she thinks, "Your pride cannot blind God! You tempt Him to wring [your heart and nerves], till He forces a cry of humiliation" (ch. 16). When Heathcliff is near death, she urges him to send for a minister— "you have lived a selfish, unchristian life" —and is "shocked at his godless indifference" (ch. 34). She sides with Edgar against Cathy, "for he was kind, and trustful, and honourable," whereas she has "little faith" in Cathy's "principles, and still less sympathy for her feelings" (ch. 10). She compares Hindley's moral deterioration after the death of his wife to Edgar's pious resignation: "Linton . . . displayed the true courage of a loyal and faithful soul: he trusted God, and God comforted him. One hoped, and the other despaired" (ch. 17). The novel is so full of Nelly's pious reflections that she seems to many to speak for Emily Brontë.

One of Nelly's dicta is that "people who do their duty are always finally rewarded" (ch. 25); and this, with its corollary, that the wicked are punished, is borne out by the novel. Heathcliff and Cathy are, as Schorer says, "a devastating spectacle of human waste" (1950, xi). They are miserable and self-destructive. The novel ends with the good people triumphant. Brontë seems to be trying to provide through Cathy II and Hareton a more desirable alternative to the personalities and actions of Cathy and Heathcliff. Her mother's spirit and rebelliousness are present in Cathy II, but much softened and combined with her father's moderate compliant traits: "her anger was never furious; her love never fierce; it was deep and tender" (ch. 18). She seems to combine the best of the Heights and the Grange. It is Cathy who breaks the cycle of injury and revenge by her movement toward Hareton after she has treated him scornfully. She is prompted to this by Nelly's scolding and by her guilt for having put an end to Hareton's efforts at self-improvement. Her alliance with Hareton is crucial in leading Heathcliff to relinquish his quest for revenge, as we have seen. Hareton is able to respond to her because, despite his degradation at the hands of Heathcliff, he does not have a vindictive personality. The members of the second generation are better, in part at least, because they have been better treated. The marriage of Hareton and Cathy represents the triumph of love and forgiveness over hatred and revenge, and it is "the crown" of Nelly's wishes: "I shall envy no one on their wedding-day—there won't be a happier woman than myself in England!" (ch. 33). The fact that Cathy and Hareton are going to move to the Grange seems to be a final endorsement of the values for which it stands.

Plausible as the preceding interpretation is, it is not the dominant view of the novel, which tends, rather, to see it as celebrating the intensity of Cathy and Heathcliff's love for each other and justifying, to some extent at least, Heathcliff's revenge. Nelly surrounds Cathy and Heathcliff's story with a haze of disapproval, but their glamour somehow shines through her moralizing and makes her and the people she favors seem dull and commonplace by comparison. As many critics have pointed out, Emily Brontë makes it quite evident that Nelly is frequently obtuse in her dealings with Cathy and sometimes drives her into frenzies of self-destructive behavior. It is not difficult to make a case that Nelly is an object of satire in the novel and the source of much of the mischief.

Although self-effacing traits and values are often glorified, they are also mocked and scorned, especially by Cathy and Heathcliff. Cathy has contempt for Edgar's "weak nature" (ch. 11) and Heathcliff for his "puny being" (ch. 14). Edgar's attendance on Catherine during her illness is scoffed at by Heathcliff: "that insipid, paltry creature attending her from *duty* and *humanity!* From *pity* and *charity!*" These are feeble motives compared to Heathcliff's all-consuming passion. As we have seen, Heathcliff has enormous contempt for Isabella's "sighing and wheedling." Although she talks of her vindictive impulses to Nelly, Isabella is incapable of taking revenge when she has the opportunity to do so. Hindley tries to enlist her as an ally, but when Heathcliff appears Isabella warns him of Hindley's plans. When Hindley abuses her for her "base spirit," we tend to agree and to sympathize with his contention that "treachery and violence are a just return for treachery and violence!" Many critics have argued that Heathcliff's victims are getting what they deserve. Brontë often makes vindictiveness seem justified.

In addition to the scorn of Cathy and Heathcliff, there are other things that make humane or compliant behavior seem weak or foolish. The kindhearted Mr. Earnshaw harbors Heathcliff "to his bane" (ch. 34), and Edgar's parents die as a result of caring for Catherine when she is ill. Edgar is caught when Cathy strikes him and then threatens to cry herself sick if he leaves. Nelly tries to encourage him to depart: " 'Miss is dreadfully wayward, sir!' I called out. " 'As bad as any marred child—you'd better be riding home, or else she will be sick, only to grieve us' "(ch. 8). But "the soft thing" is "doomed, and flies to his fate!" A blow to the pride is often what precipitates love in a self-effacing person, and a display of suffering usually has a coercive effect. Cathy, like Heathcliff, understands the weaknesses of those she wishes to manipulate and skillfully exploits them. The scorn for Edgar comes here from Nelly, who stands up to aggressive people but is herself a soft touch for self-effacing ones. She urges Edgar to confront Heathcliff after his return, since "there's harm in being too soft" (ch. 11); but a good deal of mischief is caused by her inability to be firm with Cathy II. When Heathcliff puts pressure on Cathy to come to see Linton despite her father's prohibition, Nelly gives in: "I couldn't bear to witness her sorrow" (ch. 23). Cathy is likewise compelled by Linton's sufferings. Her "indulgent tenderness" (ch. 27) toward that repulsive young man puts her in his power, and in Heathcliff's. It is an unsavory spectacle that does not win admiration for self-effacing behavior. Nelly and Cathy are happy in the end, as their virtue is rewarded; but so is the unrepentant Heathcliff, who dies in a state of exultation. God never forces a cry of humiliation from him.

Miriam Allott argues that *Wuthering Heights* "is an effort to explore and, *if possible,* to reconcile conflicting 'attractions' " (1970, 186). Whereas Allott sees Emily Brontë as drawn "by different parts of her nature toward both storm and calm," I would say that she was drawn toward both the arrogant-vindictive and self-effacing solutions at the same time that she saw their destructiveness. Our inability to determine where she stands in the system of contrasts results from the fact that her inner conflict is expressed but not resolved by the novel. She sees each solution not only from within but also from the perspective of the other, and she feels for each the scorn that is generated by the opposing set of attitudes. She manages to give coherent expression to her very mixed and complicated attitudes by means of her narrative technique. She allows the aggressive side of her nature to be expressed through the story of Cathy and Heathcliff, but she combines with it a continuous commentary from the self-effacing point of view, making it impossible for us to accuse her of approving these monsters. Her scorn for her self-effacing side is expressed through Cathy and Heathcliff, and in other ways as well, while having Nelly tell the story permits her to pass moral judgment and to satisfy her self-effacing shoulds.

The detached side of Emily Brontë is also expressed through her narrative technique. Lockwood is usually seen as the representative of civilization, but he may also be seen as a representative of detachment. He comes to the region in order to get away from his fellows and finds it "a perfect misanthrope's heaven" (ch. 1). He tells us a great deal about himself in his reaction to Heathcliff's reserve. At first he attributes Heathcliff's moroseness to "an aversion to showy displays of feeling," but then he realizes that he may be bestowing his "own attributes over-liberally on him." Lockwood despises himself for his detachment: "Let me hope my constitution is almost peculiar: my dear mother used to say I should never have a comfortable home, and only last summer I proved myself perfectly unworthy of one." He was attracted to "a most fascinating creature" until she showed signs of reciprocating his interest, and he then "shrunk icily into [himself], like a snail." Lockwood longs for human companionship but is terrified of emotional involvement. He visits Heathcliff a second time because Heathcliff's own greater reserve makes him safe to be with. After his painful experience, however, Lockwood curses himself for his social impulse and reminds himself that "a sensible man ought to find sufficient company in himself" (ch. 3). He seeks Nelly's company despite his determination to hold himself "independent of all social intercourse" and then feels himself to be a "weak wretch" for doing so (ch. 4).

The outermost frame of the novel is Lockwood's flirtation with the idea of a romance with Cathy II, but he is very much afraid of "the fascination that lurks" in her eyes (ch. 14) and does not want to "venture [his] tranquillity by running into temptation" (ch. 25). When he returns to find Cathy engaged to Hareton, however, he bites his lip, "in spite, at having thrown away [his] chance" (ch. 32). It seems clear at the end that Lockwood will never be able to form a loving relationship and have a comfortable home.

Nelly's narrative enables Lockwood to engage in a characteristically detached way of experiencing life, that is, through other people's passions. Lockwood is afraid of his feelings and is constantly defending himself against them. The result of his detachment is boredom, however, a sense of the emptiness of life. Nelly's story is of people who are acting out their impulses all the time, in an intense, uninhibited way. Cathy and Heathcliff are not emotionally dead, the way Lockwood is; and through them he gets a vicarious sense of being alive: "I could fancy a love for life here almost possible" (ch. 7). What makes Cathy and Heathcliff appealing to the reader is, in part, their juxtaposition with Lockwood. They have the vitality and intensity he lacks. Their grand passion is self-consuming, but his tepid little romance never gets off the ground, and he goes away with nothing. In comparison to theirs, his life is sterile.

The detached side of Emily Brontë is attracted by the intensity of Cathy and Heathcliff, just as Lockwood is; but, like him, she is also frightened by it. Cathy and Heathcliff are fascinating creatures; but they confirm Lockwood's worst fears, that if you lose control of your emotions, especially in relation to the opposite sex, you will be destroyed. Their fate reinforces his detached solution, just as it does Nelly's self-effacing one, at the very same time that it challenges its validity. Detachment is treated with the same ambivalence as are the aggressive and compliant solutions.

Given Emily Brontë's inner conflicts, it is amazing that *Wuthering Heights* is not as thematically confused as *The Awakening*. The difference lies in the narrative technique. By having the story told by Nelly and Lockwood, with much internal quotation from other characters, Emily Brontë can give expression to all of her trends, and to the crossfire of conflicting shoulds they generate, without having any one position emerge as normative, and therefore as inadequate to her ambivalence. Each set of trends can be at once expressed, justified, and criticized from the point of view of the others. Chopin's inner conflicts wreak havoc in a novel that employs omniscient narration; but *Wuthering Heights* is an impressionistic novel, like *Lord Jim* (see Paris 1974), in which interpretation is dramatized. All of the value judgments and attitudes belong to the characters and are appropriate to their personalities. This creates a problem of narrative reliability in the sense that we do not know where in the novel's system of conflicting values the author stands, but it avoids the problems that would have resulted from the establishment of a moral norm. Brontë's narrative technique serves the needs of her detachment by preserving her privacy, by enabling her to disappear. She does not want us to know where she stands. It is a way of managing her inner conflicts that does much to produce the novel's richness and complexity, its elusiveness and never-ending fascination.

Conclusion

I have tried to show that Karen Horney's mature theory has an important contribution to make to the study of literature. Like any other theory, it does not apply to all texts, but it fits many works from a wide range of periods and cultures, and it illuminates a variety of issues. It yields a distinctive set of insights and is a valuable critical tool.

One use of Horney is in the analysis of mimetically drawn characters. Such characters have always been appreciated by readers, but their study is one of the least developed areas of literary criticism, in part because we have lacked conceptual systems that would permit us to see and talk about them in detail. For many characters, Karen Horney's theory supplies this deficiency. It helps us to make sense of their often puzzling behavior and to see them, however different their cultures, as imagined human beings who are very much like ourselves. It permits us to recover the psychological intuitions of the great realistic writers and to appreciate their genius in mimetic characterization. Horneyan theory is especially suitable for character analysis because of its emphasis on the current structure of the psyche rather than on infantile origins, about which there is rarely much information. If childhood material is present it can be utilized, but if it is absent it need not be invented.

When we analyze characters in motivational terms, we often sense a disparity between rhetoric and mimesis. Authors tend to glorify characters whose solutions are close to their own while realistically portraying the adverse effects of their defenses. A Horneyan approach can help us to distinguish between the implied author's view of a character and the character actually portrayed and to understand the defenses that govern the rhetoric.

Such an approach can also help us to see how patterns of action are driven by defensive strategies. Some plots celebrate or vindicate a preferred strategy, some deflate a despised strategy or show it leading to a character's downfall, and some show a change from a failed strategy to a favored one. Plots ending in disenchantment portray irreconcilable inner conflicts and the inability of protagonists to find a viable solution.

Two of the most frequent patterns of action in Western literature are education plots, in which flawed characters grow as a result of their mistakes, and vindication plots, in which noble but devalued protagonists prove their worth and receive the recognition they deserve. From a Horneyan perspective, education plots portray the collapse of narcissistic and arrogant-vindictive solutions, which are usually replaced by self-effacement. Sometimes self-effacing characters must learn to be even more self-effacing, and sometimes detached characters discover the sterility of their solution. These plots do not portray psychological growth but rather create the illusion of education by replacing a failed or condemned defensive strategy with one approved by the author and better adapted to the culture. Vindication plots justify perfectionistic, self-effacing, and, occasionally, detached protagonists, who are not as wonderful as plot and rhetoric suggest. Mimetic characters are "creations inside a creation" who often escape their thematic roles and subvert the patterns of action within which they exist.

There are sometimes disparities not only between plot and rhetoric on the one hand and mimesis on the other but also between different strands of the rhetoric. An author may have contradictory attitudes toward a character because of his or her own inner divisions. One of the virtues of Horney's theory is that it enables us to make sense of inconsistencies as part of a system of inner conflicts, without resorting to the sort of rationalization that is common in literary criticism.

The psychological analysis of character, plot, and rhetoric can help us to understand the personality of the author. When we speak of "the author," we can mean one of three things: the "implied author" of a particular work, the "authorial personality" we can infer from some or all of a writer's works, or the historical person who creates the works but also has a life independent of them. We can take a Horneyan approach to all these forms of "the author."

A Horneyan approach can help illuminate authors through their works because in the course of artistic creation their defensive strategies tend to express themselves in a variety of ways. Their works are, among other things, efforts to reinforce their predominant solution and to resolve their inner conflicts by showing themselves, as well as others, the good and evil consequences of the various trends that are warring within them. They will tend to glorify characters whose strategies are similar to their own and to satirize those who embody their repressed solutions. Their rhetoric will affirm the values, attitudes, and traits of character that are demanded by their dominant solution, while rejecting those forbidden by it. Their plots will often be fantasies in which their claims are honored in magical ways, while their repressed strategies are shown to bring misery and retribution.

Because authors cannot help also expressing their subordinate trends, their works will frequently manifest their inner conflicts. Their attitudes, values, and beliefs will often be inconsistent or self-contradictory. Their conflicting trends will lead them to criticize each solution from the point of view of the others and to have toward their characters the mixed feelings they have toward the aspects of themselves the characters embody. Moreover, the relationships among their solutions may vary in the course of their lives, and this will be reflected in shifts in the kinds of characters they portray, in their rhetoric, and in their dominant fantasies.

In this book I have analyzed the implied authors of a number of works, and elsewhere I have described the authorial personalities of Thomas Hardy (1976a), Jane Austen (1978b), and Shakespeare (1991a). To illustrate the kinds of conclusions we can reach about an authorial personality, I shall draw on *Bargains with Fate* for a brief account of a basic conflict in Shakespeare's personality that can be inferred from a study of his corpus.

From *1 Henry VI* to *The Tempest,* a frequent concern of Shakespeare's plays is how to cope with wrongs and remain good in an evil world. In the histories and the tragedies, the tendency of the main characters is to respond to wrongs by taking revenge, but this contaminates the revengers and eventually results in their destruction. In Horney's terms, the arrogant-vindictive solution, with its emphasis on retaliation and vindictive triumph, does not work. But in these plays the self-effacing solution does not work either, as many innocent, well-intentioned, but weak characters perish. Hamlet's problem, as I see it, is how to take revenge and remain innocent. The problem is insoluble and nearly drives him mad. In a number of the comedies and romances, Shakespeare explores a different response to being wronged—namely, mercy and forgiveness. Because of the conventions of these genres, with their providential universe and miraculous conversions, wronged characters do not have to take revenge: either fate does it for them or they forgive their enemies, who are then permanently transformed. In these plays, the self-effacing solution, with its accompanying bargain, works very well, but only because the plays are unrealistic.

What I infer about Shakespeare from his plays is that he has strong vindictive impulses, but even stronger taboos against those impulses and a fear of the guilt and punishment to which he would be exposed if he acted them out. He does act them out imaginatively in the histories and tragedies and is purged of them through the destruction of his surrogate aggressors. He also has a fear of his self-effacing side, however; and he shows both himself and us through characters like Henry VI, Hamlet, Desdemona, and Timon of Athens that people who are too good and trusting cannot cope and will be destroyed. In the tragedies he portrays the inadequacy of both solutions. In some of the comedies and in the romances he fantasizes the triumph of good people and avoids guilt either by glorifying forgiveness or leaving revenge to the gods. In *The Tempest,* through Prospero's magic, he imagines a solution to Hamlet's problem; for Prospero is at once vindictive and noble, vengeful and innocent. He takes his revenge through his magic by raising a tempest and inflicting various psychological torments, but he does not really hurt anybody, and when he has had his vindictive triumph, he gives up his magic and forgives everyone.

From a Horneyan point of view, one of Shakespeare's major projects was to find a way of giving expression to the hostile, vindictive, aggressive side of his personality without violating his stronger need to be noble, loving, and innocent. Recognizing this helps us to understand many of his plays and also a number of the sonnets. *The Tempest* is perhaps the most brilliant solution he ever imagined to this essentially insoluble problem, and it is not surprising that it was his last great play. In *Henry VIII,* which followed, the self-effacing side of Shakespeare is overwhelmingly predominant, and we no longer feel ourselves to be in the presence of a complex and fascinating personality. Shakespeare's inner conflicts have much to do, I suspect, with the richness and ambiguity of his greatest art.

The relation between authors and their works is a vexed question, of course. We must always make allowances for artistic motivations, for generic requirements, and for the inner logic of individual works. Even so, it is possible to tell a good deal about authors from their literary creations when we examine such things as their recurring preoccupations, the personal element in their fantasies, the kinds of characters and relationships they habitually create, and their rhetorical stance.

In order to determine what the implied author and the authorial personality tell us about the writer as a person, we must test our inferences against biographical data that are not drawn from the works—the sort of information that is not available for Shakespeare. So far I have not attempted a biography of a literary artist, but I am convinced that there are many instances in which a Horneyan analysis of the authorial personality could contribute a great deal to our understanding of the writer's inner life, and I hope to undertake such a study in the future. It might throw a good deal of light on the relation between art and neurosis and the nature of the creative process (see chapter 8, note 1).

Such a study has been undertaken by Lawrance Thompson in his monumental biography of Robert Frost. Thompson accepted Frost's invitation to be his official biographer in 1939, when Frost was 65, with the understanding that nothing was to be published until after Frost's death, which did not occur until 1963. As he collected material in the intervening years, Thompson became aware of Frost's many cruelties, self-contradictions, and inner conflicts, which he set out to describe in his biography.

After completing a draft of the first volume, Thompson read *Neurosis and Human Growth* and found in it the analytic concepts he needed to make sense of his bewildering subject. If "it mentioned Frost on every page," he wrote in his notebook, "it couldn't have come closer to giving a psychological framework to what I've been trying to say in the first volume of the biography" (Sheehy 1986, 398). Thompson's notebook contains one hundred and thirty pages of notes and excerpts from Horney interspersed with such applications to Frost as the following: "Frost's pattern involved . . . an affectionate clinging to his mother; a fear of beatings (which he got) from his father and a consequent attempt at compliant appeasement; but more than these, his 'conflict' caused him to 'keep aloof.' The first story he ever tried to write, he said, was the story of his running away to the Happy Valley where the Indian tribes were so nice to him" (quoted by Sheehy 1986, 405). Although Horney's ideas give an interpretive structure to the biography, she is not mentioned in the text, the footnotes, or the index of any of the volumes. We owe a knowledge of Thompson's use of Horney to the work of Donald Sheehy (1986).

After studying *Neurosis and Human Growth,* Thompson revised his first volume to reflect his Horneyan interpretation of his subject. He saw Frost as a man who developed a search for glory in response to early humiliations and who longed to triumph over and retaliate against those who had hurt him. Frost's contradictory accounts of his life were a product both of his inner conflicts and of his need to confirm his idealized image by mythologizing himself. His poetry reflects these dynamics. Sometimes Frost used it to "escape from his confusions into idealized postures," while at other times it served "as a means of striking back at, or of punishing" those he considered his enemies (Thompson 1966, xix). Horney argues that works of art, like dreams, can originate in our effort to "create solutions for an inner conflict that is disquieting us" (1950, 330), and Thompson claims that Frost's poetry often had such a genesis. The central problem of his life "was to find orderly ways of dealing with the dangerous conflicts he found operative within himself or between himself and others" (1966, xxii). "At his artistic best," he "tried to make his poems provide an effective way of coming to grips with his inner and outer confusions, honestly, for purposes of resolving them" (xix–xx). Thompson concludes that the widespread appeal of Frost derives from the fact that "no themes are more universal and attractive than those which try to offer affirmative resolutions for the conflicts dramatized in his life and in his poetry" (1970, xix). To many, Horney's theory has a similar appeal.

When I first began developing a Horneyan approach to literature, I felt that authors with inner conflicts were bound to produce works full of inconsistencies, but I have come to see that disparities between rhetoric and mimesis and thematic contradictions can be exacerbated, reduced, or even eliminated, in fiction at least, by the choice of narrative technique. Although convention calls for omniscient narrators to be authoritative in their interpretations and judgments, they are often misleading, confused, or defensive, thus frustrating the reader's expectations. In first person narration, similar inconsistencies, misjudgments, and blind spots belong to the character rather than to the work, and they can be strengths rather than weaknesses if they contribute to the richness and accuracy of the psychological portrait. If the first person narrator's perspective is endorsed by the implied author, however, as is the case with Pip and Jane Eyre, the problems are the same as in omniscient narration. The best solution seems to be first person narration in which the implied author cannot be identified with the narrator, as in *Notes from Underground* (Paris 1974) and *The End of the Road*, or narration from several dramatized perspectives, as in *Lord Jim* (Paris 1974) and *Wuthering Heights*. If we are to understand what motivates the telling of the story, we must analyze both omniscient and dramatized narrators, along with the implied author. With many works, a Horneyan approach can help us to accomplish this.

If the telling of the story is psychologically motivated, so also is the reader's response. We tend to react to works in terms of our own defenses, inner conflicts, and struggles toward growth. Horney observed that analysts have a "personal equation" that leads them to respond to the solutions and conflicts they encounter in patients in terms of their own personality structures, and the same thing is true for readers responding to texts. An interpretation often tells us as much about the critic as it does about the work. Readers are bound to have different reactions; but, while recognizing the subjectivity of perception, a Horneyan approach can help us make sense of conflicting interpretations by seeing each one as responding to some aspects of the text while suppressing awareness of others.

In the criticism of *Vanity Fair*, for example, most commentators feel that Amelia and Dobbin are presented in a favorable light and that Becky is consistently portrayed as a villain. However, an important minority feel that Thackeray has contempt for Amelia and Dobbin, that he admires Becky, and that he is inconsistent toward the end when he characterizes her as a monster. In *A Psychological Approach to Fiction* (1974), I argued that the implied author of *Vanity Fair* has a personality in which self-effacing trends predominate but in which suppressed aggressive drives get themselves expressed in disguised or indirect ways. The self-effacing side of Thackeray exalts Amelia and Dobbin and condemns Becky, while his aggressive side delights in Becky's triumphs and scorns Amelia as a parasite and Dobbin as a spooney. Both groups of critics can find evidence to support their interpretations, but those who are sympathetic to self-effacing behavior are likely to emphasize Thackeray's glorification of Amelia and Dobbin, while more expansive critics will dwell on his secret admiration of Becky.

There is also a good deal of detachment in *Vanity Fair*, which is manifested by the theme that all is vanity and by the narrator's often unfocused irony, which is the means by which the implied author negates what he has affirmed and protects himself from being identified with the folly of his characters. There are critics who defend Thackeray against charges of sentimentality, cynicism, and inconsistency by pointing to his irony. The irony is there, but these critics ignore the self-effacing and expansive components of the novel.

I have found a similar state of affairs in the criticism of Shakespeare (Paris 1991a) and Jane Austen (Paris 1978b). Those who offer the orthodox Christian reading of Shakespeare are responding to the side of him that believes that right makes might and virtue is rewarded, while those who claim that his portrayal of reality is closer to the modern absurdist position are more sensitive to the expansive side of Shakespeare that sees through conventional beliefs. In the case of Jane Austen, some critics emphasize the aggressive, satirical component of her art; some stress her gentleness and conservatism; and some focus on the detached, ironic quality of her vision. Each group overemphasizes an important component of her work while showing little awareness of conflicting elements.

All of the interpretations offered in this book are instances of my own psychologically motivated responses to literature. To me, Horney seems highly congruent with the texts I have chosen, but I know that this is not the case for many other readers. Horney works for me because she is compatible with my temperament, experience, and modes of understanding, and my readings will be most appealing to those who share at least some of my premises.

Although I have wanted to focus on literature, or at least on my perspective upon it, rather than on the epistemological problems that beset all interpreters of texts, I am not unaware of those problems. The disparity between rhetoric and mimesis of which I so frequently speak is really a disparity between my interpretation of the author's view of a character and my understanding of what I regard as the mimetic portrait. I know that my approach to character, plot, rhetoric, and narrative technique will be of interest mainly to those who are receptive to Horney. It is my hope, of course, that that receptivity will be increased by my Horney-inspired readings of major works of Western literature from *Antigone* to *The End of the Road*.

Notes

NOTES TO CHAPTER 1

1. Horneyan studies have been previously published on the following authors: Jane Austen (Paris 1978b), Honoré de Balzac (Portnoy 1949), Charles Baudelaire (Van Bark 1961), Saul Bellow (Paris 1976b), Emily Brontë (Paris 1982), Charlotte Brontë (Butery 1986; Paris 1993a), Robert Browning (Lewis 1986), Pearl Buck (Vollmerhausen 1950), Frank Capra (Gordon 1994), Joseph Conrad (Paris 1974, 1993b), Anita Desai (Bande 1988), Charles Dickens (Eldredge 1986), Fyodor Dostoevsky (Van Bark 1961; Paris 1974, 1978c, 1991c, 1994b), George Eliot (Paris 1974, 1986b; Butery, 1982; Lauer 1985), William Faulkner (Haselswerdt 1986; Butery 1989; Bockting 1995), Gustave Flaubert (Paris 1981), Robert Frost (Thompson 1966, 1970; Thompson and Winnick 1976; Sheehy 1986), Graham Greene (Straub 1986), Thomas Hardy (Paris 1976a; Butery 1982), Ernest Hemingway (Yalom and Yalom 1971), Henrik Ibsen (Breitbart 1948, Paris 1978a), Henry James (Butery 1982; Lauer 1985), James Joyce (Bartlett 1993), D. H. Lawrence (Smalley 1986), Doris Lessing (Westkott 1986, Eldredge 1989), C. S. Lewis (Bartlett 1989), W. Somerset Maugham (Weiss 1973), George Meredith (Watt 1984), Arthur Miller (Becker 1987), Eugene O'Neill (Falk 1958), Samuel Richardson (Eldredge 1982), William Shakespeare (Rosenberg 1961; Rabkin and Brown 1973; Greenberg 1985; Lewis 1985; Paris 1989b, 1991a, 1991b, 1994c; Taylor 1994), George Bernard Shaw (Bartlett 1991), Lao She (You 1995), Mary Shelley (Keyishian 1989), Stendhal (Paris 1974), William Styron (Huffman 1986), William Makepeace Thackeray (Paris 1974), Edith Wharton (Lauer 1994), and Richard Wright (Fishburn 1977). See also Huffman 1994 for Horneyan observations on such American writers as Horatio Alger, Theodore Dreiser, F. Scott Fitzgerald, Carson McCullers, Robert Penn Warren, Nathanael West, Thomas Wolfe, and Budd Schulberg.

NOTES TO CHAPTER 2

1. For details of Horney's life and a fuller discussion of her ideas, see Bernard J. Paris, *Karen Horney: A Psychoanalyst's Search for Self-Understanding* (New Haven: Yale University Press, 1994).

NOTES TO CHAPTER 3

1. I am using the Eva Le Gallienne translation of *A Doll's House* and *Hedda Gabler,* published by the Modern Library.

NOTES TO CHAPTER 4

1. I should like to share with the reader the comments of my colleague Andrew Gordon in response to a draft of this chapter:

The doctor is another masterful character like Joe. Jake is torn between these two authority figures. He comes under the sway of the Doctor, who plays on his self-effacement. Then he comes under the sway of Joe and even begins to imitate Joe as a means of defying the Doctor. In the end, the Doctor triumphs, winning back total control over Jake. Jake's retreat to the Doctor's farm represents detachment, but it is also a form of self-effacement, for the Doctor confirms Jake in the notion that he has *no self.*

The Doctor, in a way, does to Jake what Joe does to Rennie and what Jake tries to do to women (when he preys on Peggy and later on Rennie). Almost everyone in this novel aggressively sets out to *subdue* people, to erase them and remake them to their heart's desire, to use them for their own ends.

It may be that all the characters in the novel secretly fear that they have no self, do not exist, are *nothing,* and that their defense against this fear is aggressively to cancel the selves of others. Jake's final stance of detachment may make him feel more aware than others, but it ironically confirms that he is nothing, for one scarcely exists who has no relations to others. He comforts himself by believing that others are nothing and do not exist.

NOTES TO CHAPTER 5

1. I am using Michael Murphy's edition of *The Canterbury Tales: The General Prologue and Twelve Major Tales in Modern Spelling* (Lanham, Md.: University Press of America, 1991). References are to line numbers. I agree with Murphy that it makes sense to provide Chaucer in modern spelling, as we do Shakespeare and other early authors.

NOTES TO CHAPTER 6

1. I am using the Kittredge-Ribner edition of *The Merchant of Venice.*

NOTES TO CHAPTER 7

1. I am using the Elizabeth Wyckoff translation of *Antigone,* published in *The Complete Greek Tragedies,* ed. David Grene and Richmond Lattimore, Vol.

2 (Chicago: University of Chicago Press, 1959). References are to line numbers.

2. I am using the David Grene translation of *Oedipus the King,* published in *The Complete Greek Tragedies,* Vol. 2.

NOTES TO CHAPTER 8

1. I suggest that Dickens is doing for Pip what his art does for Dickens, that is, normalizing his inner life by portraying external reality in a way that justifies his obsessions and anxieties. As has often been observed, *Great Expectations* is obliquely autobiographical in that Dickens seems to be drawing on the feelings of being tainted that he connected with his blacking house experience. Those feelings have seemed to some to be in excess of the occasion and to indicate previously existing problems that make the experience so traumatic. In Pip, Dickens imagines a character whose childhood explains his reactions to such an episode, a character who also needs to keep the episode secret and who cannot overcome his feelings of guilt and shame despite his social and economic elevation. Dickens seems to be trying to imagine through Pip's experiences an objective correlative that will make the irrational feelings by which he is haunted seem grounded in reality. He confirms Pip's responses because they are similar to responses of his own for which he is seeking corroboration. The hallucinatory intensity of his novels may be the result, in part, of his need to create a world to which his overreactions are appropriate. The enthusiastic reception of his work must have provided a precious validation, but it did not relieve him of his problems, any more than Pip was cured by his great expectations.

NOTES TO CHAPTER 11

1. I am using the Paul De Man translation of *Madame Bovary,* published in the Norton Critical Edition (New York: W. W. Norton, 1965).

References

Allott, Miriam. 1970. *Wuthering Heights:* The Rejection of Heathcliff. In *Wuthering Heights: A Selection of Critical Essays.* Ed. Miriam Allott. London: Macmillan.

Auerbach, Erich. 1957. *Mimesis: The Representation of Reality in Western Literature.* Garden City, N.Y.: Doubleday.

Bande, Usha. 1988. *The Novels of Anita Desai.* New Delhi: Prestige Press.

Bartlett, Sally A. 1989. Humanistic Psychology in C. S. Lewis's *Till We Have Faces:* A Feminist Critique. *Studies in the Literary Imagination* 22: 185–98.

———. 1991. Fantasy as Internal Mimesis in Bernard Shaw's *Saint Joan. Notes on Modern Irish Literature* 3: 5–12.

———. 1993. Spectral Thought and Psychological Mimesis in *A Portrait of the Artist as a Young Man. Notes on Modern Irish Literature* 5: 57–66.

Becker, Benjamin. 1987. *Death of a Salesman:* Arthur Miller's Play in the Light of Psychoanalysis. *American Journal of Psychoanalysis* 47: 195–209.

Bockting, Ineke. 1995. *Character and Personality in the Novels of William Faulkner: A Study in Psycholinguistics.* Lanham, Md.: University Press of America.

Bolt, Robert. n.d. *A Man for All Seasons.* New York: Vintage Books.

Booth, Wayne. 1961. *The Rhetoric of Fiction.* Chicago: University of Chicago Press.

Breitbart, Sara. 1948. *Hedda Gabler:* A Critical Analysis. *American Journal of Psychoanalysis* 8: 55–58.

Butery, Karen. 1982. The Contributions of Horneyan Psychology to the Study of Literature. *American Journal of Psychoanalysis* 42: 39–50.

———. 1986. Jane Eyre's Flights from Decision. In *Third Force Psychology and the Study of Literature.* Ed. B. J. Paris. Rutherford, N.J.: Fairleigh Dickinson University Press.

———. 1989. From Conflict to Suicide: The Inner Turmoil of Quentin Compson. *American Journal of Psychoanalysis* 49: 211–24.

Cather, Willa. 1899. Review of *The Awakening. Pittsburgh Leader* 8 July: 6.

Collins, Clifford. 1947. Theme and Conventions in *Wuthering Heights.* In Norton Critical Edition of *Wuthering Heights.* Ed. W. M. Sale, Jr. 1963. New York: W. W. Norton.

Culley, Margo, ed. 1994. Norton Critical Edition of *The Awakening,* 2d ed. New York: W. W. Norton.

de Beaugrande, Robert. 1986. Third Force Analysis and the Literary Experience. In *Third Force Psychology and the Study of Literature.* Ed. B. J. Paris. Rutherford, N.J.: Fairleigh Dickinson University Press.

De Man, Paul, ed. 1965. Norton Critical Edition of *Madame Bovary.* New York: W. W. Norton.

Eldredge, Patricia R. 1982. Karen Horney and *Clarissa:* The Tragedy of Neurotic Pride. *American Journal of Psychoanalysis* 42: 51–59.

————. 1986. The Lost Self of Esther Summerson: A Horneyan Interpretation of *Bleak House.* In *Third Force Psychology and the Study of Literature.* Ed. B. J. Paris. Rutherford, N.J.: Fairleigh Dickinson University Press.

————. 1989. A Granddaughter of Violence: Doris Lessing's Good Girl as Terrorist. *American Journal of Psychoanalysis* 49: 225–38.

Eliot, George. 1856. Belles Lettres and Art. *Westminster Review* 66: 571–78.

Falk, Doris V. 1958. *Eugene O'Neill and the Tragic Tension.* New Brunswick, N.J.: Rutgers University Press.

Fishburn, Katherine. 1977. *Richard Wright's Hero: The Faces of a Rebel-Victim.* Metuchen, N.J.: Scarecrow Press.

Forster, E. M. 1927. *Aspects of the Novel.* London: Edward Arnold.

Fox-Genovese, Elizabeth. 1979. Kate Chopin's *The Awakening. Southern Studies* 18: 261–90. Excerpt in Nancy Walker, ed. 1993. *The Awakening.* New York: Bedford Books, St. Martin's Press.

Frye, Northrop. 1957. *Anatomy of Criticism.* Princeton: Princeton University Press.

————. 1963. Myth, Fiction, and Displacement. In *Fables of Identity.* New York: Harcourt, Brace & World.

Gordon, Andrew. 1994. It's Not Such a *Wonderful Life:* The Neurotic George Bailey. *American Journal of Psychoanalysis* 54: 219–33.

Greenberg, Samuel. 1985. Shylock in *The Merchant of Venice. American Journal of Psychoanalysis* 45: 160–66.

Haight, Gordon, ed. 1955. *The George Eliot Letters.* Vol. 6. New Haven: Yale University Press.

Hart, Frances Russell. 1968. The Experience of Character in the English Gothic Novel. In *Experience in the Novel.* Ed. Roy Harvey Pearce. New York: Columbia University Press.

Haselswerdt, Marjorie. 1986. "Keep Your Muck": A Horneyan Analysis of Joe Christmas and *Light in August.* In *Third Force Psychology and the Study of Literature.* Ed. B. J. Paris. Rutherford, N.J.: Fairleigh Dickinson University Press.

Horney, Karen. 1937. *The Neurotic Personality of Our Time.* New York: W. W. Norton.

———. 1939. *New Ways in Psychoanalysis*. New York: W. W. Norton.

———. 1942. *Self-Analysis*. New York: W. W. Norton.

———. 1945. *Our Inner Conflicts*. New York: W. W. Norton.

———. 1950. *Neurosis and Human Growth: The Struggle toward Self-Realization*. New York: W. W. Norton.

———. 1967. *Feminine Psychology*, Ed. Harold Kelman. New York: W. W. Norton.

Huffman, James. 1982. A Psychological Critique of American Culture. *American Journal of Psychoanalysis* 42: 27–38.

———. 1986. A Psychological Redefinition of William Styron's *Confessions of Nat Turner*. In *Third Force Psychology and the Study of Literature*. Ed. B. J. Paris. Rutherford, N.J.: Fairleigh Dickinson University Press.

———. 1989. Young Man Johnson. *American Journal of Psychoanalysis* 49: 251–65.

———. 1994. A Horneyan Approach to American Literature. In *Dionysus in Literature: Essays on Literary Madness*. Ed. Branimir Rieger. Bowling Green, Ohio: Popular Press.

Keyishian, Harry. 1989. Vindictiveness and the Search for Glory in Mary Shelley's *Frankenstein*. *American Journal of Psychoanalysis* 49: 201–10.

Laing, R. D. 1965. *The Divided Self*. Baltimore: Penguin Books.

Lauer, Kristin. 1985. His Husband / Her Wife: The Dynamics of the Pride System in Marriage. *Journal of Evolutionary Psychology* 6: 320–40.

———. 1994. Is This Indeed "Attractive"? Another Look at the "Beatrice Palmato" Fragment. *Edith Wharton Review* 11: 26–29.

Lewis, Catherine R. 1985. Poet, Friend, and Poetry: The Idealized Image of Love in Shakespeare's Sonnets. *American Journal of Psychoanalysis* 45: 176–90.

———. 1986. Browning's Guido: The Self-Fictionalizing Imagination in Crisis. In *Third Force Psychology and the Study of Literature*. Ed. B. J. Paris. Rutherford, N.J.: Fairleigh Dickinson University Press.

Maslow, Abraham. 1970. *Motivation and Personality*. 2d ed. New York: Harper & Row.

Mathison, John. 1956. Nelly Dean and the Power of *Wuthering Heights*. *Nineteenth Century Fiction* 11: 106–29.

Mitchell, Giles. 1987. Flaubert's *Emma Bovary:* Narcissism and Suicide. *American Imago* 44: 107–28.

Paris, B. J. 1965. *Experiments in Life: George Eliot's Quest for Values*. Detroit: Wayne State University Press.

———. 1974. *A Psychological Approach to Fiction: Studies in Thackeray, Stendhal, George Eliot, Dostoevsky, and Conrad*. Bloomington: Indiana University Press.

———. 1976a. Experiences of Thomas Hardy. In *The Victorian Experience*. Ed. Richard A. Levine. Athens, Ohio: Ohio University Press.

Paris, B. J. 1976b. Herzog the Man: An Analytic View of a Literary Figure. *American Journal of Psychoanalysis* 36: 249–60.

———. 1978a. Horney's Theory and the Study of Literature. *American Journal of Psychoanalysis* 38: 343–53.

———. 1978b. *Character and Conflict in Jane Austen's Novels: A Psychological Approach.* Detroit: Wayne State University Press.

———. 1978c. The Two Selves of Rodion Raskolnikov. *Gradiva* 1: 316–28.

———. 1981. Third Force Psychology and the Study of Literature, Biography, Criticism, and Culture. *Literary Review* 24: 181–221.

———. 1982. "Hush, Hush! He's a human being": A Psychological Approach to Heathcliff. *Women and Literature* 2: 101–17.

———, ed. 1986a. *Third Force Psychology and the Study of Literature.* Rutherford, N.J.: Fairleigh Dickinson University Press.

———. 1986b. Third Force Psychology and the Study of Literature, Biography, Criticism, and Culture. In *Third Force Psychology and the Study of Literature.*

———. 1989a. Interdisciplinary Applications of Horney. *American Journal of Psychoanalysis* 49: 181–88.

———. 1989b. The Not So Noble Antonio: A Horneyan Analysis of Shakespeare's *Merchant of Venice. American Journal of Psychoanalysis* 49: 189–200.

———. 1991a. *Bargains with Fate: Psychological Crises and Conflicts in Shakespeare and His Plays.* New York: Plenum Press.

———. 1991b. *Character as a Subversive Force in Shakespeare: The History and Roman Plays.* Rutherford, N.J.: Fairleigh Dickinson University Press.

———. 1991c. A Horneyan Approach to Literature. *American Journal of Psychoanalysis* 51: 319–37.

———. 1993a. *Jane Eyre* as a Novel of Vindication. In *Approaches to Teaching Brontë's* Jane Eyre. Ed. Diane Hoeveler and Beth Lau. New York: Modern Language Association of America.

———. 1993b. Marlow's Transformation. *Aligarh Journal of English Studies* 15: 65–72.

———. 1994a. *Karen Horney: A Psychoanalyst's Search for Self-Understanding.* New Haven: Yale University Press.

———. 1994b. Pulkheria Alexandrovna and Raskolnikov, My Mother and Me. In *Self Analysis in Literary Criticism.* Ed. Daniel Rancour-Laferriere. New York: New York University Press.

———. 1994c. Petruchio's Taming of Kate: A Horneyan Perspective. *American Journal of Psychoanalysis* 54: 339–44.

———. 1997. The Search for Glory in *Madame Bovary:* A Horneyan Analysis. *American Journal of Psychoanalysis* 57: 5–24.

Portnoy, Isidore. 1949. "The Magic Skin": A Psychoanalytic Interpretation. *American Journal of Psychoanalysis.* 9: 67–74.

Rabkin, Leslie Y., and Jeffrey Brown. 1973. Some Monster in His Thought: Sadism and Tragedy in *Othello. Literature and Psychology* 23: 59–67.

Robinson, James K., ed. 1977. Norton Critical Edition of *The Mayor of Casterbridge.* New York: W. W. Norton.

Rosenberg, Marvin. 1961. *The Masks of* Othello. Berkeley: University of California Press.

Rubins, Jack. L. 1978. *Karen Horney: Gentle Rebel of Psychoanalysis.* New York: Dial Press.

Saint-Beuve, Charles Augustin. 1857. *Madame Bovary,* by Gustave Flaubert. In Norton Critical Edition of *Madame Bovary.* Ed. Paul De Man. 1965. New York: W. W. Norton.

Sale, William M., Jr., ed. 1963. Norton Critical Edition of *Wuthering Heights.* New York: W. W. Norton.

Scholes, Robert, and Robert Kellogg. 1966. *The Nature of Narrative.* New York: Oxford University Press.

Schorer, Mark. 1950. Introduction to *Wuthering Heights.* Rinehart edition. New York: Rinehart.

Sheehy, Donald. 1986. The Poet as Neurotic: The Official Biography of Robert Frost. *American Literature* 58: 393–410.

Smalley, Barbara. 1986. Lawrence's "The Princess" and Horney's "Idealized Self." In *Third Force Psychology and the Study of Literature.* Ed. B. J. Paris. Rutherford, N.J.: Fairleigh Dickinson University Press.

Straub, Joe. 1986. A Psychological View of Priesthood, Sin, and Redemption in Graham Greene's *The Power and the Glory.* In *Third Force Psychology and the Study of Literature.* Ed. B. J. Paris. Rutherford, N.J.: Fairleigh Dickinson University Press.

Taylor, Mark. 1994. Farther Privileges: Conflict and Change in *Measure for Measure. Philological Quarterly* 73: 169–93.

Thompson, Lawrance. 1966. *Robert Frost: The Early Years 1874–1915.* New York: Holt, Rinehart & Winston.

———. 1970. *Robert Frost: The Years of Triumph 1915–1938.* New York: Holt, Rinehart & Winston.

Thompson, Lawrance, and R. H. Winnick. 1976. *Robert Frost: The Later Years 1938–1963.* New York: Holt, Rinehart & Winston.

Van Bark, Bella S. 1961. The Alienated Person in Literature. *American Journal of Psychoanalysis* 21: 183–97.

Vollmerhausen, Joseph. 1950. "Pavilion of Women: A Psychoanalytic Interpretation. *American Journal of Psychoanalysis* 10: 53–60.

Walker, Nancy, ed. 1993. *The Awakening.* New York: Bedford Books, St. Martin's Press.

Watt, Stephen. 1984. Neurotic Responses to a Failed Marriage: George Meredith's *Modern Love*. *Mosaic* 17: 49–63.

Weiss, Frederick. 1973. Of Human Bondage. *American Journal of Psychoanalysis* 33: 68–76.

Westkott, Marcia. 1986. *The Feminist Legacy of Karen Horney*. New Haven: Yale University Press.

———. 1989. Female Relationality and the Idealized Self. *American Journal of Psychoanalysis* 49: 239–50.

Yalom, Irvin D., and Marilyn Yalom. 1971. Ernest Hemingway—A Psychiatric View. *Archives of General Psychiatry* 24: 485–94.

You, Wenjia. 1995. A Horneyan Analysis of Lao Li in Lao She's *Divorce*. *Chinese Culture* 36: 89–99.

Index

Abraham, Karl, 17
Absolom, Absolom! (Faulkner), 29
Actual self, 30–31
Adler, Alfred, 3
Aggressive women in Shakespeare, 93
Alexander, Franz, 17
Alger, Horatio, 271 n. 1
Alice Mellings *(The Good Terrorist)*, 22
Allott, Miriam, 259
Amelia Sedley *(Vanity Fair)*, 5, 22, 268
Anne Elliot *(Persuasion)*, 27
Antigone (Sophocles): analyzed, 105–16
Antigone, 212; analyzed, 105, 106, 110–16
Antonio *(Merchant of Venice)*, 112; analysis of, 93–104
Antony *(Antony and Cleopatra)*, 22, 93
Antony and Cleopatra (Shakespeare), 22, 93, 212
Arrogant-vindictive (aggressive) solution: defensive strategies of, 22–24, 253–54; examples of in literature, 24. *See analyses of* Catherine Earnshaw; Creon; Hedda Gabler; Michael Henchard; Pip; Shylock
Auerbach, Erich, 196
Austen, Jane, 5, 13, 22, 27, 29, 264, 271 n. 1; criticism of, 269
Author: as historical person, 263–64; implied, 263–64; inner conflicts of, 263–65; meanings of the term, 263
Authorial personality: Horneyan approach to, 263–67; of Jane Austen, 13, 264; of Thomas Hardy, 13, 264; of Shakespeare, 13, 264–66
Awakening, The (Chopin), 240, 261; analysis of, 215–39; thematic confusions of, 215–22
Axel Heyst *(Victory)*, 65

Balzac, Honoré de, 271 n. 1
Bargains with Fate: Psychological Crises and Conflicts in Shakespeare and His Plays (Paris), 33, 93, 103, 264
Bargain with fate: defined, 33
Barth, John: analysis of *The End of the Road*, 64–81
Basic anxiety, 18
Basic needs, 18
Baudelaire, Charles, 271 n. 1
Beach, Joseph Warren, 168
Becky Sharp *(Vanity Fair)*, 5, 24, 268
Bellow, Saul, 22, 65, 271 n. 1
Bennet, Mr. *(Pride and Prejudice)*, 29
Biography: Horneyan approach to, 266–67
Bleak House (Dickens), 22
Booth, Wayne, 255
Brontë, Charlotte, 271 n. 1; analysis of *Jane Eyre*, 144–67
Brontë, Emily, 271 n. 1; analysis of *Wuthering Heights*, 240–61; psychological conflicts of, 256–61
Browning, Robert, 24, 271 n. 1
Brutus *(Julius Caesar)*, 27
Buck, Pearl, 271 n. 1

Caine Mutiny, The (Wouk), 115
Capra, Frank, 22, 271 n. 1
Cassius *(Julius Caesar)*, 24
Cather, Willa, 215
Catherine Earnshaw *(Wuthering Heights)*, 244–51
Characterization: aesthetic, 6; E. M. Forster on, 6–10; illustrative, 6–7; mimetic, xii 7, 9–10; taxonomy of, 6–7
Characters: as "creations inside a creation," 7, 10, 144; formal analysis of, 6; a Horneyan approach to, xi, 8–9; as imagined human beings, xi, 10; mimetic

About the Author

BERNARD J. PARIS is the leading authority on Karen Horney and the application of her psychoanalytic theories in literary criticism. His first book, *Experiments in Life: George Eliot's Quest for Values*, reflects his training in thematic analysis and the history of ideas. He has subsequently published a series of studies that employ Karen Horney's theories to examine a variety of authors and critical issues. These include *A Psychological Approach to Fiction: Studies in Thackeray, Stendhal, George Eliot, Dostoevsky, and Conrad; Character and Conflict in Jane Austen's Novels: A Psychological Approach; Bargains with Fate: Psychological Crises and Conflicts in Shakespeare and His Plays;* and *Character as a Subversive Force in Shakespeare: The History and Roman Plays.* He has edited *Third Force Psychology and the Study of Literature* and coedited *Shakespeare's Personality* (with Norman Holland and Sidney Homan). His most recent book, *Karen Horney: A Psychoanalyst's Search for Self-Understanding*, was selected as a Notable Book of the Year by the *New York Times Book Review*.

Paris received his Ph.D. from The Johns Hopkins University and has taught at Lehigh University, Michigan State, and the University of Florida, where he is Emeritus Professor of English and former director of the Institute for Psychological Study of the Arts. He has been Visiting Professor at the Victorian Studies Centre of the University of Leicester and has held NEH and Guggenheim fellowships. He is an Honorary Member of the Association for the Advancement of Psychoanalysis, a Scientific Associate of the American Academy of Psychoanalysis, and a member of the editorial board of *The American Journal of Psychoanalysis*. He is founder and director of the International Karen Horney Society.

About the Author